FIELD BOOK OF ✤ AMERICAN ✤ WILD FLOWERS

FIELD BOOK OF AMERICAN WILD  FLOWERS

BEING A SHORT DESCRIPTION OF THEIR
CHARACTER AND HABITS, A CONCISE
DEFINITION OF THEIR COLORS, AND IN-
CIDENTAL REFERENCES TO THE INSECTS
WHICH ASSIST IN THEIR FERTILIZATION

BY F. SCHUYLER MATHEWS

MEMBER OF THE NEW ENGLAND BOTANICAL CLUB
AND AUTHOR OF
FAMILIAR FLOWERS OF FIELD AND GARDEN
FAMILIAR TREES AND THEIR LEAVES, FAMILIAR
FEATURES OF THE ROADSIDE, ETC.

WITH NUMEROUS REPRODUCTIONS OF WATER
COLORS AND PEN-AND-INK STUDIES FROM NATURE
BY THE AUTHOR ❋ ❋ ❋ ❋ ❋ ❋ ❋

A MAIN STREET BOOK

ORIGINALLY PUBLISHED BY
THE KNICKERBOCKER PRESS, NEW YORK, NY

© 1902 BY
F. SCHUYLER MATHEWS

———————

2001 FACSIMILE EDITION
Published by Sterling Publishing Company, Inc.
387 Park Avenue South, New York, NY 10016
Distributed in Canada by Sterling Publishing
Canadian Manda Group, One Atlantic Avenue, Suite 105
Toronto, Ontario, Canada M6K 3E7
Distributed in Great Britain and Europe by Cassell PLC
Wellington House, 125 Strand,
London WC2R 0BB, England
Distributed in Australia by Capricorn Link (Australia) Pty Ltd.
P.O. Box 704, Windsor, NSW 2756 Australia

Printed in Hong Kong

STERLING ISBN 0-8069-9043-0

To

C. A. M.

IN REMEMBRANCE OF

MANY JOURNEYS AFIELD IN

THE BEAUTIFUL VALLEY OF THE PEMIGEWASSET

THIS BOOK IS AFFECTIONATELY

INSCRIBED

CONTENTS.

CONTENTS.

CONTENTS.

COLORED ILLUSTRATIONS.

FACING PAGE 266

TECHNICAL TERMS.

Corolla.   The flower-cup composed of one or more divisions called petals.

Petal.   One of the divisions of the corolla.

Calyx.   A flower-envelop, usually green, formed of several divisions called sepals, protecting the bud.

Sepal.   One of the divisions of the calyx.

Stamen.   Anther and filament combined.

Anther.   The pollen-bearing organ, usually yellow.

Filament.   The stalklike support of the anther.

Pistil.   Ovary, style, and stigma combined.

Ovary.   The seed-bearing organ.

Style.   The stalklike projection proceeding from the ovary and terminated by the stigma.

Stigma.   The generally sticky and sometimes branching termination of the pistil through which fertilization by the pollen is effected.

Rostellum.   See Orchid Family description, page 68.

Regular Flower.   Generally symmetrical and uniform in the number of its parts.

Perfect Flower.   A flower complete in all the common parts.

Staminate.   With stamens and without pistils.

Pistillate.   With pistils and without stamens.

Polygamous.   Pistillate, staminate, and perfect flowers on the same plant or on different plants.

Spathe.   A leaflike formation enclosing a floral growth.

Spadix.   A fleshy spike of flowers.

Bracts.   Small leaflike formations.

Stipule.   Small leaflike formations confined to the base of the leaf.

Pubescent.   Covered with soft short hairs.

Cleistogamous Flower.   A flower closed to all outward agencies and self-fertilized in the bud.

COLORS.

xi

COLORS.

Papilio ajax.

Anosia plexippus
or Danais archippus.

Brenthis bellona.

Papilio troilus.

Pieris rapæ.

Colias philodice.

Junonia cœnia.

Papilio asterias.

BUTTERFLIES
CONCERNED IN THE CROSS-FERTILIZATION OF FLOWERS.

xiii

The Bumblebees.   Various.   The Syrphid Flies.

Bombus vagans.

The Honeybee.
Apis mellifica.

Eristalis flavipes.

Bombus ternarius
(Orange-banded)

Bombylius fratellus.

(These two flies much enlarged)

Syrpus Lesueurii.

Bombus frigidus.
(Orange-banded)

Bombylius atriceps.

Polydonta cardus.

Bombus Virginicus

Megachile latimana.
(Leaf-cutter bee)

Helophilus similis.

Bombus terricola

Halictus confusus.

Bombus Pennsylvanicus

Andrena vicina.

Halictus & Andrena
are ground bees.

Syrpus diversipes.

BUMBLEBEES, BEES, AND FLIES CONCERNED IN THE
CROSS-FERTILIZATION OF FLOWERS.

xiv

INTRODUCTION.

PERHAPS it is not too much to say that the wild flower of late has become popular. If such is the case I am presumably justified in presenting it in a new light, or, to speak more to the point, in the position it occupies according to the light of one who loves to draw it.

Quite recently, in a conversation about art with Mr. Fosdick, the artist, he remarked to me that those who followed our profession were legitimately and continually seeking after expression regardless of limitation. I have since thought this was a very happy truth. Perhaps, therefore, it is sufficient to account for the existence of a volume on our American flora, fully one half of which is pictures.

This is a field-book of wild flowers; it originated in the fields and it is intended to go back there, I trust, in the hand of its good reader. Of course, not all of it was written on sunny meadow and in shady wood, nor were all of its illustrations made at once from specimens gathered during various botanical rambles; but, in the truest sense of the word, nearly all of the book is a direct result of field work, ranging from New Hampshire to Virginia.

Not many years ago, my highly esteemed friend, the late William Hamilton Gibson, in the course of an address he was delivering before the Society of American Florists, said that some day he hoped to write a botany in plain English. It is unnecessary to add that if he had lived to do so, in all probability he would have contributed as much to our happiness as the father of American botany, Dr. Asa Gray. Undoubtedly he felt, as the rest of us have felt, the great need of simple, untechnical English in direct connection with botany. But there are difficulties to face in even a modest attempt to avoid bothersome technicalities. We must necessarily retain the Latin names and surrender the advantage of those direct, crisp terms which express volumes to students who understand them and nothing at all to others who do not. On the other hand, we can resort to the drawing, which often expresses more at the glance of the eye than the best turned phrase, technical or otherwise; so with plain English and the plainer drawing, one ought to be able to identify a plant without great difficulty.

To be sure, one is continually running into "snags"; it is not all plain sailing even for the botanist. Rules are all very well in their way, but unfortunately Nature abides by them only when it suits her convenience. There are hybrids and extreme forms galore; there are puzzling groups, difficult families, and differences of expert opinion; in fact there are so many problems for one to solve that the very interest in botany lies in their solution. The roses seem to be indifferently separated. The genus *Polygonum* is simple only to one who is satisfied to know about three species. The *Epilobiums* are not all easily distinguished apart. *Sisyrinchium*, that beautiful little blue-eyed grass, shows signs of complications relative to species which prove that it is not as simple as it looks. *Pentstemon* occasionally puzzles one by taking a half-way form. *Sagittaria*, the genius of the sluggish river, tries to be everything it ought not to be in leaf and flower, so Mr. J. G. Smith settles the matter by calling the forms a, b, c, d, etc. Even the dandelion and the strawberry have lost their simplicity, and now each poses as one of two very distinct species. Then there is *Lactuca* — what a puzzler! Anyone who knows *Lactuca* despairs about its leaves; a third of the way up the plant-stem they represent one species, half-way up they represent another, and at the finish the flowers take up the disagreement where the leaves leave off, and declare for a third. I have known one plant, *Lactuca Canadensis*, to look like three things all at once! When one reaches the mints, whatever trouble existed before seems child's play; here is an order of plants which was apparently created for the express purpose of convincing the amateur that he can never master botany.

INTRODUCTION.

What is particularly hard, too, is the fact that the botanists have apparently shaken the names up in a bag and sorted them out afresh.

Regarding that bugbear of the botanical student, nomenclature, it may be well to make a plain statement of the facts of the case. Neither the older system of plant arrangement according to Dr. Gray nor some of his names can remain as they have been. At present the botanists prefer the system of Engler and Prantl. It certainly shows more distinctly the character of development in plant form by placing TYPHACEÆ first and COMPOSITÆ last, not to speak of the satisfactory character of the arrangements in between. As for names, few, after all, of Dr. Gray's choosing are to be displaced. His successors are now engaged with such revision as is really necessary. Through the courtesy of Mr. Merritt L. Fernald I am able to adopt most of these names, and the extreme care with which the system they represent has been worked out inclines me to believe it will be ultimately and universally accepted.

At the present time there is no international agreement regarding nomenclature by the scientists of the new and the old world. From what I know of the so-called Rochester Code, I should say it is a disturbing influence among already agitated conditions, and its lack of consistency does not entitle it to unreserved acceptance. Perhaps its instability is more clearly attested by the two articles from Mr. Fernald's pen which appeared in the *Botanical Gazette*, vol. 31, March, 1901, and vol. 32, Nov., 1901, and by the action long since of most of our eminent botanists, who have published a signed protest against it.

In reference to the color names used in this book it would be advisable to concisely explain the principle upon which they are based. There is always one unfailing source where one may obtain color properly labeled ; that is at the color dealer's. Perhaps I must modify this statement and say *most generally* properly labeled. It is upon a purely scientific basis that the flowers are given their proper color names ; this is the list in simple form :

INTRODUCTION.

Pure yellow	Pure pink	Violet
Deep yellow	Crimson	Blue-violet
Golden yellow	Crimson-pink	Ultramarine
Pure orange	Magenta	Pure blue
Scarlet	Magenta-pink	Madder purple
Pure red	Pure purple	Madder brown

Beyond various modifications of these hues there are no color names of any value whatever in relation to the wild flower. We have in the color dealer's catalogue numerous conditions of these hues indicated by standard names : there is Naples yellow, a dilute form of golden yellow ; crimson lake, a subdued rendering of crimson ; and vermilion, which is a synonym for scarlet. These are standard colors which have never varied, and which will probably last with many others as long as painting does.

In botanical and ornithological works we find such color names as fuscous, rufous, vinaceous, ferruginous, rose-purple, greenish purple, etc.; they mean nothing at all to one who is not a scientist, and I half suspect they mean but little to one who is. Purple (botanically speaking) is a dreadfully abused term which is made to stand for half the rainbow ; it means anything from crimson to violet. As an actual fact it is fairly represented by *Mimulus ringens*, and one jot to the right or left of that hue is *not* purple. Pure yellow is perfectly represented by *Œnothera biennis*, and no tint to the right or left of that is a true yellow. Magenta is a crimson-purple ; the list of flowers which represent it is too long to give here. Blue in its pure form only exists (dilutely) in *Myosotis*. But I find that if I disturb *all* the botanists' color names I may complicate matters and add to the confusion which already exists in plant names, so I am content to let *Ranunculus* stand in plain yellow, although the color is *not* pure yellow, and it ranges through eight distinct deep or golden tones. In many other instances, also, I have refrained from making a change, although I am compelled to draw the line at rose-purple, and call it by its proper title, light magenta.

INTRODUCTION.

I have found myself indebted to many authors of botanical lists for the information I give regarding the distribution of plants, and I have had frequently to congratulate myself upon the possession of that excellent work, Brainerd, Jones, and Eggleston's *Flora of Vermont*. But it seems as though I am most indebted, for many things, to the late gifted Dr. E. Newlin Williams, who, while this book was going to press, lost his life in an excursion during a bitter cold wave in February among the White Hills we both loved so well. He would have made his mark as a botanist if he had chosen that profession, and he was more than well informed in many other departments of knowledge. Not long ago we trudged together on a botanical excursion over the slopes of Mt. Washington, and I found myself depending upon him for the identification of many an alpine species ; he knew them all at a glance, and their whole history as well. From him I received the specimen of *Belamcanda* which is drawn here, together with much information regarding the flora of eastern Pennsylvania. I had looked forward to the time when I should place this book in his hands and say, " Here is one of the results of our pleasant mountain rambles together."

I am also indebted to others for help in the writing of this volume. I soon found my " wild garden " a field of work too narrow to enable me to record all that might be recorded regarding the visitations of insects ; hence I was glad to turn to those remarkable essays on the subject by Prof. Charles Robertson which appeared in the *Botanical Gazette*. Then, too, by the courtesy of Dr. Robinson, Curator of the Gray Herbarium, practically the whole magnificent collection of valuable specimens and the splendid library have been open to me for reference.

One must always ask for the indulgence of the reader and apologize if mistakes appear, but if they do it will be in spite of great vigilance. Again, much of the descriptive text may seem somewhat bald and brief through the effort to sustain the portable character of the book ; thus the brilliant and extensive Composite family suffers for want of elbow-room. But, on the whole, I considered that we all know that family best of all, and we would be glad to give it all the room it needed on our highways, if not in our book, which must fit the narrow limits of our pocket at all hazards.

F. SCHUYLER MATHEWS.

BOSTON, MASS.,
     March, 1902.

FIELD BOOK OF AMERICAN WILD FLOWERS.

CAT-TAIL FAMILY. *Typhaceæ.*

CAT-TAIL FAMILY. *Typhaceæ.*

Perennial marsh herbs with stemless, ribbonlike leaves, and with flowers of two kinds, staminate and pistillate on the same plant, lacking petals or flower-cup. Naturally not dependent upon insects for fertilization.

Cat-tail
Typha latifolia
Yellow-brown
June–July
The light olive green leaves usually exceed the flower-stem in height. The upper half of the cylindrical flower-spike consists of the stamens, and the lower half of the pistils; the abundant, yellow, powdery pollen of the staminate flowers scattering itself over the pistillate flowers below, fertilizes them.

It is the compact down of the bractless pistillate flowers tipped with red-brown that forms the familiar cat-tail of August and September. At that time only a few lingering remnants of the staminate flowers remain on the withering tip of the stem above. The completely developed cat-tail measures fully 1 inch in diameter. In June it is important to note that the two kinds of flowers are not appreciably separated by a gap as in the next species described. The color of the staminate flowers is a variable olive yellow-brown, or brownish yellow, according to age.

Typha is the Greek *Τύφη*, meaning fen or bog, and *latifolia* refers to the broader leaf of this species. The plant is 4–8 feet high, and is common in swamps everywhere.

Narrow-leaved Cat-tail
Typha angusti-folia
Yellow-brown
June–July
The slenderer species known specifically as *angustifolia*, that is, narrow-leaved, is remarkable for the distinct and considerable separation, on the stem, of the two groups of flowers; this is usual, but not without exception. The structure of the pistillate flowers is also different from that of the same flowers on *Typha latifolia;* under a glass it will be seen that they possess a hairlike bractlet slightly swollen at the top. This cat-tail is narrow, rarely measuring over ¾ inch in diameter. The plant is 4–9 feet high, and grows, not invariably, near the coast from Me., south; it is sometimes found as far west as Mich. and Mo.; it is common

Cat-tail.
Typha latifolia.

Narrow-leaved Cat-tail.
Typha angustifolium.

in Nantucket, and along the N. J. coast, and is reported at Mt. Equinox, Vt., by Miss Mary A. Day.

BUR REED FAMILY. *Sparganiaceæ.*

Marsh herbs with flowers arranged like those of *Typha* but collected in separate spherical heads. Largely self-fertilizing, but assisted in the process by aquatic insects and flies.

Great Bur Reed
Sparganium eurycarpum
Brown-white
May-August

The deep green leaves are similar to those of the foregoing species and are about ⅝ inch wide. The downy flowers are in dense round heads scattered along the top of the stem, and like those of the cat-tails consist of the two kinds, staminate and pistillate, absolutely separated. The green fruit is a burlike sphere composed of nutlets wedge-shaped below, and flattened above with an abrupt point in the centre, so that the general appearance of its surface is not unlike that of the pineapple. The name is from σπάργανον, a band, in allusion to the ribbonlike leaves. The plant is 3–7 feet high, and is common on the borders of ponds and rivers from Me., south to Va., and west.

Smaller Bur Reed
Sparganium simplex
Brown-white
June-August

This is a much smaller species with narrower leaves, and a simple stem and row of flower-heads. The green fruit is about ¾ inch in diameter, with a decidedly burlike appearance, the nutlets tapering to a point at either end, and the upper point being *much* longer than that of the fruit in the preceding species. The plant is 1–2 feet high, and is generally in the water, erect or sometimes afloat; it is found from Me. to N. J., and west to Minn.

Branching Bur Reed
Sparganium androcladum
Brown-white
June-August

This familiar variety, which is common in all bogs, is larger than the foregoing in many respects, and it is distinguished for its branching and somewhat angular flower-stem; the latter grows out at the point where the leaf is joined with the plant-stem. The plant is 1–2 feet high, and is distributed from Me., south, and west to Minn. The sparganiums are all peculiarly decorative plants.

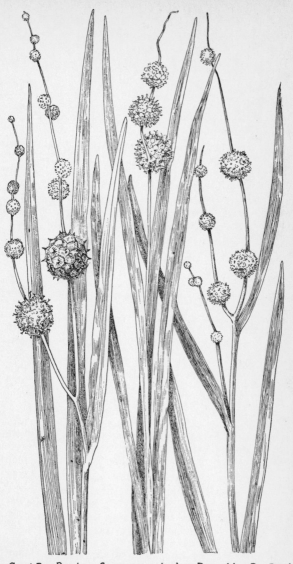

Great Bur Reed.   Sparganium simplex. Branching Bur Reed.
Sparganium eurycarpum.   Sparganium androcladum.

WATER PLANTAIN FAMILY. *Alismaceæ.*

Marsh herbs with long-stemmed leaves, and flowers of three orders, thus :

1. With stamens and pistil, 2. Staminate and pistillate growing on one plant, 3. Staminate and pistillate growing on different plants. The flowers have three conspicuous petals and generally six stamens ; they are visited by numerous insects which undoubtedly assist in the process of fertilization.

Water Plantain
Alisma Plantago
White or pale pink
July–September

The leaves, all from the root, are olive green, strongly veined, and elliptical but very variable in shape, broader or longer, and sometimes heart-shaped at the base. The flower-stem is tall and symmetrically branched, displaying the three-petaled, very small white or rarely delicate pink flowers to great advantage. The flowers are perfect, with six stamens and a pistil ; they are possibly self-fertilized, but more probably cross-fertilized by the beelike drone-flies (*Syrphidæ*), all pollen-eaters and honey-drinkers. The plant is 1–3 feet high, and is found in the shallow water of ponds and sluggish streams everywhere. The name, which is of uncertain Greek origin, is supposed to refer to the occurrence of the species in salt marshes.

Arrowhead
Sagittaria variabilis
White
July–September

This genus is remarkable for its manifold variations ; hence it is called *variabilis*. *Sagittaria* is derived from the Latin *sagitta*, an arrow, referring to the shape of the leaves. There are fourteen native species recorded by Britton and Brown, and over twenty by Jared G. Smith, while Gray recognizes but seven. However, until botanists arrive at a united opinion regarding this group, it will be a safe and therefore preferable course to accept the fewer species recognized by Gray. It is an unreliable method of procedure to rely upon leaf character for the foundation of a species, and unfortunately this has a great deal to do with the separation of *Sagittaria* into many species or groups. The particular species called *variabilis*

6

Water Plantain.　　　　Alisma Plantago.

shows, according to Gray, four variations as follows: var. *obtusa* (*S. latifolia*, Form a, of J. G. Smith) has flowers mostly of the third order above described, and broad, blunt-pointed leaves: var. *latifolia* (*S. latifolia* proper of J. G. Smith) has the second, or imperfectly the third order of flowers above described, and varying broad or narrow, acute leaves : var. *angustifolia* (*S. latifolia*, Form d, of J. G. Smith) has flowers of the second order, and leaves with narrow, divergent lobes ; found in mountain districts : var. *diversifolia* (*S. latifolia*, Form e, of J. G. Smith) has flowers of the second order, and lance-shaped or broader leaves, variably arrow-pointed. These are mere *forms*, not varieties.

Sagittaria vari-abilis **var.** *pu-bescens*   A well established type with very broad blunt leaves, is pubescent, or woolly-coated, especially the flower-stem. This is the *S. latifolia pubescens* of J. G. Smith. It is found from Me., south, usually east of the Alleghanies.

Sagittaria En-gelmanniana **J. G. Smith**   This is also a well established type, the flowers of which are scarcely 1 inch across, and the leaves remarkably narrow and linear. The fruit is a narrow wedge-shaped nutlet tipped with a small erect beak. Somewhat rare. Mass., N. Y., N. J., south. The leaves of the arrowhead are shiny dark green, and the three-petaled flowers are pure white relieved by the charming bit of golden yellow contributed by the large anthers. The flowers grow in clusters of three, the staminate ones above, and the pistillate below. The pollen is distributed by a variety of agents, not least of which are the insects which frequent wet places, among them the beautiful glassy-winged dragon-fly. The tendency of some of the types to develop only staminate flowers on one plant and pistillate on another, suggests the probability that *Sagittaria* is beginning to rely entirely upon insects for fertilization. Remarkably decorative in every part of its structure, the arrowhead like the cat-tail is a great favorite among artists. Common everywhere. The three forms *angustifolia, latifolia* (2nd order), and *obtusa* (3rd order), are reported in Neb. by H. J. Webber.

Narrow-leaved   Arrowhead.
Sagittaria variabilis var. angustifolia. of Asa Gray.
or Sagittaria latifolia form d. of J. G. Smith.

ARUM FAMILY. *Araceæ.*

ARUM FAMILY. *Araceæ.*

Perennial herbs possessing a sharp, peppery juice, and with sometimes perfect, but generally only two orders of flowers ; i. e., 1. Staminate and pistillate on the same plant, 2. Staminate and pistillate on different plants. The flowers crowded on a club or spadix enclosed within a hood or spathe. Fertilization assisted by insects.

Indian Turnip or Jack-in-the-pulpit
Arisæma triphyllum
Purple-brown and green
April–July

Generally with two long-stemmed, tri-parted dull green leaves without a gloss, which overshadow the hooded flower below at the junction of the leaf-stems. The flowers, on the clublike spadix within the hood, are grouped at the base of the spadix and are generally staminate and pistillate on separate plants, that is to say, the stamens are abortive on one plant and the pistils are abortive on another ; thus small insects (the gnat of the genus *Mycetophila* especially) are a means of fertilization, and frequently they may be found imprisoned in close quarters between the bases of spathe and spadix. It is possibly developing a dependence upon insects for fertilization ; but often one plant develops both staminate and pistillate flowers. The novel and beautiful green and purple-brown striped spathe is variable in depth of color ; exposed to sunlight it is usually quite pale, while in the dark woods it is exceedingly purple ; as a rule the plant prefers the shaded, wet woods. The handsome clustering berrylike fruit is at first green and finally, in late August, brilliant scarlet. The plant attains a height of 1–2½ feet. It is common in the woods in wet situations, everywhere. The exceedingly peppery bulb becomes edible after boiling.

Green Dragon, Dragon-root, or Dragon Arum
Arisæma Dracontium
Dull white-green
May–June.

This species generally has a single compound leaf with seven or more obovate-lance-shaped, pointed, dull green leaflets. The long spadix is usually composed of both staminate and pistillate flowers, and it tapers to a slender point, reaching far beyond the rolled-up, greenish, pointed spathe. The berries are red-orange. The

Dragon Arum.
Arisæma Dracontium.

Jack-in-the-pulpit.
Arisæma triphyllum.

ARUM FAMILY. *Araceæ.*

plant is 1–3 feet high, and grows in wet woods or low grounds from Me., south, and west to Minn.

Arrow Arum
*Peltandra
undulata*
Green
May–June
The rich green leaves are arrow-shaped with one prominent vein or nerve. The flowers are staminate and pistillate on the same plant, covering the long tapering spadix ; the pointed green spathe, rolling and wavy on the margin, is 4–7 inches long. The cluster of berries is green, and is at first enclosed in a green sheath, the fleshy base of the spathe. The plant grows 1–1½ feet high, in shallow water, from Me. south, and west to Mich. It derives its name from πέλτη, a target or shield, and ὑνηρ, stamen, from the targetlike form of the latter.

Water Arum
Calla palustris
White
June
A little swamp flower resembling the so-called calla-lily ; the latter is, of course, not a lily, and, curiously enough, not a true calla, it is a *Richardia.* The deep green leaves of the water arum are long-heart-shaped with long stems. The open and rolling edged spathe is white above and greenish beneath. The yellow spadix is entirely covered with flowers, the lower ones perfect, i. e., with all the parts complete, and the upper ones *often* staminate. Fertilization is assisted by insects and pond-snails. The berries, red and distinct, in a head like those of the Jack-in-the-pulpit, are ripe in August. The plant grows 5–10 inches high and is at home in cold bogs, from Me., south to Va., and west to Minn. The name *Calla* is ancient and obscure, *palustris* is the Latin name for swamp.

Arrow Arum.
Peltandra undulata.

Water Arum.
Calla palustris.

Skunk Cabbage
Symplocarpus
fœtidus
Dark purple-red and green
March–April

A single species, of the earliest appearance in spring, having a fetid odor, which attracts numerous insects, and a closely coiled purple-red streaked and blotched, green, leathery spathe which entraps them to their death. The stout spadix is compactly set with perfect lavender-flesh-colored flowers, i. e., flowers with stamens and pistil. The conspicuous anthers are a grayish straw-color. The fruit is the enlarged and fleshy spadix enclosing round bulletlike seeds immediately beneath its surface which ripen in September. The name is from συμπλοκή, connection, and καρπός, fruit, alluding to the connection of the ovaries forming compound fruit. The color of the shellike spathe is not without æsthetic interest ; the madder purple, green, and yellow-green are blended and streaked with a peculiar charm ; inside, the red is darkest. The leaves will at first be found in a compactly coiled, pointed spike close beside the ruddy spathe. Later when the coarse 1–2 feet long, cabbagelike leaves are unfolded the origin of the common name becomes evident. The odor of the flower is *imitative* of decaying flesh, but it is not wholly bad, it reminds one of the smell of a mustard plaster, and raw onions ; the cut stem *decidedly* suggests the latter. The plant is found in swamps, beside brooks, and in wet glades. Common from Me., south to Ga., and west to Iowa and Minn. Found at Clarendon Hills, Mass.

Skunk Cabbage.   Symplocarpus fœtidus.

ARUM FAMILY. *Araceæ.*

Golden Club
Orontium
aquaticum
Golden yellow
April-May

A single species, perennial and aquatic, whose prominent golden yellow spadix (the club) scarcely larger around than its long, snaky stem, is thickly clustered with the completely developed flowers of generally six sepals, as many golden stamens, and a pistil. The spathe is undeveloped and removed from the spadix, appearing like a mere leaflet on the flower-stem. Fruit green and bladderlike. The long-stemmed, oblong, dark green leaves float upon the water. It is a beautiful aquatic plant whose flowers deserve close examination under the glass, 1–2 feet high, common in the shallows of ponds, from Mass., south, and generally found near the coast. Name from the Syrian river Orontes.

Calamus or
Sweet Flag
Acorus
Calamus
Yellow-green
June-July

The stiff, swordlike, light green leaves give the plant a rigid character. It has inconspicuous flowers compactly covering a tapering cylindrical spadix which grows angularly from the side of a two-edged stem resembling the flat ribbonlike leaves. The individual flower has a pistil, six stamens, and as many sepals of a dull yellow-green color. The fruit is a small berry, at first gelatinous and finally dry, but the plant is mostly propagated by its stocky roots. Name, "Ἄκορας of unknown meaning, from Pliny. The horizontal, pungent, and pleasantly aromatic rootstalk is a familiar commodity of the apothecary. There is a striped-leaved variety. The plant grows 1–4 feet high, or more, and is found beside small streams and in wet ground, from Me., south, and west to Minn., Iowa, and Kan.

Golden Club.
Orontium aquaticum.

Sweet Flag.
Acorus Calamus.

YELLOW-EYED GRASS FAMILY. *Xyridaceæ.*

YELLOW-EYED GRASS FAMILY. *Xyridaceœ.*

Perennial herbs with narrow, grasslike leaves, and perfect, regular flowers, with three spreading lobes and a slender tube. Fertilized largely by insects.

Yellow-eyed Grass
Xyris flexuosa
Yellow
July–August

A little swamp plant with grasslike, or rather slender rushlike, light green leaves which twist as they grow old, and flowers about ⅓ inch across, of three yellow petal-like divisions, three stamens, and as many sepals, the flowers proceeding from a conelike head composed of light green leafy scales. The fruit is an oblong many-seeded capsule. The name is from Ξυρίς an unknown Greek plant with two-edged leaves. The plant grows 6–16 inches high, in sandy bogs or morasses, from Me. to Minn., and south to Ga. and Tex. There is a mountain variety barely 1 foot high, with very slender leaves, which rarely twist, known as var. *pusilla*. It is found in bogs from the White Mts., south to the Pocono Mts. of Penn., and in N. J. It blooms in the same season.

Carolina Yellow-eyed Grass
Xyris Caroliniana
Yellow
June–August

A tall species, with a slender flower-stem, and leaves reaching nearly an inch in width. The conelike head also longer and measuring nearly ⅔ inch. It grows 1–2 feet high, and is found in swamps near the coast from Mass., south to Fla. and La.

SPIDERWORT FAMILY. *Commelinaceœ.*

Herbs with jointed and often leafy branching stems, the leaves sheathed at the base, and generally perfect flowers, i. e., flowers with stamens and pistil. Cross-fertilization assisted by insects.

Day Flower
Commelina hirtella
Light violet-blue
August–September

The grass green leaves are lance-shaped, and brown-sheathed at their junction with the plant-stem; the sheath is hairy-edged. The flowers are three-parted and irregular, that is, unequal in size, form, and structural parts; for instance, two of the blue petals are larger than the third. The leaf

Yellow-eyed Grass.
Xyris Caroliniana.   Xyris flexuosa.

SPIDERWORT FAMILY.   *Commelinaceæ.*

immediately below the flowers is heart-shaped, and clasping, forming a hollow from which the flower-stem proceeds. The flowers expand only in the morning. The plant is erect, stout-stemmed, and grows 2–3 feet high. It is named for the early Dutch botanist Kaspar Commelin. Fond of damp and shady, but warm places, it distributes itself along river banks and streams from southern N. J., south, and west to Mo.

Virginia Day Flower
Commelina Virginica
Light violet-blue
June–September

This is a much commoner species in the northeastern section of the country, and it differs from the foregoing species in the following particulars. The leaves and stem are slenderer, the stem taller, but branching and reclining, frequently taking root at the joints, and the whole plant is frequently slightly rough to the touch. The third petal is also particularly inconspicuous and abortive. The plant grows 1½–3 feet high, and is found on river banks or wet shaded places, from southern N. Y., south, and west to Neb. and Tex.

Spiderwort
Tradescantia Virginica
Light violet-blue
May–August

This species has mucilaginous, upright stems, with light green, narrow, and linear leaves. The flowers are regular with three purplish ultramarine blue petals which richly relieve the golden anthers within; the latter are widely removed from the prominent stigma. It is unquestionably cross-fertilized by the earlier queen bumblebees *Bombus pennsylvanicus* and *B. separatus*, who are attracted by the plentiful pollen, and evidently come in contact with the exposed stigma before stumbling among the yellow anthers. It is also a familiar, old-fashioned garden flower, common beside the farm-houses of the north. It is named for John Tradescant, gardener to Charles I. of England. It grows 1–1½ feet high, usually in rich or moist ground, from Me., south, and west to the Rocky Mts. There are variable forms of this species, as well as another slenderer southern species with smaller *pink* flowers, 6–12 inches high, named *Tradescantia rosea*. It is distributed from Md., south, and west to Mo. There are garden varieties of *Tradescantia* also white and purple.

Virginia Day Flower.   Spiderwort.
Commelina Virginica.   Tradescantia Virginica.

PICKEREL WEED FAMILY. *Pontederiaceæ.*

PICKEREL WEED FAMILY. *Pontederiaceæ.*

Aquatic herbs with perfect (i. e. having stamens and pistil), more or less irregular flowers issuing from a spathe or leaflike envelop, which are mostly fertilized by insects.

Pickerel Weed
Pontederia cordata
Light violet-blue
June–September

A tall plant with one blunt arrowhead-shaped, dark green, thick leaf, varying to a very elongated triangle shape, and a showy flower-spike about 4 inches long, crowded with ephemeral, violet-blue flowers which are marked with a distinct yellow-green spot. Immediately below the spike is the small spathe. Sometimes the flowers are white. The flower-cup is funnel-formed and six-divided, the upper three divisions united, and the three lower ones spread apart. The six stamens are three of them long and protruding, and three short which are often abortive ; the blue anthers are so placed that it is impossible for an insect to enter the flower-cup without brushing against them and detaching the pollen. The fruit is a bladderlike receptacle containing one seed. The plant is named for Giulio Pontedera, a professor of botany at Padua about 1730. Pickerel weed grows 1–3 feet high, and is commonly found in the shallows of ponds and sluggish streams, sometimes associated with the arrowhead. The deer in the Adirondack region frequent the lake shores to feed upon it.

Mud Plantain
Heteranthera
reniformis
White or bluish
July–August

A small water plant with deep green, floating, round-kidney-shaped leaves on long stems, and 2–5 white or pale blue perfectly developed flowers, which, like those of the preceding species, are exceedingly short-lived. The tiny flowers proceed from a spathe or leafy enclosure projecting from the sheathed side of a leaf-stem. The flower-cup shows six nearly equal divisions spread above its slender tube. The plant is named for its unlike anthers, ἑτέρα different, and ἀνθηρά anther ; the specific *reniformis* means kidney-formed, in allusion to the shape of the leaf. It grows about 12 inches high, in mud or shallow water, from Conn. to N. J., and west to Kan., Neb., and La.

Pickerel Weed.   Mud Plantain.
Pontederia cordata. Heteranthera reniformis.

LILY FAMILY. *Liliaceæ.*

Mostly perennial herbs with a flower-cup of generally six parts remarkable for its simplicity and beauty. Flowers with six stamens each of which stands before one of the divisions. In the case of *Allium* the flowers spring from a spathe or leafy inclosure, like the flowers of most of the species already described.

Carrion Flower
Smilax herbacea
Green-yellow
May–July

The light green veiny-corrugated leaves are mostly round-ovate and heart-shaped at the base, pointed at the tip, and devoid of gloss, their stems greatly varying in length, measuring $\frac{1}{3}$–3 inches; with a tendril at either side. The long flower-stem, proceeding from between the tendrils, is topped by a hemispherical flower-cluster with spokelike stemlets. The greenish-yellow flowers are insignificant and putrid-odored; they are staminate and pistillate on separate plants, thus showing their dependence upon insects for fertilization, particularly upon those flies which are attracted by carrion. The cluster of berries is first green and finally blue-black with a bloom. It is, indeed, a beautiful and decorative vine, most unfortunate in the repellent odor of its flowers at the time of bloom. It is very variable, grows to a length of 4–15 feet, and frequents river banks and thickets. Common from the coast west to Dak. and Neb.

Green Brier
Smilax rotundifolia
Light green
May–June

The slightly zigzag stem and branches, the latter more or less squarish, are covered with scattered prickles, and the broadly ovate, short-stemmed, light green leaves are 2–3 inches long and pointed. The leaf-stalk is bent upward at a right angle; in the angle are the slender tendrils. The flower-stalk bears fewer flowers than that of the preceding species. The berries are blue-black. It is common in most thickets, and closely connects with a western form, var. *quadrangularis*, the branches of which are quite perceptibly square. Common from the coast west to Minn. and Tex. It is a familiar vine on Long Island, N. Y., and at North Easton, Mass., but it is not found in the mountain region of N. H.

Carrion Flower.
Smilax herbacea.

Green Brier.
Smilax rotundifolia.

LILY FAMILY. *Liliaceæ.*

Clintonia
*Clintonia
borealis*
**Cream-color,
greenish
June-early
July**

A handsome woodland plant with from two to four (usually three) shiny, light green, large oval-oblong leaves ; a slender flower-stalk, about 7 inches high, bears from three to six cream-colored drooping flowers greenish on the outside. The flower is formed of six distinct sepals, and is perfect, having six stamens and a pistil ; its form is lilylike and dainty. It was named for DeWitt Clinton, once governor of New York. It unfortunately lacks odor and color to make it perfectly attractive, but it is not without a subtle and delicate grace. The berries, which are ripe about the middle of August, turn a beautiful pure blue, a color devoid of any purplish tinge, and therefore one which is rare and remarkable in nature. Prussian blue mixed with a little white will exactly match the unique color of the Clintonia berry. The plant grows 6–16 inches high, and is common in the northern woods, especially where they are cold and moist. Me., south to N. C., and west to Minn.

*Clintonia
umbellata*
**White, spotted
May-June**

A far less common species, with a woolly flower-stem, and flowers half the size of those of the foregoing species, borne in a thick cluster. The flowers are also very different in color ; they are mostly 'white speckled with madder purple, and possess a sweet odor. The berries are globular and black. Height 8–22 inches. Rich woods of the Alleghanies from N. Y. to Ga. ; not in New Eng.

Clintonia borealis.

LILY FAMILY. *Liliaceæ.*

Twisted Stalk
Streptopus amplexifolius
Greenish white
May-July
The leaves, strongly clasping the zigzag stem, are smooth and light green, with a whitish bloom beneath. The curly-sepaled, greenish flower is about ½ inch wide, and hangs by a long, crooked, threadlike stem from beneath the leaves. The flower is perfect and regular, with six lance-shaped sepals, and is either solitary or (rarely) in pairs. The name is from the Greek, for *twisted*, and *stalk* or *foot*. The usually solitary berry is red, round, and nearly ½ inch in diameter. 2–3 feet high. Cold moist woods. Me., west to the Rockies, and south to N. C., in the mountains.

Streptopus roseus
Dull purple-pink
May–early July
Differs from the preceding in its dull purple-pink flower, its leaves which are not whitened with a bloom beneath, but are altogether green and finely hairy at the edge, and its earlier period of bloom. 1–2½ feet high. In the same situations, but extending farther south to Ga., and west to Ore.

The genus *Streptopus* is dependent in part upon insects for cross-fertilization. Some of the most frequent visitors are the bumblebees, the beelike flies *Bombylius*, and the bees of the genus *Andrenidæ*, still, their effect upon the flower is mere probability. It takes much time and attention to make sure of the *results* of such insect visitations. Certainly the delicate green-white coloring of one species and the magenta of the other directly indicate the adaptation of the flowers to insect visitors.

Twisted Stalk.   Streptopus roseus.

LILY FÁMILY. *Liliaceæ.*

Asparagus
Asparagus officinalis
Green-yellow
June

This beautiful perennial, so well known as a vegetable, is not quite as familiar to us in its æsthetic dress. Its leaves (or properly, its branchlets), are threadlike; and it assumes a bushy, almost larchlike figure as it grows older, and becomes decorated with round, scarlet berries. The tiny green-yellow flowers are six-parted, and rather inconspicuous. The name is ancient. Adventive from the old country, and a frequent escape from kitchen gardens everywhere. It is a favorite among the farmers' wives who use it decoratively in their homes; certainly it is not less decorative than the florist's famous *Asparagus plumosus.*

False Spike-nard
Smilacina racemosa
White
May

A really beautiful woodland plant slightly resembling Solomon's Seal, but bearing its Spiræalike cluster of fine white flowers at the tip of the stem. The light blue-green leaves are oblong and ovate-lance-shaped, taper-pointed, and with very short stems—hardly any, in fact. The tiny flower has six distinct white sepals, and is perfect, with six stamens and a pistil. The flower cluster is pyramidal, and the zigzag plant-stem gracefully inclines. The berries, smaller than peas, are at first greenish then yellowish white speckled with madder brown, and finally, in late September, a dull ruby-red of translucent character. They possess an aromatic taste. A familiar plant of the White Mt. region The name is a diminutive of Smilax, without appropriate application. Common in moist copses and beside woodland roads. 1–3 feet high. Me., south to S. C. and west to Minn. and Ark.

False Spikenard. Smilacina racemosa.

LILY FAMILY. *Liliaceæ.*

False Solomon's Seal
Smilacina stellata
White
May–early June

A much smaller species than the foregoing, with a very small but pretty starry cluster of white flowers at the tip of the stem. The leaves, light blue-green and very firm, clasp the zigzag stem. The flower is ¼ inch wide. The berries, which are few, are at first spotted and finally dull ruby-red. 8–16 inches high. Moist banks and meadows. Me., south to N. J., and west.

Three-leaved False Solomon's Seal
Smilacina trifolia
White
May–early June

A still smaller species, with generally three leaves, but sometimes two or even four, tapering to a sheathing base ; flowers smaller than those of the preceding species, and the berries red like those of the next species. 2–6 inches high. In bogs or wet woods. Me., south to Penn., west to Mich.

Although the resemblance of *Smilacina trifolia* to *Maianthemum Canadense* (the next species described) is close, the differences are easily detected by a close observer. The (usually) three leaves of *Smilacina trifolia* clasp the stem but are in no way heart-shaped at the base. This species also has *six* sepals and as many stamens, and the whole plant is invariably smooth, not fine-hairy as is *sometimes* the case with the next species. The berries of *Smilacina* and *Maianthemum* are closely similar, but those of *Smilacina stellata* are in a measure harder, more opaque than any of the others, and certainly *not* blackish, as described in Gray's Manual, 6th Edition, but dull red.

False Solomon's Seal.
Smilacina stellata.

Smilacina trifolia.

LILY FAMILY. *Liliaceæ.*

☙

Canada Mayflower
Maianthemum Canadense
White
May–June

A tiny woodland plant resembling *Smilacina trifolia*, with small white flowers which differ from those of the genus *Smilacina* in having only four sepals and as many stamens. It has two to three light green, shiny leaves which are ovate-lance-shaped or broader, with a somewhat heart-shaped base. The berries are yellow-white, spotted with madder brown, until early fall when they turn a dull translucent ruby-red.

A familiar plant in the woods of the White Mts. ; generally in moist places. 3–6 inches high. The name is from *Maius*, May, and ἄνθεμον, flower. Me., west to Minn. and Iowa, south to N. Car.

Lily of the Valley
Convallaria majalis
White
May–early June

This is the only one true species, familiar in cultivation. It has two oblong leaves, shiny and smooth, and a slender stalk bearing a one-sided row of tiny white flowers, extremely sweet-scented and dainty. Flower-cup bell-shaped, with six lobes recurved, and six stamens. It is apparently cross-fertilized by bees who collect the *pollen*, as there is little or no honey at the base of the bell ; in the absence of insects it is self-fertilized (Hildebrand). Berry red. The name is from the Latin *convallis*, valley, and the Greek for lily. Identical with the European flower of the gardens, it also grows on the higher Alleghanies, from Va. to S. Car.

☙

Canada Mayflower.
Maianthemum Canadense.

Lily of the Valley.
Convallaria majalis.

LILY FAMILY. *Liliaceæ.*

The pendulous position of the flowers of this genus, is in a great measure protective; the wind and weather can not injure or uselessly scatter the pollen. The flowers, moreover, have short styles and long anthers, and are unquestionably cross-fertilized by the larger bees; the bumblebees *Bombus vagans*, and *Bombus pennsylvanicus* are common visitors, together with innumerable small insects.

Solomon's Seal
Polygonatum biflorum
Pale green
April–June

The oblong-ovate, light green leaves smooth or finely hairy and paler beneath, arranged alternately either side of the slender, smooth stem; the cylindrical and tassellike perfect flowers (each having six stamens) depend in clusters of two, rarely three, below them. An extremely pretty and graceful plant when under cultivation. The fruit, at first a green berry with a whitish bloom, at last becomes blue-black and resembles a small Concord grape; it imparts an additionally decorative appearance to the plant. 1–3 feet high. Common in thickets beside woodlands, and on hillsides. Me., south, and west to E. Kan., Neb., and Tex.

Great Solomon's Seal
Polygonatum giganteum
Pale Green
May–early July

The plant is taller and smooth, *without* the fine hairiness. Leaves ovate, pointed, and partly clasping the plant-stem, 3–8 inches long, and many-ribbed. Flowers in clusters of from two to eight. Stem stout and round. 2–8 feet high. Meadows and river banks. Me., south to Va., and west to the Rocky Mts.

Solomon's Seal.   Polygonatum biflorum.

LILY FAMILY. *Liliaceæ.*

Bellwort
Uvularia per-foliata
Pale corn yellow
May–June

A graceful woodland plant, smooth throughout, with a forking stem (one to three leaves below the fork), the deep green ovate-lance-shaped leaves appearing as if perforated by it. The delicately fragrant flower-cup, granular-rough inside, is attenuated but lilylike, with six distinct pale corn yellow sepals. Flowers perfect, with six short stamens and a pistil. Sepals with a deep honey-bearing groove within ridged on either edge.

Seed pod a three-parted capsule, appearing as if chopped off at the end, and in this respect entirely different from that of the *Oakesia* following. Name from *uvula*, palate, referring to the way the flower hangs. It grows 6–18 inches high, in rich woods, from Me. to the Dakotas, and south.

Large-flowered Bellwort
Uvularia gran-diflora
Pale corn yellow
April–June

This is the commoner bellwort from western New Eng., west and south. The deep green leaves are fine-white-hairy beneath ; the large pale, corn yellow flower, inclining to green, at the summit, is fully 1½ inches long, and *smooth* inside. Stem with a single leaf or none below the fork. A more limited distribution, south to Ga. and west to Minn., Iowa, and S. Dak.

Oakesia
Oakesia sessili-folia
Corn or cream yellow
May–June

Similar in some respects to the foregoing genus, but with marked differences. Stem angled. The deep green leaves, fine-hairy beneath, conspicuously three-grooved, sharp-pointed, and stemless, or slightly clasping. The six divisions of the flower less pointed, no ridges within the flower-cup, the latter more buffish cream-colored, but still near corn yellow. The seed capsule three-sided, resembling a beech nut. The one or two flowers on slender stems, at first terminating the plant stem, but finally appearing opposite the leaves by reason of the growth of the branches. Named for William Oakes, an early botanist of New England.

Stem 6–13 inches high. It is very common in the north woods. Me., south to Ga., and west to Minn. and

Large-flowered Bellwort.   Oakesia
Uvularia grandiflora.   sessilifolia

LILY FAMILY. *Liliaceæ.*

Ark. *Uvularia* and *Oakesia* are both slender drooping-leaved plants, early in the season at the time of bloom; later they expand to a broader figure.

Stemless Trillium, or Wake-robin
Trillium sessile
Dull magenta-red
April–May

The trilliums are handsome woodland plants with stout stems, ruddy purple at the base; their perfect flowers have three green sepals which remain until the plant withers, three petals much larger, and six stamens. *T. sessile* has stemless, slightly fragrant flowers with narrow petals and sepals, the former rather erect and spreading, dull magenta-red, varying to a greenish tone. Leaves stemless, somewhat four-sided but ovate, and often blotched with lighter and darker green. Red berry spherical or nearly so, ½ inch deep. The name is from *triplum*, triple, a characteristic of all parts of the plant. 5–10 inches high. Moist woods. Penn., south, and west to Minn. and Ark.

Trillium recurvatum

Differs from the preceding in the following particulars. The leaves are narrowed at the base into a stem, and the flower has reflexed sepals, and pointed petals narrowed at the base. 6–16 inches high. Rich woods. Ohio and west.

Wake-robin, or Birthroot
Trillium erectum
Maroon, or white, etc.
April–June

A very common eastern species, with four-sided ovate leaves scarcely stemmed, and abruptly pointed, and flowers, with a reclining stem, varying in color from white to pink, brownish purple-red or maroon, with flat, ovate, spreading petals nearly 1½ inches long, the sepals a trifle shorter. Sometimes the flower is dull pink, of a brownish purple tone, and rarely it is greenish. It is ill-scented, and as a consequence attracts the carrion-loving green fly (*Lucilia carnicina*), commonly called the flesh-fly, who finds the raw-meat color of the flower as acceptable as the odor. According to Clarence M. Weed this fly is the most useful pollen disseminator of *Trillium erectum*. Berry darker red, round-ovate. 7–15 inches high. Rich woods, New Eng. to N. C., west to Minn. and Mo.

Wake Robin.
Trillium erectum.

Berry of
T. undulatum

Painted Trillium.
Trillium undulatum.

LILY FAMILY. *Liliaceæ.*

❦

Large Flowering Trillium
Trillium grandiflorum
White
May–June

A handsome, large-flowered species flowering later, and cultivated by the florists. The waxy-white petals 1½–2 inches long, larger than the sepals, curve gracefully backward, and, as they grow older, turn pink. 10–18 inches high. The red berry fully 1 inch long. Rich woods. Vt. to N. C., west to Minn. and Mo.

Nodding Trillium
Trillium cernuum
White
April–June

Leaves almost stemless and broadly four-sided ovate. Flower with white or pinkish wavy petals ¾ inch long, and with a short stem recurved so that the blossom is often hidden beneath the leaves. 8–14 inches high. Moist woods. New Eng. to Minn., south to Ga. and Mo.

Dwarf White Trillium
Trillium nivale
White
March–May

A very small species with ovate leaves, 1–2 inches long, and flowers whose white petals, less than 1 inch long, are scarcely wavy. Berry red, about ⅓ inch in diameter, flattened and spherical, with three rounded divisions. A dwarf plant 2–5 inches high. Rich woods. Pa. and Ky. to Minn. and Iowa.

Painted Trillium
Trillium undulatum
White, crimson-striped
May–June

One of the most beautiful of the genus, and very common in the rich woodlands of the north. Leaves ovate and tapering to a sharp point. Green sepals quite narrow, and the gracefully recurved, wavy-edged white petals strongly marked with a crimson V deep or pale, as the case may be ; it is never *purple*. The dark scarlet ovate berry ¾ inch long, ripe in September, and falling at a touch. 8–16 inches high. Cold damp woods and beside woodland brooks. New Eng. to Ga., west to Minn. and Mo.

❦

Nodding Trillium.
Trillium cernuum

Dwarf White Trillium.
Trillium nivale.

LILY FAMILY. *Liliaceæ.*

**Indian
Cucumber**
Medeola Virginica
**Green and
terra-cotta
May–June**

The only species, the thin, circling, long-ovate, light green leaves of which are arranged around the middle, and the three ovate ones around the top of the thin stem. The inconspicuous nodding, but perfect flower is $\frac{2}{3}$ inch wide, green, and accented by the reddish terra-cotta color of the six stamens, and the three long, recurved terra-cotta brown stigmas, i. e., the three divisions of the tip of the pistil ; the three petals and three sepals are also recurved.   In September about two or three purple-black berries replace the flowers at the apex of the plant. Named for the sorceress Medea on account of its sup-posed medicinal virtue.   The common name alludes to the succulent, horizontal, white tuberous root which tastes like cucumber, and was in all probability relished by the Indians.   1–3 feet high.   Rich damp woods.   Me., west to Minn., and south.

Medeola Virginica is a characteristic woodland plant, common in the White Mountain woods.   It is adapted to subdued sunlight, and is interesting in both flower and fruit.   The blossoms, often beneath the three upper leaves, are thus protected from the dripping of the trees in wet weather ; their colors are æsthetic.   Crawling insects cannot easily mount the (at first) woolly stem and rob the flower of its pollen, flying insects readily find the blossom, and in September the three crowning leaf-lets beneath the berries are stained with dull crimson, the color attracting birds to the fruit.   It is therefore evident that the plant depends in some measure upon visitors.

Indian Cucumber.   Medeola Virginica.

LILY FAMILY. *Liliaceæ.*

Blazing Star, or Devil's Bit
Chamælirium Carolinianum
White
June-July

The stem bearing light green, flat, lance-shaped (blunt) leaves at the base with several shorter, narrower ones farther up, and terminated by a feathery spike 4–10 inches long of small, fragrant flowers, white with a tinting of the yellow stamens characterizing the staminate, and in conspicuous white the pistillate ones. It is quite dependent upon insects for cross-fertilization, the staminate flowers growing on one plant and pistillate on another; the flower-cup has six narrow, spreading white sepals. The pistillate plant is more leafy. Fruit an oblong capsule. The name, which was first applied to a half-grown, low specimen, is from χαμαί, on the ground, and λείριον, lily. The wandlike stem is 1–4 feet high. Low grounds and swamps, from Mass. to Ga., west to Neb. and Ark.

Bunch Flower
Melanthium Virginicum
Cream yellow, turning brown
June-August

The lowest leaves nearly 1 inch wide, the few upper ones small, and linear or grass-shaped. Flowers polygamous, i. e., staminate, pistillate, and perfect on the same plant. It does not, therefore, rely fully upon insects for fertilization. Flower-cup of six separate, greenish cream yellow sepals turning brown with age. Fruit, an ovoid-conical capsule, three-lobed. The name is from μέλας, black, and ἄνθος, flower, in allusion to the dark color which the flower assumes upon withering. The leafy, slender stem is 3–5 feet high. It grows in wet woods and meadows, from Conn., south to S. Car., west to Minn. and Tex.

Indian Poke or American White Hellebore
Veratrum viride
Dull yellow-green
May-June

A leafy perennial herb with very poisonous coarse roots, remarkable in the early stage of its development for its beautiful pure yellow-green color, which becomes darker and dull within four weeks, and finally withers to an unsightly brown before the summer is in its prime. The broad ovate, clasping leaves are scored with numerous ribs, and crinkled in parallel lines. The uninteresting large flower-spike is dull yellow-green turn-

Devil's Bit.   Chamælirium Carolinianum.

ing brownish with age; the flowers, like those of the preceding genus, are polygamous, but small, with six green sepals. Capsule also like that of *Melanthium.* Name from *vere*, truly, and *ater*, dead black, in allusion to the blackening (really turning brown) of the plant upon withering. The plant is poisonous in all parts for sheep and cattle. It grows 2–7 feet high, in wet meadows and low grounds, everywhere.

Stout
Stenanthium
Stenanthium
robustum
White or green
July–August

Stem leafy, stout and erect, with grasslike leaves. Flower-spike sometimes 2 feet long; the flowers are also polygamous. Flower-cup whitish green or white with six narrow spreading lance-shaped sepals, ⅓ inch long. Leaves grasslike. Fruit capsule pointed long-ovate. The name is from σrενόs, narrow, and ἄνθos, flower, alluding to the slender sepals and flower-cluster. 3–5 feet high. Penn. to S. C., west to Ohio and Tenn.

The lily group is distinguished for its handsome bell-shaped flowers, of six distinct spreading sepals with a honey-bearing groove at the base of each. Flowers perfect with six prominent stamens, and a long pistil the tip of which is a three-lobed stigma. Fruit an oblong capsule containing many flat seeds. The bulb scaly. The name Latinized from the Greek λείριον.

Wood Lily or
Wild Orange-
Red Lily
Lilium
Philadelphicum
Orange=scarlet
July

The most beautifully colored wild lily of all, with bright green leafy stems, flower-cup opening *upward*, and the six sepal divisions narrowing to a stemlike slenderness toward the base. The color varying from orange-scarlet to scarlet-orange or paler, and spotted with purple-brown on the inner part of the cup. The sepals do not recurve. From one to three flowers are borne at the branching summit of the plant-stem. A small form common in Nantucket bears a single lighter-colored flower. 1–3 feet high. Dry and sandy soil, common in the borders of thin woods. Me. to N. C., west to Minn. and Mo.

Wood Lily.   Lilium Philadelphicum.

LILY FAMILY. *Liliaceæ.*

Yellow Meadow Lily or Canada Lily
Lilium Canadense
Buff yellow spotted purple-brown
June–July

The common lily of the north, found most often upon low meadows. The stem is slender or stout, very light green and smooth, and bears the light green lance-shaped leaves in circles. The stem divides into several branches (really flower-stems) each of which bears a pendulous flower, buff yellow on the outside, and a deeper orange-buff spotted purple-brown on the inside. The nectar is protected from the rain by the pendulous position of the flower-cup; it is gathered mostly by the wild honey-bee, and the leaf-cutter bee (*Megachile*), who visit the flower to gather the brown pollen as well. These insects are therefore the most potent means of fertilizing this lily. It grows 2–5 feet high, and frequents moist meadows and copses, from Me., south to Ga., and west to Minn. Neb., and Mo.

Lilium Canadense is probably the most popular wild lily of our range. However, it certainly does not possess the beauty of color that characterizes the wood lily, nor the subtle delicacy of the Turk's Cap; but the graceful curves of its pendulous bells are unsurpassed in any wild or cultivated flower, and it must always command the greatest admiration for that matchless quality. Of the three wild lilies this one is also the most prodigal of its charms; it is not only in the meadow, it is everywhere.

As for the Carolina Lily described farther on, I am disposed to consider it a *questionable variety.* Until all botanists agree upon its right to varietal rank, it would be best to count it as a mere *form.* But as that form is absolutely distinct I give the lily the benefit of the doubt.

Yellow Meadow Lily.   Lilium Canadense.

LILY FAMILY. *Liliaceæ.*

Turk's Cap Lily
Lilium superbum
Buff orange-yellow
July–early August

A less common, but most beautiful species remarkable for its completely reflexed petals, or rather sepals, which leave the handsome stamens, tipped by the brown anthers, fully exposed to view ; the flower-cup is thickly freckled with brown, and hangs in a half-drooping position. It is also largely fertilized by bees, but is frequently visited by the monarch butterfly (*Anosia plexippus*) of a tawny and black color, whose favorite plant is the common milkweed. The light green leaves of this lily hold alternating positions at the upper part of the stem, but are more or less in circles at the lower part. 3–7 feet high. It is oftenest found in wet meadows not very far from the coast, and it is distributed from Me. (rather rare) and Mass., south to N. Car. and Tenn., and west to Minn.

Carolina Lily
Lilium superbum, var. *Carolinianum*
Buff orange-yellow
August

A similar species the flowers of which have far less reflexed sepals, with perhaps fewer spots. The leaves are darker green and broader, rather blunt-lance-shaped. 2–3 feet high. Commonly found in the dry woods and among the mountains. Va., south to Fla. and La.

Tiger Lily
Lilium tigrinum
Orange-scarlet
July–August

A Japanese species escaped from gardens, and commonly found beside old farmhouses. Its leaves are lance-shaped and scattered along a stiff, straight, cottony, dark-colored stem, with black bulblets at the point where they join the plant-stem. The flower sepals are strongly spotted and reflexed. Me. to N. Y.

Turk's Cap Lily.   Lilium superbum.

LILY FAMILY. *Liliaceæ.*

Dogtooth Violet or Yellow Adder's Tongue
Erythronium Americanum
Dull gold yellow
April–May

A small, lilylike flower distinguished for its brown-purple-tinged (outside) gold yellow color ; sometimes the purple tinge is wanting in the flower, but the two leaves are almost always strongly mottled with it ; these are elliptical, pointed, nearly stemless, and proceed from the root. The flower is perfect, with six stamens and a pistil, and it is especially adapted to long-tongued insects ; it is undoubtedly cross-fertilized by the early bees, chief among which are the queen bumblebees (*Bombus pennsylvanicus*) whom I have often observed enter the flower-bell and issue plentifully besprinkled with pollen. Other occasional visitors are the small butterflies *Colias philodice*—yellow, and *Pieris rapœ*—white. It is probable, too, that many species of flies are attracted to this plant on account of its mottled color ; but the majority of flies are poor pollen disseminators. The name, Greek, for *red*, in allusion to the European species which is purple-red. The little plant, 5–10 inches high, is common in moist woods and beside brooks in swampy places, from Me., south, and west to Minn. Found in Campton, N. H.

White Adder's Tongue
Erythronium albidum
White or violet-white
March–May

A very similar species with narrower leaves mottled less distinctly or not at all, smooth, thick, and whitish green. The flowers are white, or dull, pale violet-tinged outside, and yellow-tinged at the heart, inside ; the six divisions of the flower-cup strongly recurved. As the white stigma in *Erythronium* matures in advance of the golden anthers, it is, generally speaking, cross-fertilized ; its most frequent visitor is the bumblebee (*Bombus virginicus*). 5–8 inches high. Common only in the west and south. N. J., south to Ga., and west to Minn. Found near Carlinville, southern Ill. (Prof. Robertson).

Yellow Adder's Tongue.
Erythronium Americanum.   Erythronium albidum.

LILY FAMILY. *Liliaceæ.*

Star-of-Bethlehem
Ornithogalum umbellatum
White
May–June

A slender ornamental plant of Europe, escaped from gardens. The dark green leaves are narrow and linear, and the flowers are borne in a branched cluster; they are white inside, green-lined outside, and they open only in the sunshine. Name from the Greek, meaning *bird's milk*, supposed to allude to the egg-white color of the flower. 4–12 inches high. Found most often in fields and meadows near farm-houses. Mass. to Pa. and Va.

Wild Leek
Allium tricoccum
Greenish white
June–July

In spring the wild leek develops two or three light green, flat, oblong-lance-shaped leaves 8–10 inches long, and about 1 inch wide or more, and by summertime when these are withered, the white or greenish white flowers begin to bloom, in a spokelike cluster from a spathe or leaflets at the top of a naked stem. The perfect flowers with stamens and pistil, are six-parted, with six green-white sepals. The flowers are rich honey-bearers and undoubtedly are *mostly* fertilized by bees. It is an onion-scented herb whose name is the Latin for garlic, and it is not remarkable for its beauty. It grows 4–15 inches high, in rich woodlands from west N. E., west to Minn. and Iowa, and south among the Alleghanies to N. Car.

Wild Garlic
Allium Canadense
Pale pink or white
May–June

A more commonly distributed, extremely narrow-leaved species frequenting wet meadows, the flower-cluster of which is sparse in bloom or else is replaced by a thick cluster of bulblets—a frequent occurrence with *Allium*. The flower's sepals are narrow and obtuse, and quite as long as the stamens. 8–24 inches high. Me. to Minn., and south to the Gulf. The Alliums are mostly assisted by flies, bees, moths, and butterflies in the process of fertilization.

Wild Garlic.
Allium Canadense.

Wild Leek.
Allium tricoccum.

LILY FAMILY. *Liliaceæ.*

Day Lily
Hemerocallis
fulva
Tawny orange
July–August

A native of Europe and Asia, escaped from gardens. Leaves angled in section, tapering to a sharp point, narrow and light green. The flower-stalk tall bearing usually eight or nine blossoms which open one or two at a time. The flower divisions six, three narrow, and three wide and blunt, very fragile, and rusty or tawny light orange, with a veined texture. The name is from the Greek, and means *beautiful for only a day.* 2–5 feet high. Found usually on meadows and upon the borders of streams. I gathered it not far from the Arondack Spring, Saratoga, where it was growing wild and plentiful. Mass. and N. Y., south to Va. and Tenn.

Yellow Day
Lily
Hemerocallis
flava
Yellow
June–July

A beautiful but far less common species, occasionally escaped from country gardens, with narrow leaves, and pure bright yellow flowers more delicate and slender in form, having a delightfully fragrant odor. 2–3 feet high. The leaves of both these plants grow thickly, and are characterized by graceful, drooping curves.

Hemerocallis fulva is rapidly becoming established as a wild flower in many parts of the country. Its tenacity of life under apparently adverse conditions is remarkable. It propagates rapidly by its spreading roots, and sometimes takes complete possession of by-ways and spare corners where the environment is favorable. In various parts of New York State the plant is abundant. Less attractive in figure than the delicate yellow *Hemerocallis flava*, and odorless besides, it makes up for such discrepancies by a magnificent tawny orange matched by few if any members of the Lily Family. The flowers bloom for one day only.

Star-of-Bethlehem.   Ornithogalum umbellatum.

AMARYLLIS FAMILY. *Amaryllidaceæ.*

Perennial herbs, with generally showy, perfect flowers—with stamens and pistil—having six generally equal divisions of the flower-cup. Mostly fertilized by bees, the beelike flies (*Syrphidæ*), and small butterflies (*Hesperia*).

Atamasco Lily
Zephyranthes
Atamasco
Pink or white
April–July

Leaves somewhat thick, blunt, and shining deep green, long and straight. The flower perfect with six stamens and a pistil, the former very much shorter than the flower-cup. The flower-cup is symmetrical and divided into six distinct lobes, crimson pink, white with a magenta tinge, or white ; it is rarely eight-lobed. Unquestionably the plant is cross-fertilized by insects, chiefly by bees, the honeybee (*Apis mellifica*) visiting the flower most frequently, and generally early in the morning. The low position of the anthers in the flower-tube makes it impossible for the bee to pass them without powdering herself with pollen. The name is from the Latin and Greek, *Zephyrus*, the west wind, and ἄνθος, a flower. The fruit is a depressed capsule. 6–15 inches high. In moist localities. Del. to Fla. and Ala.

Star Grass
Hypoxis
erecta
Yellow
April–July

The leaves are deep green, linear, grasslike, and covered with hairs. The perfect flower is six-parted, with six stamens of unequal lengths ; it is deep yellow inside, and hairy and greenish outside. There are perhaps three flowers at the top of the hairy stalk, which, by a plentiful supply of pollen, attract both smaller bees (*Halictus*) and smaller butterflies, notably the Meadow Fritillary (*Brenthis bellona*). Prof. Robertson says the plant depends mostly upon the genus *Halictus* for fertilization, and that it is self- as well as cross-fertilized. *Hypoxis* is commonly found in the meadow grass, in dry situations. The name is of Greek origin, alluding to some unknown plant with sour leaves. 3–6 inches high. Me., south, west to Minn., E. Kan., and Tex.

Atamasco Lily.
Zephyranthes Atamasco.

Star Grass.
Hypoxis erecta.

IRIS FAMILY. *Iridaceæ.*

Perennial herbs found in damp or moist situations, having straight straplike leaves and showy, perfect flowers of three and six parts. Commonly cross-fertilized by honeybees, bumblebees, and the beelike flies (*Syrphidæ*).

Larger Blue Flag or Fleur-de-lis
Iris versicolor
Violet-blue
May–July

A handsome, and decorative plant, with light green, straight, flat leaves, and three-parted perfect flowers blooming one by one from a green bract or leaflet at the tip of a somewhat irregular stalk. The stamens are hidden and inserted at the base of the three larger and more showy divisions of the flower, which are beautifully veined with deep violet over a whitish ground tinted at the base with yellow. The stamens are under each of the three straplike divisions of the style (the middle portion of the pistil) which directly overlie the showy purple-veined petals or divisions. Thus the insect, generally a bee, in order to reach the honey, must alight upon the showy petal, crawl beneath the overhanging style-division, and brush past the anther hidden below it, dislodging the yellow pollen in its passage. At the tip of each style-division is the stigma, and upon this some of the pollen is deposited as the bee passes ; but it is really the pollen from some previously visited flower which possesses the greater fertilizing power, therefore the iris is a plant which has especially adapted itself to cross-fertilization. It is, however, robbed of its nectar by the little yellow butterfly (*Colias philodice*), who goes straight to the base of the flower between the divisions, and reaches the honey with its long tongue, and also, according to the testimony of C. M. Weed, by the tiny skipper butterfly (*Hesperia*). Fruit a long three-lobed capsule. The name is from Ἶρις, the rainbow, in allusion to the prismatic colors of the species. 16–30 inches high. On the wet margins of ponds, and in swamps, from Me., south, and west to Minn., Ark., and Neb.

Blue Flag.   Iris versicolor

IRIS FAMILY. *Iridaceæ.*

Slender Blue Flag
Iris prismatica
Violet-blue
May-June

A slender-stemmed species with very narrow grasslike leaves, and a smaller flower with generally narrower proportions, and an extremely short tube, but a long slender stem proceeding from smaller bracts or leaflets. The fruit capsule narrowly three-lobed and angular. This species is mainly found near the coast in brackish swamps, or wet grounds. 1-3 feet high. Me. to Penn. and N. Car.

Dwarf Iris
Iris verna
Violet-blue and yellow
April-May

A usually one-flowered, small, slender-stemmed species with grasslike leaves scarcely over seven inches long, the flower with the three principal divisions narrowed toward the base, slightly woolly, and deep gold yellow at the narrowing part. Sometimes the flowers are white. The fruit capsule is obtusely triangular and short. 4-8 inches high. On wooded hillsides, from south Penn. to Ga. and Ky.

Crested Dwarf Iris
Iris cristata
Light Violet
April-May

A lance-shaped leaf tapering at both ends distinguishes this species from all others; the leaf is bright green, 4-9 inches long, and about $\frac{1}{2}$ inch wide. The flowers are very light violet with the broad outer divisions *crested;* i. e., they are marked with three raised parallel flutings along the centre, the middle one of which is orange yellow. The flower is exceedingly delicate in color and dainty in form. The fruit capsule is sharply triangular and ovate in outline, hardly twice as long as it is wide. 3-6 inches high. It is a very dwarf plant common on the hillside and along streams, from Md. south to Ga., and west to southern Ind. and Mo.

Blackberry Lily
Belamcanda Chinensis
Golden orange, magenta-spotted
August-September

A Chinese plant escaped from cultivation, similar to the iris, but much more branched. The leaves flat and light green, like those of the iris, the perfect flowers with six even divisions of a light golden orange color mottled with dull magenta spots. Three prominent stamens. Several flowers in bloom at once. The fruit capsule is fig-shaped, 1 inch long, and when the scales or

Crested Dwarf Iris.   Blackberry Lily.

Iris cristata.   Belamcanda Chinensis.

IRIS FAMILY. *Iridaceæ.*

divisions of the shell fall in August, the blackberrylike, fleshy-coated, black seeds are exposed to view. The name is East Indian. 2–4 feet high. The plant has escaped from gardens to roadsides and low hills, from south N. Y. and Pa., south to Ga., and west to Ind. and Mo.

Blue-eyed Grass
Sisyrinchium angustifolium
Deep violet-blue
May–July

A stiff grasslike little plant with linear, pale blue-green leaves less than the somewhat twisted and flat flower-stem in height. The flowers are perfect, with a prominent pistil, and three stamens; the six divisions are blunt and tipped with a thornlike point; they are violet-blue, or sometimes white; the centre of the flower is beautifully marked with a six-pointed white star accented with bright golden yellow, each one of the star-points penetrating the deeper violet-blue of the petallike division. The flower is mostly cross-fertilized by bees, and the beelike flies (*Syrphidæ*). Seed capsule globular. The name is Greek in origin, and is meaningless. 6–13 inches high. In fields and moist meadows, common from Me., south to Va., and west.

Stout Blue-eyed Grass
Sisyrinchium anceps
Deep violet-blue
May–June

A similar species which has usually two unequal branches springing from a conspicuous grasslike leaf; the leaves a trifle woolly and very light green; less stiff than those of the preceding species, and somewhat wider. The flower petals are also sparsely woolly on the outer surface. 8–16 inches high. In grassy places, and sometimes on the borders of woods, from Mass., south, and southwest to La.

Eastern Blue-eyed Grass
Sisyrinchium Atlanticum
Violet-blue
May–June

A tall, bending species, similar to the preceding, but lighter green and somewhat woolly; a slenderer and weaker stem, sometimes nearly 2 feet long, and reclining, terminating in two or three almost equal branches. Leaves very narrow, bracts somewhat purplish and dry papery; the flower a trifle smaller, the outside somewhat woolly. The seeds but slightly pitted or nearly smooth. In wet meadows or brackish marshes or sandy soil, from Me. to Fla., near the coast. (Bicknell, Torrey Bot. Club Bull. 23 : 134. 1896.)

Blue-eyed Grass.

Neither species nor S. Atlanticum are as yet absolutely determined.

Sisyrinchium angustifolium   Sisyrinchium anceps.

ORCHID FAMILY. *Orchidaceæ.*

Perennial herbs having perfect flowers, the various parts of which are irregular in structure but symmetrical in arrangement. There are three similar sepals colored like petals, two lateral petals, and below these a third unique petal called the *lip*, conspicuously colored, often spurred, and containing nectar for the attraction of insects. The latter in the effort to reach the nectar invariably dislodge the peculiarly adhesive pollen-clusters and eventually carry them to the next blossom. The ingenious mechanical device of the flower to insure cross-fertilization is simple but effective. The orchids, except the *Cypripedium*, have but one stamen which is united with the style into one common column placed at the axil of the flower facing the lip. The stigma, the usual termination of the style, is a gummy surface located directly below the so-called rostellum, the receptacle of the anther, and the *actual* termination of the style. In the two anther-cells above the rostellum there are two pollinia, or stemmed pear-shaped pollen-clusters, each composed of several packets of pollen tied together by elastic threads ; these threads running together form the stem terminated by a sticky disc. It is these discs which attach to the tongues or heads of insects and insure the transportation of the pollen-masses to the gummy stigma of another flower. The orchids as a general rule are incapable of self-fertilization, and are wholly dependent upon long-tongued insects for the transportation of their pollen. In *Cypripedium*, the stigma is not a gummy surface but is in a cavity between the anther-cells.

Green Adder's Mouth
Microstylis ophioglossoides
Whitish green July

A small species with tiny white-green flowers in a small cluster about the size of mignonette. A single oval, pointed leaf clasps the slender stem about half-way up. The sepals are oblong, and the lip three-pointed. Fruit capsule oval. The name from the Greek, meaning *small* and *column* or style. 4–9 inches high. In cold woods or bogs, from Me., south, and west to Minn. and Mo. Found at Jackson,

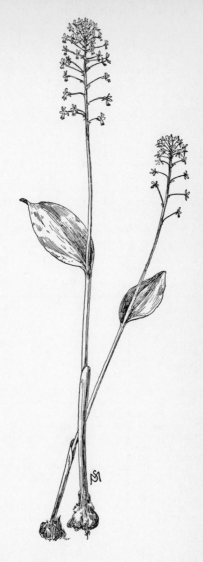

Green Adder's Mouth   Microstylis ophioglossoides.

ORCHID FAMILY. *Orchidaceæ.*

Bethlehem and Campton, N. H., in the region of the White Mountains.

Large Tway-blade
Liparis lilii-folia
Madder purple
June–July

A small but showy species with rather large shiny leaves. 2–4 inches long, light green. The flowers showy, brownish or madder purple, with reflexed sepals and petals, the latter exceedingly narrow, the lip ½ inch long and broad. Flowers numerous, the cluster sometimes 5 inches tall. The Greek name in allusion to the shining leaves. 4–9 inches high. Me., south to Ga., west to Mo.

Early Coral Root
Corallorhiza innata
Dull madder purple
May–June

A small species commonly found in evergreen woods, with a ruddy, irregular root resembling coral, and a straight yellowish brown leafless but scaly stem bearing small, uninteresting madder purple flowers, with tiny sepals and petals and a whitish lip; the seed capsule nearly ½ inch long. The name, Greek, meaning *coral* and *root*. Common in swamps and damp woods, from Me., south to N. J. in the mountains to Ga., and west to Neb. Found in Shelburne and Dublin, N. H.

Small-flowered Coral Root
Corallorhiza odontorhiza
Dull madder purple
July–September

A slender but generally taller species with very small, dull purple-brown flowers, drooping on a stiff stem; the lip whitish, spotted, and the sepals and petals marked with purple lines. The flower-stem purplish brown. 6–12 inches high, leafless, but with one or two sheathing scales. In evergreen woods, especially under arborvitæ. Common from Mass. to Mich., south to Fla., and southwest to Mo.

Large Coral Root
Corallorhiza multiflora
Madder purple
July–September

A taller, large-flowered species, the stem of which has several close scales. Many slightly fragrant flowers, with the white lip spotted and lined with purple-brown. Common in spruce woods. 10–18 inches high. Me., south to Fla., and west to Neb. and Cal. Found at Mt. Agassiz, Bethlehem, and Sandwich, N. H., and the White Mt. Notch.

Large Twayblade.
Liparis liliifolia.

Early Coral Root.
Corallorhiza innata.

ORCHID FAMILY. *Orchidaceæ.*

Heart-leaved Twayblade
Listera cordata
Madder purple
June–July

A delicate plant with a very slender stem bearing two opposite light green, stemless leaves shaped somewhat like the *ace of spades*, and a loose cluster about 2 inches long of *tiny* dull purple flowers. The flower is without a spur but possesses a very long two-cleft lip, bearing nectar in a furrow ; the slightest disturbance of a visiting insect causes the delicate rostellum above the lip to explode and forcibly eject a sticky fluid which is sure to hit the pointed tops of the pollen-masses lying just over the crest of the rostellum. Thus, the insect coming in contact with the sticky fluid withdraws fluid and pollen-masses. Smaller members of the family *Hymenoptera*, the bees, etc., most frequently visit the flower, also those of the order *Diptera*, flies, notably the tiny beelike ones. 3–10 inches high. Named for Martin Lister an early English botanist. Moist woods, Me. to N. J., and west to Ore. Found in the woods about Mt. Washington.

Broad-lipped Twayblade
Listera convallarioidis
Greenish yellow
June–July

A similar species with leaves less heart-shaped and flowers with a wedge-oblong lip, much longer than the narrow sepals and petals. Sepals purplish. In damp woods. Me., south to N. Car., in the mountains, and west to Minn.

Ladies' Tresses
Spiranthes cernua
Yellowish white
August–September

A marsh orchid, with a peculiarly twisted or spiral flower-spike and very light green linear leaves not nearly as tall as the flower-stem. The flowers translucent yellowish white, or variably cream white, odorless or fragrant, the whiter ones generally most fragrant, the lower sepals not upturned or joining with the upper, the latter arching and joined to the petals; all these parts with the curly-edged broader lip forming the bugle-horn-shaped tiny flower. It is fertilized by some of the smaller bees, moths, and butterflies. In *Spiranthes* the rostellum holds in its centre a narrow boat-shaped disc containing a sticky fluid ; it is covered by a membrane easily ruptured by an insect. After the rupture the exposed sticky fluid glues itself to the tongue of the insect and the boatlike disc is with-

Heart-leaved Twayblade.   Listera cordata.

drawn together with the pollinia which are already attached to it at the back. When the flower first opens the tube or passage between the rostellum and the lip is exceedingly narrow, hence, the former is easily ruptured by visitors. Later the space widens as the column topped by the rostellum moves upward in the maturer development of the flower. As a consequence, only those flowers which are mature are sufficiently open for the insect to reach the stigma and thereon leave the pollen of a younger flower. The name is from the Greek, for *coil* and *flower*, alluding to the spiral growth of the flowers. 6–24 inches high ; not more than 9 inches in northern N. H. In wet meadows and grassy swamps. Me., south, and west to Minn. and Neb.

Grass-leaved Ladies' Tresses *Spiranthes præcox* **Yellowish white July-August** A slender and tall species with grasslike light green leaves, and a leafy stem bearing a much twisted flower-spike of yellow-white spreading blossoms. The lateral sepals free, the upper one closely connected with the two petals, the lip often dark-striped. 10–30 inches high. In moist grassy places. Mass. and southern N. Y., south and southwest to La.

Slender Ladies' Tresses *Spiranthes gracilis* **Cream white August-October** An exceedingly slender and tall species, smooth or rarely woolly above, bearing small withering bracts or leaflets along the flower-stem which is terminated by a very-much twisted cluster of very many slender flowers, translucent cream white, and very fragrant. The odor of *Spiranthes* is peculiarly aromatic, reminiscent of the horse-chestnut, but remarkably sweet. The sepals of the flower are a little longer than the lip, which is greenish above with white margins. The ovate leaves at the root, wither before the flowers bloom. Visited by the bumblebee (*Bombus Americanorum*) and the small bee, *Calliopsis andreniformis* (Prof. Robertson). 10–22 inches high. Common in dry situations, in pastures, fields, and half-wooded hillsides. Me., south, and west to Minn. and Kan. It is rare in central N. H., where *S. cernua* is plentiful.

Ladies' Tresses.
Spiranthes cernua   Spiranthes Romanzoffiana   Spiranthes gracilis.

ORCHID FAMILY. *Orchidaceæ.*

Spiranthes Romanzoffiana **White, creamy or greenish July–August** *Spiranthes Romanzoffiana* replaces it in northern regions. This shorter species has a thick and short flower-spike, with very fragrant greenish cream white flowers somewhat hooded by the combined sepals and petals. Leaves linear. 6–12 inches high. Me., N. Y., and Pa., west to Minn. and Cal.

Rattlesnake Plantain *Goodyera repens var.ophioides (Fernald)* **White, creamy or greenish July–early August** A remarkably odd and attractive little orchid, with the very dark blue-olive green leaves marked with darker cross-veins. It has a scaly, slender, slightly woolly flower-stem, set on *one side only* with translucent greenish or creamy white small flowers; the saclike lip of the flower has a recurved wavy margin. The pollen-masses, called pollinia, are made up of numerous packets connected by threads which run together and form a single flattened brown ribbon the end of which is fastened to the rostellum. The rostellum when rubbed is removed and carries with it a bit of *membrane* to which the pollinia are attached ; this clings to the tongue of the bee, and all is properly withdrawn, and carried to another probably more mature flower, whose stigma is easily accessible, as in the case of *Spiranthes.* Named for John Goodyear an early English botanist. 5–8 inches high, rarely higher. Under hemlocks and spruces, in the northern woods. Me., N. H. (frequent in the White Mts.), south to the Great Smoky Mts. of N. Car., west to Mich. The original species *G. repens* is definitely known only in the extreme north and in the Rocky Mts.

Goodyera tesselata **White, creamy or greenish August** The commonest species in northern New England, with a stouter stem than that of the preceding species, and a little taller. Leaves 5–9 ribbed, the veins bordered by pale green pencilings, the whole leaf irregularly mottled with light and dark green, rarely without the markings. The lip of the flower is less sac-shaped, with a less recurved margin. In hillside woods. Me., northern N. Y., south to the Catskills and Hartford, Conn. (M. L. Fernald, *Rhodora*, vol. i., No. 1, p. 6.)

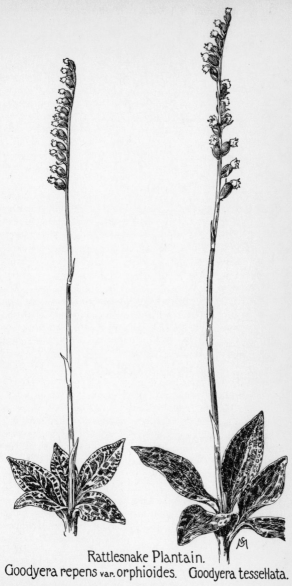

Rattlesnake Plantain.
Goodyera repens var. orphioides.   Goodyera tessellata.

ORCHID FAMILY. *Orchidaceæ.*

Goodyera Menzieii
White, creamy or greenish
August

Stem stout, leaves stiff, plain green or indistinctly marked, often with broad white ribs, or *rarely* mottled as in the foregoing species. The flower-spike *thick* and *one-sided;* the lip of the flower is large at the base and tapers to the point with the edges *curved inward.* 8-20 inches high. In dry woods, generally among evergreens. Aroostook Co., Me., Que., N. B., and along the Great Lakes from Lake Huron westward. (M. L. Fernald, *Rhodora*, vol. i, No. 1., p. 7). This is the largest of all the species.

Goodyera pubescens
White, creamy or greenish
July–August

This is the commoner rattlesnake plantain of southern New England; its flower-spike is thick, blooms upward, and is *not* one-sided. The flower-stem is stout, densely woolly, and bears several lance-shaped scales. The flower has a pronounced sac-shaped blunt lip the margin of which is not recurved. Leaves dark blue-olive green, white-veined, the middle vein broad. 6-18 inches high. In dry evergreen woods, southern Me., and central N. H., south and west to Minn.

Arethusa
Arethusa bulbosa
Magenta-crimson
May–June

A large single-flowered and delicate scented orchid, the light magenta-crimson petals and sepals of which point upward like the fingers of a half-open hand viewed in profile. The lip of the flower is recurved and spreading, with the broad apex often fringed, magenta blotched, and crested in three white hairy ridges; this forms a conspicuously colored landing platform for the visiting insect, usually a bumblebee, who, after pressing beneath the column and sipping the nectar, backs out brushing against the edge or lid of the anther, opening it and emptying the enclosed pollen upon his head, as is also the case with *Pogonia ophioglossoides.* The column is topped by the lid-like anther instead of the usual rostellum, and the pollen-masses are not pearl-like and stemmed. The solitary leaf is linear, and hidden in the sheathed scape; it appears after the flowering season. Rarely a plant produces two flowers; these vary from 1–2 inches in length. Fruit capsule elliptical,

Rattlesnake Plantain.
Goodyera pubescens.

Arethusa bulbosa.

about 1 inch long. 5–10 inches high. Common in bogs, from Me., south to N. Car., west to Minn. and Ind. Named for the fountain nymph Arethusa.

Grass Pink
Calopogon
pulchellus
Magenta-pink
June–July

A smaller-flowered, but very beautiful orchid, slender-stemmed, and with one linear bright green leaf. Flower-stem bearing 3–9 magenta-pink sweet-scented flowers with a long spreading lip crested with yellow, orange, and magenta hairs; the anther and pollen are as in *Arethusa*. Name from the Greek, *beautiful* and *beard*, referring to the handsome bearded lip. 10–16 inches high. In bogs, from Me., south, and west to Minn. and Mo. Often found in company with the next.

Snake Mouth
Pogonia
ophioglossoides
Crimson-pink
June–July

A most delicate little orchid bearing generally solitary, raspberry-scented crimson-pink flowers with a small light green lance-shaped leaf half-way up the stem, and a tiny one just below the blossom; sometimes a long-stemmed leaf proceeds from the root. The flower has sepals and petals of equal length overhanging a beautifully crested and fringed lip, curved like the hollow of one's hand, which furnishes an alighting platform for the visiting insect, who pushes forward in the narrow space between the stigma and the lip, scraping pollen off its back in its progress. The pollen attaches to the gummy stigma. In retreating, the lid of the anther catches on the back of the visitor, swings open, and fresh pollen is deposited for the benefit of the next flower. This orchid has no rostellum and its pollen is not in stemmed pearlike masses. The name, Greek, *bearded*, from the bearded lip of some of the species. 8–13 inches high. In wet meadows and swamps. Me., south, and west to Kan.; also in Japan. Frequently found in company with *Calopogon*.

Nodding
Pogonia
Pogonia
pendula
Light magenta
August–
September

A local species less showy than the foregoing, but remarkable for its dainty pendulous flowers, which are considerably smaller. With 2–8 tiny leaves, alternating, and clasping the stem. There are 1–6 long-stemmed flowers which proceed from

Grass Pink.
Calopogon pulchellus.

Snake Mouth.
Pogonia ophioglossoides.

between the stem and leaf. 3–8 inches high. In rich woods, from R. I. to Fla., Wis., and Kan.

Pogonia verticillata
Purple and green-yellow
May–June

Distinguished by its circle of five light green leaves at the summit of the stem. Flower dull purple with long stem and long narrow greenish sepals, erect or inclining above the circle of leaves. 8–12 inches high. Moist woods. Me., south, west to Ind. and Wis. Rare in the east. Found in Middlesex Co., Mass. (Miss M. P. Cook.)

Showy Orchis
Orchis spectabilis
Magenta and white
May–June

This, with another more northern species, is our only true *orchis*. There are two light shiny leaves proceeding from the base of the stem ; the latter is thick and angular in section, bearing at its summit a few showy flowers with magenta sepals and petals united in a hood, and beneath them the conspicuous, almost white lip ; behind the lip is the rather long spur, in which is secreted an abundant supply of nectar for the thirsty, visiting insect ; the latter, generally a queen bumblebee (*Bombus Americanorum* is a common visitor), thrusts its head into the spur, brushing carelessly past the rostellum at the top of the column, and, rupturing its thin membrane, exposes the two sticky round discs attached to the pear-shaped pollen-clusters. These discs immediately fasten upon the bee's face or forehead, and when the creature retires it carries with it discs and pollen-clusters. Finally when the next flower is visited the pollen is scraped off upon its sticky stigma. *Orchis spectabilis* is 5–10 inches high, and frequents rich moist woods, especially hemlock groves, from Me., south to Ga., and west to Minn. and Neb. It is found in the valley of the Connecticut west of the White Mts. The name is Latin, meaning a plant with oblong roots. (Pliny.)

Orchis rotundifolia
Magenta and white
June–July

Orchis rotundifolia is a less common species with but one leaf, oval or nearly round, and smaller flowers about the same color but deeper than those of *O. spectabilis*. From northern Me. and Vt., westward.

Showy Orchis.   Orchis spectabilis.

ORCHID FAMILY. *Orchidaceæ.*

Green Wood Orchis
Habenaria tridentata
Greenish White
June–July

A slender species with a single obtuse lanceolate leaf less than ⅓ of the way up the stem, and two or three tiny scalelike ones above it. The insignificant very small greenish 5–12 white flowers with tiny sepals and petals, a wedge-shaped lip, and a characteristic long slender spur curved *upward*, and around to one side. The pollen-clusters of the *Habenarias* are short-stemmed and terminated with a sticky gland which is so arranged that it easily fastens upon the heads or faces of visiting insects. The plant is 6–18 inches high. Name from the Latin, *habena* a bridle or rein, alluding to the narrow lip of some species. Me., west to Minn., and south in the mountains to N. Car. Found in Campton and Jaffrey, N. H., and in the White Mts.

Habenaria integra
Orange-yellow
July

This southern species has *several* leaves upon its slender stem, and a dense flower-cluster, orange-yellow. 10–20 inches high. Wet pine-barrens. N. J., south.

Habenaria nivea
White
July–August

Is another southern species, with several very narrow leaves low on the stem, and a loose many-flowered spike of small, fragrant, slightly greenish white flowers, each with an exceedingly slender curving spur. Wet pine-barrens. Del., south to Ala. and Fla.

Habenaria virescens
Yellow-green
June–July

A very common yellow-green-flowered species, with a stout stem, several lance-shaped leaves, and small flowers with yellow-green sepals and petals, the blunt lip toothed on either side and slightly protuberant in the centre at the base, the slender spur twice its length. 10–24 inches high. Common in all wet places, from Me., south, and west to Minn.

Habenaria bracteata
Light green
June–August

Characterized by the numerous bracts or leaflets from the bases of which the tiny flowers spring. The lower leaves broadly ovate, the upper ones mere long bracts scarcely three times the length of the pale green flowers. The lip of the flower toothed at the tip and oblong, twice as long as the white spur. 6–20 inches high. **Damp**

Green Wood Orchis.
Habenaria tridentata.

Habenaria virescens.

woods and meadows, from Me., south in the mountains
of N. Car., west to Minn., and reported in Neb. (Webber).

Habenaria
hyperborea
Green, yellow-
green
June-July

A tall and leafy northern species, with
green, or yellow-green flowers, erect lance-
shaped leaves, and a dense narrow flower-
spike sometimes 12 inches long, or longer.
Flower-spur short and incurved, petals,
sepals, and lip much shorter than the ovary.   8-30 inches
high.   Cold, wet woods.   Me., to N. J. and Iowa.

Habenaria
dilatata
Greenish white
June-July

A very similar species with much narrower leaves and greenish white flowers
with small obtuse sepals.   Flower-lip
lance-shaped from a lozenge-shaped base.
Cold, wet bogs.   Conn., to Mich. and Minn.

Hooker's
Orchis
Habenaria
Hookeriana
Whitish
yellow-green
June-August

The two large, shining, nearly round, or
broadly oval light green leaves usually lie
upon the ground, but are sometimes raised
above it.   The somewhat twisted and *bare*
stem bears 10-20 upright flowers, with
green lateral sepals curving backward,
narrow yellow-green petals, and the throat
accented by two lateral spots of yellow-ochre.   The lip
is lance-shaped, incurved, and pointed; the slender white-
green spur nearly 1 inch deep is especially adapted to
the long tongues of the moths.   8-15 inches high.
Woods and borders of wooded swamps from Me., south
to N. J., west to Minn. and Iowa.

Green Round-
Leaved Orchis
Habenaria
orbiculata
Whitish
yellow-green
July-August

A larger species, the two nearly round
leaves of which are sometimes 7 inches
across, and lie flat upon the ground; they
are light green and shining above, and
silvery white beneath.   The stem is *not*
bare, but bracted; the whitish yellow-
green flowers in a loose cluster, with the
upper sepal nearly round, the lateral ones ovate, and
the narrow lip obtuse and drooping, almost three times
the length of the small lance-shaped petals; the slender,
curved, whitish spur nearly 2 inches long thickened
toward the blunt point is peculiarly adapted to the long
tongue of one of the lesser sphinx-moths.   " A larger in-

Habenaria hyperborea.

dividual might sip the nectar it is true, but its longer tongue would reach the base of the tube without effecting the slightest contact with the pollen " (Wm. Hamilton Gibson). The pollen is usually withdrawn fastened upon the moth's eyes. 1-2 feet high. Rich evergreen woods. Me., south to N. Car., in the mountains, west to Minn.

Yellow Crested Orchis
Habenaria cristata
Orange-yellow July-early August

This is a southern species among a group of *fringed Orchises*, with narrow lance-shaped leaves below diminishing to the size of bracts above, and orange-yellow flowers with narrow fringed petals, and a very deeply fringed lip. Spur about ¼ inch long. The anther cells widely separated at the base. 8-20 inches high. In bogs, from N. J., south. Rather rare in N. J.

Yellow Fringed Orchis
Habenaria ciliaris
Orange-yellow July-early August

An exceedingly handsome slender species, with lance-shaped leaves, and a large many-flowered spike of showy golden or orange-yellow flowers with ovate sepals, narrow fringed petals, and a deeply fringed lip. The spur long and slender, and the anther cells as in the preceding species. 12-24 inches high. In meadows and wet sandy barrens, from Mass., south, and west to Mich.

White Fringed Orchis
Habenaria blephariglottis
White July-early August

A similar species. The white fringed flowers a trifle smaller, with a less deeply fringed lip ; the latter ⅓ the length of the spur. 12-21 inches high. In swamps and bogs from Me., south to N. J., west to Minn. Blooms a few days earlier than *H. ciliaris* where the two grow together.

(Britton.)

Habenaria leucophœa
White, greenish June-July

A western species with fragrant large greenish white or white flowers, the fan-shaped lip three-parted, broad, and fringed. Spur 1½ inches long, so it is especially adapted to the long-tongued sphinx-moths (*Sphingidæ*). 18-30 inches high. Western N. Y., south to Ky., west to Minn. and Ark.

Yellow Fringed Orchis   Habenaria ciliaris.

ORCHID FAMILY. *Orchidaceæ.*

Ragged Fringed Orchis
Habenaria lacera
White, greenish
June–July

A common species remarkable for its lacerated three-parted flower-lip, and unsubstantial translucent white which is sometimes greenish and sometimes yellowish. Leaves lance-shaped, smaller above. The long flower-spike crowded with the inconspicuous deep-spurred flowers. The pollen-cells are not widely separated. Wm. Hamilton Gibson describes the structure of the flower thus, after remarking that no botanist has mentioned its distinct peculiarity. " The nectary instead of being freely open is abruptly closed at the central portion by a firm protuberance or palate which projects downward from the base of the stigma, and closely meets the lip below." The opening is thus divided into two lateral ones, each lying directly beneath a sticky elongated pollen-disc. Thus the insect, generally a butterfly, inserts its tongue exactly where the latter will touch the disc which is sure to clasp it and be withdrawn together with the pollen. *H. lacera* is 10–22 inches high, and is found in bogs and wet woods from Me., south to Ga., and west to Minn. and Mo.

In appearance this white orchis is distinctly different from all others. Although its similarity to the next species is marked, it is *structural* and therefore not so evident to a casual observer. The flower is well named; its lacerated flower-lip is literally torn to divisions of threadlike fineness, and the general effect is accordingly unique. No other orchis is like it; the flower of *H. psycodes* has a compact settled figure; that of *H. tridentata* is distinct and has a swirling appearance due to the curving spur, while that of *H. blephariglottis* is a characteristically fringed affair of orderly appearance. But *this* orchis is a thing of " shreds and tatters."

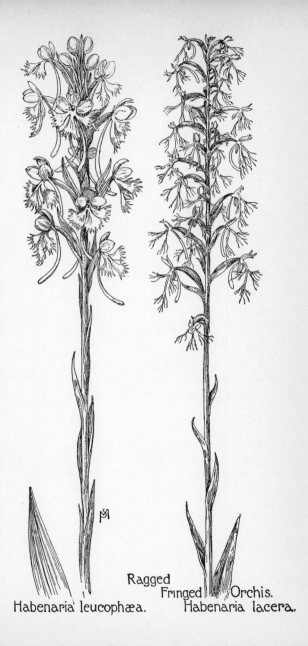

Ragged Fringed Orchis.

Habenaria leucophæa.   Habenaria lacera.

ORCHID FAMILY. *Orchidaceæ.*

Smaller Purple Fringed Orchis
Habenaria psycodes
Magenta-pink
July-early August

A similar species but of more imposing proportions, with elliptical and lance-shaped leaves, and fragrant magenta-pink or lilac-pink flowers variably pale or deep, with the fringed lip three-parted, and a spur ⅔ inch long. 1–3 feet high. Commonly found in swamps and wet woods from Me., south to N. Car.; west to Minn.

Large Purple-Fringed Orchis
Habenaria fimbriata
Magenta-pink
June-early August

A similar but much larger species with flowers twice the size of those of *H. psycodes*, fragrant, and variable in magenta-pink from a deep tone even to white. The upper sepal and petals close together, the lateral sepals small, ovate and acute. The three divisions of the broad lip more deeply fringed. Flower-spike sometimes 12 inches long and 2½ inches across. Anther cells separated at the base. In both flowers, *H. psycodes* and *H. fimbriata*, fertilization is generally effected by moths and butterflies whose heads and eyes are often decorated by the pear-shaped pollen-masses. The crowded flower-spike allows the butterfly to land indiscriminately here or there among the spreading fringed lips, and inserting its tongue obliquely in the nectary it brushes the pollen-disc on the side approached and the pollen-mass is withdrawn (Wm. Hamilton Gibson).

The difference between *H. psycodes* and *H. fimbriata* is distinct and absolute; there is no need for confusion in the identification of the two species, although it must be evident to a close observer that intergrading types are not infrequent. *H. psycodes* has more conventional, compact flowers with an even (not ragged) very short fringe, and they are about half the size of those of *H. fimbriata*. They are also distinctly muscat-scented.

Purple Orchis
Habenaria peramœna
Purple
July-August

This is a truly *purple flowered* species, found in the south and southwest. The fan-shaped lip is toothed but not fringed, and the leaves are somewhat narrower. The long spur curved. 12–30 inches high. Wet meadows, N. J., south to Va., west to Ill. and Ky.

Smaller Purple Fringed Orchis.   Habenaria psycodes.

ORCHID FAMILY. *Orchidaceæ.*

White Lady's Slipper
Cypripedium candidum
White
May–early July

A handsome but rather small-flowered orchis, with 3–4 light green narrow elliptical leaves ; the flower with two wavy and twisted narrow green petals, three broader, green, purple-blotched sepals, and a pouch or lip open at the top by a fissure, white outside, purple-streaked inside, containing nectar at its base. Two of the sepals are joined together under the lip. The column of *Cypripedium* is flanked on either side by a fertile stamen bearing a two-celled anther, opening lidlike, the pollen loose and sticky-powdery within—in this respect the genus is distinctly different from those already described. The stigma is hidden beneath the third sterile stamen crowning the column, exactly between the anthers ; it is moist and roughish. In the process of fertilization by the insect, generally a bee, the latter enters the pouch by the fissure, sucks the nectar from its base, and escapes by crowding through the small opening immediately beneath one of the anthers, receiving upon its back the sticky pollen in the exit. In the next flower the insect brushes *first* against the stigma, leaving some of the pollen, as it takes its departure in the manner described. The rather rare *C. candidum* is 6–10 inches high, and is found in bogs and wet meadows from N. Y. and N. J., west to Minn. and Mo. The name is from Κυπρις, Venus, and πόδιον, buskin,—Venus's buskin.

Yellow Lady's Slipper
Cypripedium pubescens
Yellow
May–July

This is a taller species, with a slender leafy stem, and showy fragrant yellow flowers the petals and sepals of which are madder purple streaked ; the narrow petals are usually twisted, and the bright golden yellow lip as well as the summit of the column is more or less blotched and striped with madder purple. 12–24 inches high. Woods and woodland bogs, Me., south among the mountains to Ala., and west. *C. parviflorum* is a mere *form* of this species, characterized by its smaller size and stronger color. (See Gray's *Manual*, pg. 511, 6th edition.)

Yellow Lady's Slipper   Cypripedium pubescens.

Showy Lady's Slipper
Cypripedium spectabile
White, crimson-magenta
June-July

This is perhaps the most beautiful plant of the whole genus. The stem is stout and leafy to the top, the flower fragrant; its pouch is white more or less blotched or stained with velvety light crimson-magenta, the sepals and petals white, broad and not longer than the rotund pouch. The sterile stamen long-heart-shaped, stained yellow at the tip and spotted crimson, crowns the column (see *C. acaule*). 1-2 feet high. Swamps and wet woods Me., south to Ga., west to Minn.

Moccasin Flower or Stemless Lady's Slipper
Cypripedium acaule
Crimson-pink
May-early July

The commoner and more familiar lady's slipper, with two large leaves from the root, without a plant-stem, the slightly fragrant flower terminating a long slender stem with a green leaflet or bract at the point of junction; the pouch crimson-pink (rarely white) veined with a deeper pink, sepals and petals greenish and brown, more or less curved and wavy. The third, or sterile stamen of *Cypripedium* crowning the column and overhanging the stigma is variable according to the species; in *C. acaule* it is angularly six-sided, in *C. candidum* lance-shaped, in *C. pubescens* long-triangular, and in *C. spectabile* heart-shaped; beneath these is the hidden stigma which receives pollen from the backs of visiting bumblebees or honeybees, or most frequently from the smaller bees, members of the tribes *Andrena* and *Halictus* (C. M. Weed). In *My Studio Neighbors* Wm. Hamilton Gibson describes at length the fertilization of *C. acaule* by the bumblebee. 8-12 inches high. Me. to N. Car. and Ky., west to Minn.

Moccasin Flower.   Cypripedium acaule.

BIRTHWORT FAMILY. *Aristolochiaceæ.*

A small family of twining or low herbs, having **perfect** flowers—with six or more stamens and a pistil. The leaves stemmed, and either alternate or proceeding from the root. The flower-cup or calyx, without petals, united with the ovary or fruit receptacle, and lobed or irregular. Assisted in the process of fertilization by various smaller insects.

Wild Ginger
Asarum
Canadense
Brown-purple
April-May

The two long-stemmed deep green veiny leaves soft woolly, and heart-shaped, their stems hairy ; the flower with three distinct pointed brownish or madder purple divisions to the calyx which is closely united to the solid seed receptacle or ovary, green outside ; the cup white below marked by a hexagon in purple-brown. A curious woodland plant whose odd flower is half concealed by its low position and its sober color which not infrequently resembles the leaf-mould just beneath it. Its proximity to the ground and the frequent visits of the fungus gnats and the early flesh-flies suggest that these have most to do with the fertilization of the plant. 6–12 inches high. Common in rich woods from Me., south to N. Car., west to Mo. and Kan.

Asarum
arifolium
Green-purple
April-June

A southern species with evergreen leaves arrow-heart-shaped, and urn-shaped flowers dull green outside, dull purple-brown inside, with three short blunt lobes. One leaf only put forth each year. In woods from Va., south to Tenn., Ala., and Fla.

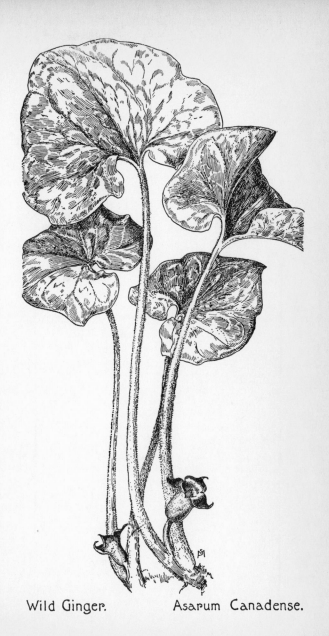

Wild Ginger.   Asarum Canadense.

BIRTHWORT FAMILY. *Aristolochiaceæ.*

Virginia Snakeroot
Aristolochia Serpentaria
Dull green
June–July

A woolly stemmed and familiar medicinal herb, the long heart-shaped leaves thin and green on both sides, and the dull greenish flowers with curving crooked long stems, near the root, as in *Asarum*, the calyx curved like the letter S. Sometimes the flowers are fertilized in the bud without opening (Britton), but often they trap many of the smaller insects—notably gnats who possibly assist fertilization. Fruit an ovoid ribbed capsule. 8–20 inches high. Conn. and N. Y., south to Fla., west to Mich. and Mo.

Dutchman's Pipe
Aristolochia Sipho
Dull green, purple-brown
May–June

A familiar tall vine in cultivation from New York south, trailing most frequently over arbors, porches, and piazzas. Smooth heart-shaped light green leaves, and hook-shaped flowers, the yellow-green veiny tube with a flat, three-lobed purple-brown throat, resembling a Dutch pipe; it entraps early small insects — gnats and flies. 10–25 feet high. In rich woods southern Pa., south to Ga., west to Minn.

The Dutchman's pipe is one of those vigorous, stolid, and satisfactory vines, big leaved and curiously flowered, which commends itself to the horticulturist. It responds readily to cultivation.

Aristolochia tomentosa
Dull green, purple-brown
May–June

A similar vine, but characterized by an extreme woolliness; leaves round-heart-shaped, veiny, and smaller than those of *A. sipho.* The flowers a yellower green, with calyx exceedingly woolly, the deep purple-brown throat nearly closed and oblique. N. Car., south, and west to Mo.

Virginia Snakeroot.　　　Aristolochia serpentaria.

BUCKWHEAT FAMILY. *Polygonaceæ.*

Herbs with alternate toothless leaves and swollen-jointed stems, usually a stipule or leaflet above each joint, and small, generally perfect flowers (or sometimes diœcious, monœcious, or polygamous ones) without petals, the calyx 2–6 parted.

Patience Dock
Rumex
Patientia
Green
May–June

The docks are mostly uninteresting northern weeds that cumber fertile ground, and decorate waste places; many of them like the patience dock come from the old country. This species has smooth broad lance-shaped leaves, broadest just above the base, and the flowers are green, tiny, inconspicuous and drooping, replaced by seed-wings or heart-shaped discs, resembling miniature palm-leaf fans. 2–5 feet high. Vt., N. Y., and Pa., west to Wis. and Kan.

Great Water Dock
Rumex
Britannica
Green
July–August

Dark green smooth leaves, the lowest very long, a branching, stout stem, and densely flowering, circling clusters; the tiny flowers nodding, replaced by seed-wings similar to those of the preceding species. 3–6 feet high. In wet situations, Me., Pa., west to Minn., Iowa, and Neb.

Swamp Dock
Rumex
verticillatus
Green
May–July

A smooth deep green species, similar to the above, with a grooved stem, and long-stemmed lance-shaped leaves. Flowers in dense circles, the outline of the seed-wing top-shaped. 2–5 feet high. Swamps. Common from Me., south, and west to Iowa.

Curled Dock
Rumex crispus
Green
June–August

This is the very common curled leaf dock throughout the U. S., a troublesome weed from the old country. Leaves wavy on the margin, flowers replaced by heart-shaped pointed seed-wings 1–4 feet high.

Winged seed R. crispus.

Winged seed R. Patientia.

Curled Dock.   Rumex crispus.

BUCKWHEAT FAMILY. *Polygonaceæ.*

Bitter Dock
Rumex obtusi-folius
Green
June–August

Another weed from the old country, common in fields and waste places. A loose and thinly flowered spike; the stem rough and stout and the somewhat wavy leaves oblong and wider than those of the other species. The seed-wings with a few spines on either side. 2–4 feet high. Me., south, and west to Ore.

Golden Dock
Rumex persi-carioides
Green
July–October

A sea-shore species, an annual; with light green, narrow, lance-shaped leaves, the plant more or less woolly, and greatly branched, the circles of the flowers crowded together into a compact spike, the seed-wings narrow and pointed, golden yellow in autumn, bearing 2–3 long spines on either side. In the sand along the shores. Me., south to Va., and from Kan. and Minn., west and north. It has been confused with *R. maritimus* of the old country.

Field or Sheep Sorrel
Rumex Aceto-sella
Green, Brown-red
June–September

A most troublesome small weed from the old world, with long-arrowhead-shaped leaves, acid to the taste, and inconspicuous flowers in branching spikes, green, or later brown-red; the whole plant sometimes turning ruddy in dry, sterile fields. It will generally flourish in one place for two or three years and then die out. The flowers are diœcious, that is, the staminate and pistillate ones are found upon separate plants, and are therefore fertilized by insects ; bumblebees, honeybees, and the smaller butterflies are the commonest visitors. 6–12 inches high. Growing everywhere.

The genus *Polygonum*, the name from πολύς, *many*, and γονυ, *knee*, alluding to the many joints of the plants, comprises about twenty-five distinct species, all of which may be characterized by the term *weed !* They are æsthetically uninteresting and many are extremely troublesome in the farmer's vegetable garden. They mostly bear pink perfect flowers grouped in a slender grasslike spike.

Sheep Sorrel   Rumex Acetosella.

BUCKWHEAT FAMILY. *Polygonaceæ.*

Knotgrass
Polygonum aviculare
Greenish yellow
June–September

A slender species with a weak stem, bluish green, small lance-shaped leaves, scaly joints, and greenish pink-tipped flowers. Common everywhere in cultivated and waste ground. The blue-green leaves, alternate, or are in appearance clustered, and issue from tiny brown sheaths.

Erect Knotweed
Polygonum erectum
Greenish yellow
July–September

A stouter and a yellowish green stem, leafy; the leaves nearly oval, and the flowers greenish yellow. A common wayside weed north of Tenn. and Ark., east and west. The stem of this species is noticeably erect with no tendency to sprawl.

Pennsylvania Persicaria
Polygonum Pennsylvanicum
Pink or white-green
July–September

A somewhat red-jointed species, at home in wet waste places, with shiny lance-shaped leaves, and pink or white-green flower-clusters; the upper branching stems and flower-stems beset with tiny hairlike glands. Common everywhere. It has a branching, sprawling habit.

Lady's Thumb
Polygonum Persicaria
Crimson-pink
June–September

A smooth-stemmed species, from the old world, with similar leaves and crimson-pink or deep magenta flowers, the leaves rough and generally marked with a darker green triangle in the middle. Very common in waste damp places.

Smartweed
Water Pepper
Polygonum Hydropiper
Green
July–September

A common weed in all wet waste places, indigenous in the far northwest, but naturalized from Europe in the east. Leaves narrow lance-shaped, very acrid and pungent, and fringed with tiny bristles. Flowers mostly green in a slim long cluster, nodding. An annual 1–2 feet high. The indigenous species *P. hydropiperoides* with an equally wide distribution has pink or flesh-colored or greenish flowers, branching stems, and very narrow leaves, not acrid. Common south, and reported in Neb. (Webber).

Smartweed.
Polygonum
hydropiperoides.

Lady's Thumb.
Polygonum Persicaria.

BUCKWHEAT FAMILY. *Polygonaceæ.*

Halberd=leaved Tearthumb
Polygonum arifolium
Pink, greenish
July–September

A perennial species with broad-arrow-head-shaped leaves, and a ridged reclining stem beset with fine teeth curved backward. Leaves long-stemmed, and prickle nerved. Insignificant pink or greenish flower-clusters. In pulling up the weed the thumb and fingers are apt to be torn with the saw-edged stems, hence the common name. 2–6 feet high. Common everywhere in wet soil.

Arrow=leaved Tearthumb
Polygonum sagittatum
Pink
July–September

An annual species climbing over other plants, with a weak four-angled reclining stem beset with prickles only at the angles; the narrow-arrowhead-shaped leaves, far apart, sometimes blunt-pointed, short stemmed, or the smaller leaves without stems. Flowers five-parted, pink, in small dense clusters. Common in low, wet ground, everywhere.

Climbing False Buckwheat
Polygonum dumetorum var. *scandens*
Green-white, pink
July–September

A perfectly smooth species, with slender climbing, reddish stem, arrowhead-shaped leaves, and leafy flower-spikes, the tiny flowers green-white or pink, the calyx five-parted. Climbing over rocks and bushes 6–12 feet high. In moist places, common everywhere. A rather decorative vine but often troublesome in the vegetable garden.

Buckwheat
Fagopyrum esculentum
Greenish white
June–September

The familiar buckwheat in cultivation escaped to waysides. From the old world; with arrowhead-shaped leaves, and greenish white flowers sometimes pinkish, the calyx five-divided, and with eight honey-glands alternating with the stamens; the flowers fertilized mostly by honeybees; the honey of a peculiarly fragrant character but dark in color. Seed beechnut-shaped. Common everywhere. The name from *fagus*, beech, and πυρός, wheat.

Leaf of Polyganum arifolium.

Arrow-leaved Tearthumb.   Polygonum sagittatum.

GOOSEFOOT FAMILY. *Chenopodiaceæ.*

Uninteresting herbs—*weeds*, many of which are from the old country; with minute, green, perfect flowers with a persisting calyx. The spinach and beet are members of this family.

Lamb's-quarters, or Pigweed
Chenopodium album
Green
June–September

The family is divided into nine tribes, chief among which is *Chenopodium*. Some of these are quite western, others are of the old world and have been introduced in the east. Lamb's-quarters is common east and west. Leaves mealy-white beneath, varying from rhombic-oval to lance-shaped or narrower, the lower ones coarse-toothed. The green flower-clusters dense, and dull green. Var. *viride*, commoner eastward, is less mealy, and has a less dense flower-spike (Gray's *Manual*). 1–4 feet high. Waste places. The name from the Greek meaning *goose* and *foot*, in allusion to the shape of the leaves of some species.

Jerusalem Oak, or Feather Geranium
Chenopodium Botrys
Green
July–September

An annual species, from the old country, not mealy, but with an aromatic odor. Leaves smaller, slender stemmed, and deeply subdivided. The flowers green in dense heads, the spike leafless, the calyx three-parted. 1–2 feet high. In autumn the leaves fall off and leave the stem and seed-spike naked. *C. ambrosioides*, or Mexican Tea, is a similar introduced species, with a densely flowered *leafy* spike; the leaves lanceolate. Both are common in waste places. *C. Botrys* found in empty lots, Norfolk Ave., Roxbury, Mass.

Jerusalem Oak.   Chenopodium Botrys.

AMARANTH FAMILY. *Amarantaceæ.*

AMARANTH FAMILY. *Amarantaceæ.*

Weeds ; some of those of a ruddy color, mostly foreign, are widely cultivated. The perfect flowers with lapping scales or leaflets (generally three) which retain their color when dry ; hence the name 'Αμάραντος, meaning unfading.

Pigweed
Amarantus retroflexus
Green
August–October

An annoying weed, common in cultivated ground and in gardens, with light green roughish leaves and stem ; leaves long-stemmed and angularly ovate. The dull green flowers in a stiff bristly spike. 1–8 feet high. Common east and west, introduced from the old world.

Amarantus chlorostachys
Green
August–October

A similar species, but smoother and a darker green, with slenderer linear-cylindrical, bending spikes, branching. The flowers also similar, but with more acute sepals. 2–6 feet high. Apparently indigenous in the southwest, but introduced eastward (Gray's *Manual*). Troublesome in gardens.

Tumble Weed
Amarantus albus
Green
July–September

A low, smooth, greenish white-stemmed species with light green, small obovate leaves, obtuse at the point, and with many branches. The flowers green, and crowded in close small clusters, at the stem of each leaf. 6–20 inches high. In the west, late in autumn, the withered plant is uprooted and tumbles about in the wind, hence the popular name. Common in waste places.

Pigweed.
Amarantus retroflexus.

Tumble Weed. Amarantus albus.GRAY
or Amarantus græcizans.

PURSLANE FAMILY. *Portulacaceæ.*

A small group of low herbs with thick juicy leaves, and perfect but unbalanced flowers—that is, with two sepals and five petals and as many stamens as petals, or more sepals, or an indefinite number of stamens, or sometimes the petals altogether lacking. Cross-fertilization is largely effected by bees and butterflies. Fruit a capsule filled with several or many shell-shaped or kidney-shaped seeds.

Purslane or Pusley
Portulaca oleracea
Yellow
June–September

An annual ; a fleshy-leaved prostrate weed naturalized from the old world, and commonly found in gardens and dooryards. Stems thick and often a terracotta pink, leaves dark green, thick, and round-end wedge-shaped. The tiny, solitary yellow flowers with five petals open only in the morning sunshine, 7–12 stamens. The branches hug the ground and spread or radiate in an ornamental circle ; they are 3–10 inches long. In early days the plant was used as a pot herb. It is indigenous in the southwest, but is firmly established in the north where it flourishes under any and all conditions, and has become a very troublesome weed.

Spring Beauty
Claytonia Virginica
Pale pink or white
March–May

A charmingly delicate flower (rarely quite white) of early spring, distinguished for its flush of pale crimson-pink, and its veins of deeper pink starting from a yellow base. The deep green leaves are linear or broader, the two upper ones located at about the middle of the plant-stem. The flower has five petals and but two sepals. Its golden stamens develop before the stigma is mature, making cross-fertilization a certainty. Its visitors in search of pollen and nectar are mostly the bumblebees *Bombus vagans* and *B. pennsylvanicus*, the beelike flies called *Bombylidæ*, and the bees of the genus *Halictus* and *Andrenidæ* ; also among the butterflies are *Colias philodice*, yellow, and *Papilio ajax*, buff and black. Stem 6–12 inches high. In open moist woods, from Me., south to Ga., and southwest to Tex.

Purslane.
Portulaca oleracea.

Spring Beauty.
Claytonia Virginica.

Claytonia
Caroliniana

A species similar in all respects except that the leaves are broader, lance-shaped, and the basal ones are quite obtuse ; the flowers are also fewer and smaller. Me., south to N. Car., among the mountains, and west to Minn. and Mo. Named for John Clayton, an early American botanist.

PINK FAMILY. *Caryophyllaceæ.*

Annual or perennial herbs generally characterized by smooth stems and *swollen joints*, opposite-growing leaves without teeth, and regular, perfect flowers, with five (rarely four) sepals, the same number of petals, and twice as many stamens. Fertilized by bees and moths.

Deptford Pink
Dianthus
Armeria
Crimson-pink
June–
September

An annual escaped from gardens, naturalized from Europe, with light green narrow, erect leaves, hairy and small ; and clustered crimson-pink, white-dotted flowers whose five petals are toothed or jagged-edged, resembling Sweet-William. 6–18 inches high. Fields and waysides Me. to Md., west to Mich. Common eastward ; found in Lexington, Mass.

Maiden Pink
Dianthus
deltoides
Crimson-pink
June–August

A perennial (growing from a matlike base) smooth or somewhat hoary, escaped from gardens, naturalized from Europe. Leaves small and narrow lance-shaped, erect. The little crimson-pink or white-pink flowers *bloom singly*, and have broader petals which are pinked at the edge. 6–12 inches high. The face of the flower more nearly resembling Sweet-William. In fields and waste places. N. H., Mass., and northern N. Y. to Mich. Found in Campton, N. H.

Bouncing Bet
or Soapwort
Saponaria
officinalis
Pale magenta-pink
June–September

A very common perennial species, naturalized from Europe, the flowers of which have an old-fashioned spicy odor ; they are delicate magenta-pink and white, scallop-tipped, and grow in clusters, the single blossom remotely resembling a pink. Leaves ovate, 3–5 ribbed, and smooth. Stem, thick jointed, 1–2 feet high. Common in waste places Found in Nantucket.

Deptford Pink.
Dianthus Armeria.

Maiden Pink.
Dianthus deltoides.

PINK FAMILY. *Caryophyllaceæ.*

Starry Campion
Silene stellata
White
June–August

The lance-shaped leaves and the stem are fine-hairy; the former in distinct clusters of four. The flowers are white, arranged in a loose terminal spike, star-shaped and fringed-edged, the stamens very long. A beautiful and delicate wild flower frequently visited by *Colias philodice*, the small yellow butterfly, and many moths. 2–3 feet high. Common in wooded slopes, from R. I., south to S. Car., and west to Minn.

Wild Pink
Silene Pennsylvanica
Crimson-pink
May–June

A very low species with a somewhat sticky-hairy character immediately beneath the flowers, most of the blunt lance-shaped leaves clustered at the base; the upper leaves small. The crimson-pink flowers with somewhat wedge-shaped petals. The calyx tubular and adapted to the tongues of butterflies and moths, by which the flower is cross-fertilized. 4–9 inches high. Me., south to Ga., west to southern N. Y., Penn., and Ky.

Bladder Campion
Silene Cucubalus
White
June–August

A delicately beautiful, foreign, perennial species which has become naturalized in this country. The deep green leaves are smooth and ovate-lance-shaped. The flowers are white with the five petals deeply two-lobed; the pale green flower-cup is greatly inflated, almost globular in shape, and beautifully veined with green markings not unlike those of a citron melon. The ten anthers (on long stamens) are sepia brown when mature. 8–18 inches high. In meadows and moist hollows beside the road. Me., south to N. J., west to Ill.

Sleepy Catchfly
Silene Antirrhina
Pink
June–September

A homely but curious annual species whose small flowers open only for a short time in sunshine. The joints of the stem are glutinous (hence the common name), and evidently prevent any stealing of the nectar by creeping insects (such as ants) which are useless as pollen carriers. The flower-calyx is ovoid with the pink petals above insigni-

Bladder Campion.
Silene Cucubalus.

Starry Campion.
Silene stellata.

ficant. 10–25 inches high. Common in waste places everywhere.

Night-flowering Catchfly
Silene noctiflora
White
July–September

Like the bladder campion; a foreign species with a beautifully marked calyx resembling spun glass, but smaller, the petals similar. The plant is hairy-sticky, the leaves blunt lance-shaped. The white flowers are delicately fragrant, and open only at dusk, closing on the following morning. Probably it is exclusively fertilized by moths, as many such visitors may be seen sipping at the newly opened blossoms in the early evening. 1–3 feet high. Common in waste places everywhere. Found in Campton, N. H.

Evening Lychnis or White Campion
Lychnis alba
White
July–October

A charming plant naturalized from the old country, with densely fine-hairy, ovate-lance-shaped leaves and stem, both dark green; the leaves opposite. The sweet-scented flowers are white, closely resembling those of *Silene noctiflora;* in fact the habit and form of these two species are almost identical. Both open their blossoms toward evening and close them during the following morning. The white petals are deeply cleft and crowned at the base with miniature petallike divisions. The calyx is inflated, and often stained maroon-crimson along the ribs, which are sticky-hairy; after becoming still more inflated it withers and leaves exposed the vase-shaped light brown seed-vessel, pinked at the small opening above. 1–2 feet high. In waste places and borders of fields, from Me. to N. J. and N. Y. Probably farther west. Found at Phillip's Beach, Marblehead, Mass.

Corn Cockle
Agrostemma Githago
Magenta
July–September

A densely hairy straight-branched annual, adventive from Europe, and found mostly in grain fields. The magenta flowers, not brilliant, but broad and showy, with very long *linear* sepals much exceeding the petals in length. Fertilized by butterflies and moths. 1–3 feet high. Common or occasional throughout the country. Reported in Neb. (Webber).

Corn Cockle
Agrostemma Githago.

PINK FAMILY. *Caryophyllaceæ.*

Ragged Robin or Cuckoo Flower
Lychnis Floscuculi
Pink or crimson
June–September

A slender perennial, also adventive from Europe, found in old gardens. The plant is downy below, and slightly sticky above, the leaves slender lance-shaped above, and few, but blunt lance-shaped below. The pink, or crimson, or light violet petals of the ragged-looking flowers are deeply cut into four lobes each, the two lateral lobes very small. Fertilized in great measure by bees and butterflies, the bumblebee, perhaps, the most frequent visitor. 1–2 feet high. Common in wet and waste ground, from Me., south to N. J., and southwest to Penn.

Thyme-leaved Sandwort
Arenaria serphyllifolia
White
May–August

A tiny annual widely branched and rough-downy, naturalized from Europe ; with small ovate leaves and miniature white flowers, the sepals of which are rather long, and rough. 2–8 inches high. Common in dry sandy places everywhere.

Mountain Sandwort or Mountain Daisy
Arenaria Grœnlandica
White
June–August

Another similar tiny, dainty plant, but with arctic proclivities, having much larger flowers with translucent white petals notched at the tip. The crowding leaves are linear and threadlike, the plant grows in a dense tuft from the root, in crevices of rocks. 2–5 inches high. On Mt. Washington and the higher peaks of N. Y., Penn., Va., and N. Car. Also on river banks at Bath, Me., and on Mt. Desert Island, and near Middletown, Conn. On Mt. Washington, where it is called the " Mountain Daisy," it snuggles close to the rocks in sheltered situations, but holds its own, almost, if not quite alone, on the highest points of the bleak Presidential range, from 5000 to 6290 feet above tide-water, where snow lasts during eight months of the year.

Field Chickweed.
Cerastium arvense.

Ragged Robin.
Lychnis Flos-cuculi.

PINK FAMILY. *Caryophyllaceæ.*

Chickweed
Stellaria media
White
April–October

The commonest weed of Europe, most widely distributed through North America, but possibly indigenous in the farther north. A weak-stemmed low-lying annual, with small ovate pointed light green leaves, slightly woolly stems, and minute white flowers with five petals almost cleft in twain, and five larger green sepals much longer than the petals. 2–4 inches high. On damp ground everywhere. An especial favorite of birds and chickens.

Long-leaved Stitchwort
Stellaria longifolia
White
May–July

A tall very slender species with many branches, the stem with rough angles, and the light green leaves small and lance-shaped. The tiny flowers like white stars, with five white petals so deeply cleft that they appear as ten, sepals nearly equalling the petals in length. 10–20 inches high. In wet grassy places everywhere. Reported in Neb. (Webber).

Lesser Stitchwort
Stellaria graminea
White
May–July

A similar species with smaller lance-shaped leaves widest just above their base, a four-angled stem, and white flowers with deeply cleft petals. 12–18 inches high. In fields and grassy waysides from Me. to western N. Y. and N. J. Introduced from Europe, but said to be indigenous in Canada.

Larger Mouse-ear Chickweed
Cerastium vulgatum
White
May–September

A bothersome weed common in cultivated fields, naturalized from Europe, but probably indigenous in the farther north. Stem hairy and clammy, leaves oblong. The somewhat loosely clustered white flowers with two-cleft petals, but with *short* sepals. 6–15 inches high.

Field Chickweed
Cerastium arvense
White
April–July

A low, rather large-flowered, handsome species, the broad petals also deeply cleft, the sepals very short, the stems downy or smooth, and the leaves rather broad linear. 4–10 inches high. In dry or rocky situations, Me., south to Ga., and west to Mo., Neb., and Cal.

Chickweed.
Stellaria media.

Mountain Sandwort.
Arenaria Grœnlandica.

Long-leaved
Stitchwort.
Stellaria
longifolia.

WATER=LILY FAMILY. *Nymphæceæ.*

Sand Spurry
Buda rubra D.
Tissa rubra L.
Pink
June–August

A common little low plant in sandy waste places sometimes near the coast but not on the shore. Leaves linear and flat, in clusters about the frail stem. Tiny flowers, crimson-pink, sepals glandular-hairy. The plants grow in dense company. 2–6 inches high. Roadsides and waste places, Me. to Va., west to western N. Y.

WATER-LILY FAMILY. *Nymphœaceœ.*

Aquatic perennial herbs, with floating leaves, and solitary flowers with 3–5 sepals, numerous petals, and distinct stigmas or these united in a radiate disc. Fertilized by bees, beetles, and aquatic insects.

Water=Lily
Nymphœa
odorata
White
June–
September

The common and beautiful white pond-lily found in still waters everywhere. Leaves dark green, pinkish beneath, ovate-round, cleft at the base up to the long stem. The white flowers, often 5 inches in diameter when fully developed, open in the morning and close at noon or later ; they are frequently pink-tinged ; the golden stamens and anthers are concentric, and are luminous in quality of color. They mature after the stigma does, and cross-fertilization occurs by the agency of bees and beetles in general. The flower yields pollen only. The var. *rosea*, in southeastern Mass., and Nantucket, is deeply pink-tinged. The var. *minor* is small, with flowers less than three inches broad.

Yellow Pond-
Lily or
Spatter=dock
Nuphar advena
Golden yellow
May–
September

A common odorless yellow pond-lily found often in the same water with the preceding species. With *ovate* leaves or broader, and small, green and yellow cup-shaped flowers, with 6 green sepals, sometimes purple-tinged, yellowish inside ; the petals yield nectar ; they are small, narrow, thick, and yellow—stamenlike. The stigma is a pale ruddy or deep golden yellow-rayed disc, beneath which the undeveloped anthers are crowded. On the first opening of the flower there is a triangular orifice over

Water-Lily.
Nymphæa odorata.

Yellow Pond-Lily.
Nuphar advena.

the stigma so small that an entering insect must touch the stigma. On the following day the flower expands fully and the anthers beneath the stigma unfold, spread outward, and expose their pollen. Cross-fertilization is thus insured, and is generally effected by means of the bees of the genus *Halictus,* and (so says Prof. Robertson) the beetle named *Donacia piscatrix.* A very common and familiar plant in stagnant water, with stouter stem and coarser leaves than those of the preceding species. Var. *minus* is a slenderer form the smaller flower of which has a crimson stigma. Northern Vt. to Mich. and Penn.

Small Yellow Pond-Lily
Nuphar Kalmianum
Golden yellow
June-September

This is a very slender species, with flowers scarcely 1 inch wide. Sepals only three. The stigma disc, dark red. In ponds and sluggish streams, Me. to southern N. Y., Penn., and west to Minn.

CROWFOOT FAMILY. *Ranunculaceæ.*

A large family of perennial or annual herbs, with generally regular but sometimes irregular flowers ; with stamens and pistil, or with staminate and pistillate flowers on different plants ; 3–15 petals, or none at all ; in the last case the sepals petallike and colored. Generally fertilized by the smaller bees, butterflies, and the beelike flies.

Virgin's Bower
Clematis Virginiana
Greenish White
July-August

A most beautiful trailing vine commonly found draped over the bushes in copses and by moist roadsides. The leaves dark green, veiny, with three coarsely toothed leaflets ; the flat clusters of small flowers with four greenish white sepals and no petals, polygamously staminate and pistillate on different plants ; cross-fertilized by bees, the beelike flies (*Bombylius*), and the beautiful and brilliantly colored flies of the tribe *Syrphidæ.* In October the flowers are succeeded by the gray plumy clusters of the withered styles (still adherent to the seed-vessels), which

Virgin's Bower.
Clematis Virginiana.

Purple Virgin's Bower.
Clematis verticillaris.

appear under the glass like many tiny twisted tails. The plants presenting this hoary appearance gave rise to the popular name, Old Man's Beard. The vine supports itself by a twist in the leaf-stem, the latter revolving a number of times in the course of growth. Stem about 12 feet long. Waysides and river-banks. Me., south to Ga., and west to Kan., Neb., and S. Dak.

Leather Flower
Clematis
Viorna
Dull purple
May–July

A southern species with solitary, thick, leathery, bell-shaped, dull purple flowers without petals, the purple sepals about 1 inch long. The three or more leaflets with unbroken edges or lobed. In early autumn the hoary plume is brownish. Southern Pa., south to Ga. and Tenn., and west to Ohio.

Purple Virgin's Bower
Clematis
verticillaris
Light purple
May–June

A rather *rare* species found in rocky places among the northern hills, with leaves similar to those of *C. Virginiana*, and showy light purple flowers, downy inside and outside, sometimes over 3 inches broad ; the four purple, finely veined sepals expanding only to a cup-shape. The plumes brown-gray. Me. and Vt., south to Va., and west to Minn.

Long-fruited Anemone
Anemone
cylindrica
Greenish white
June–August

A slender tall species the leaves and stem of which are silky haired, leaves dark green and veiny, ornamentally cut (or lobed) into 3-5 parts. The solitary flowers without petals, but with 5-6 greenish white sepals, are set on a tall stem. The fruit a narrow, cylindrical, burrlike head 1 inch or more in length. 2-6 flowers are borne on each plant. 18-24 inches high. Common in dry woods and by wooded roadsides, from the lower Androscoggin Valley, Me., Vt., N. Y., and northern N. J., west to Kan., Neb., and S. Dak. The name, Greek, meaning a flower shaken by the wind.

Thimble-weed or Tall Anemone
Anemone
Virginiana
Greenish white
July–August

This is the common tall anemone of wooded roadsides and banks. The leaves and stem are more or less hairy and deep olive green, the leaves conspicuously veined. The flowers generally have five inconspicuous sepals white or greenish white inside and greener outside ; the flower-

Thimble-weed.   Large White-flowered Anemone.
Anemone Virginiana.   Anemone riparia.

head usually 1 inch or less across, is succeeded by the enlarged fruit-head similar in shape to, and about as large as, a good-sized thimble. Fertilized by the bumblebees, the smaller bees (among them the honeybee), and the brilliant little flies of the genus *Syrphidæ.* 2–3 feet high. Me., south to S. Car., west to Kan., Neb., and S. Dak. Found in Campton, N. H.

Large White-flowered Anemone
Anemone riparia (Fernald)
White
June–July

A slender, tall, and handsome plant intermediate between the two preceding species, with large white flowers maturing earlier than those of the foregoing, and with smoother stem and leaves; the latter thin, and unequally cleft into coarsely and sharply toothed segments. The five thin sepals generally obtuse and a strong white. The short cylindrical fruit-head slenderer than that of *A. Virginiana.* 12–35 inches high. Banks of rivers and streams, and on rocky banks, from the St. John River, Fort Kent, Me., Willoughby Lake and western Vt., Uxbridge, Mass., to western N. Y. and Sullivan Co., N. Y. (M. L. Fernald, *Rhodora*, vol. i., p. 51). Found on the borders of the pond near the Arondack Spring, Saratoga, N. Y.

Canada Anemone
Anemone Canadensis
White
May–August

A northern, rather coarse stemmed species, very much branched, with broad, sharply toothed, three-cleft leaves; their under surfaces rather hairy. The five white sepals quite blunt, and the flower 1–1½ inches broad. The fruit-head globular. 1–2 feet high. Low moist grounds, from western N. Eng., south to Pa., and west to Kan. and S. Dak. Common in western Vt., along the slopes of Lake Champlain.

Canadian Anemone.
Anemone Canadensis.

Wood Anemone or Wind Flower
Anemone quinquefolia
White April-June

A beautiful, delicate, and low little plant common in the early spring in woodlands, with deep green leaves of five divisions, and frail white, or magenta-tinged blossoms of from 4-9 petallike sepals; the solitary flower frequently 1 inch across. Cross-fertilized by the early bees and beelike flies (*Bombylius*). Common on the borders of the woods. 4-8 inches high. Me., south to Ga., and west to the Rocky Mts.

Liverwort or Hepatica
Hepatica triloba
Lilac white, pale purple March-May

The earliest flower of spring, appearing before its leaves, and generally found half hidden among the decaying leaves of autumn that cover the woodland floor. The blossom about $\frac{7}{8}$ inch broad, with 6-12 lustrous sepals varying in color from lilac white to pale purple and light violet, beneath which are three leaflets closely resembling a calyx, or the outer floral envelop. The three-lobed olive green leaves last throughout the winter, the newer ones together with stems and flower-stems are extremely hairy. About 3 inches high. Common from the seaboard west to Minn. and Mo.

Hepatica acutiloba

This is a species close to the preceding one and often passing into it. The leaves are three- or sometimes five-lobed, with acute tips, and the three little leaflets beneath the flower are also pointed. Range the same as *H. triloba*, in fact, both species are often found together in the same woods.

Wood Anemone.
Anemone quinquefolia.

Rue Anemone.
Anemonella
thalictroides.

Liverwort.
Hepatica triloba.

CROWFOOT FAMILY. *Ranunculaceæ.*

Rue Anemone
Anemonella thalictroides
White, or pink-tinged
March–May

A frail and delicate spring flower, usually white but rarely magenta-pink-tinged, which often blooms in company with *Anemone quinquifolia*, but readily distinguished from it by the 2–3 flowers in a cluster, the other bearing a solitary blossom. The deep olive green leaves in groups of three closely resemble those of the meadow rue; they are long-stemmed. The flower with usually six delicate white petallike sepals, but there are variations of from 5–10. The flowers are perfect (with orange-yellow anthers), and are probably cross-fertilized largely by the early bees and beelike flies. 5–9 inches high. Common everywhere in thin woodlands.

Early Meadow Rue
Thalictrum dioicum
Green, terra-cotta
April–May

A beautiful but not showy, slender meadow rue with the staminate and pistillate flowers on separate plants. The bluish olive green leaves lustreless, compound, and thinly spreading; the drooping staminate flowers with generally four small green sepals, and long stamens tipped with terracotta, and finally madder purple. The pistillate flowers inconspicuously pale green. An airy and graceful species, common in thin woodlands. 1–2 feet high. Me., south to Ala., and west to Mo., S. Dak., and Kan.

Tall Meadow Rue
Thalictrum polygamum
White
July–September

The commonest species, remarkable for its starry plumy clusters of white flowers, lacking petals, but with many conspicuous threadlike stamens. The flowers are polygamous, that is, with staminate, pistillate, and perfect ones on the same or different plants. The leaves are compound, with lustreless blue-olive green leaflets; the stout stem light green or magenta-tinged at the branches. The decorative, misty white flower-clusters are often a foot long; the delicate-scented staminate flowers are a decided tone of green-white. This species is an especial favorite of many bees, moths, and smaller butterflies, by which it is cross-fertilized. 3–10 feet high. Common in wet meadows from Me., west to Ohio, and south.

Tall Meadow Rue.   Thalictrum polygamum.

**Purplish
Meadow Rue**
*Thalictrum
purpurascens*
**Green-purple
June-August**

The stem of this species is generally stained with madder purple, but sometimes it is green with only a slight magenta tinge in parts. The leaves are thick, deep blue-olive green and similar in shape to those of the preceding species. The flowers are green, with a brown-purple tinge, and are also polygamous. 3-6 feet high. On the borders of wooded hills, and copses, in dry situations. Middle N. Eng., south, and west to S. Dak., Neb., and Ariz.

**Water Plantain
Spearwort**
*Ranunculus
ambigens*
**Yellow
June-August**

An insignificant marsh species closely allied to the buttercup, with yellow flowers $\frac{2}{3}$ inch broad, the 5-7 petals rather narrow. The lance-shaped leaves almost if not quite toothless, and clasping the jointed stem, which often sends out roots from the joints ; the lower leaves contracted into a broad stem clasping the plant stem. 1-2½ feet high. Common in wet places, from Me., south to Ga., and west to Minn. and Mo. Name from the classic *Rana*, a frog, referring to the marshy home of the genus.

**Small-flowered
Crowfoot**
*Ranunculus
abortivus*
**Yellow
April-June**

Rather an attractive biennial species, commonly found beside the woodland brook, the lower leaves of which are somewhat kidney-shaped, and the upper ones slashed like those of the buttercup, but very moderately so ; the leaves bright green and smooth. The small flowers with globular heads, and reflexed or drooping yellow petals ; the head about ¼ inch broad. 6-24 inches high. In shady and moist ground, everywhere. The var. *eucyclus* (Fernald) is a common form in Me., N. H., and Mass., with slender and zigzagged stem, and thin leaves, the lower, rounded ones with narrowed cleft ; the flowers are smaller. Found at Ammonoosuc Lake, Crawford Notch, by J. M. Greenman, and at Orono, Waterville, and Dover, Me., by M. L. Fernald. (See *Rhodora*, vol. i., p. 52.)

Water Plantain.
Ranunculus ambigens.

Small-flowered Crowfoot.
Ranunculus abortivus var. eucyclus.

CROWFOOT FAMILY.   *Ranunculaceæ.*

**Hooked
Crowfoot**
*Ranunculus
recurvatus*
**Light yellow
April–June**

A woodland crowfoot distinguished by its remarkably hooked seed-vessels which are gathered in a cluster about ½ inch broad. The light yellow flowers with the calyx (flower-envelop) curved backward, and with usually five small petals, are rather inconspicuous. The stem and olive green leaves are hairy, the latter generally three-lobed, veiny, and toothed, but the root leaves are seldom divided. 10–20 inches high. Common in woods everywhere.

**Early Butter-
cup**
*Ranunculus
fascicularis*
**Deep yellow
April–May**

Another woodland or hillside species, with deep yellow flowers almost an inch broad. The plant rather low, with fine silky hairs on stem and leaf, the latter dark green, and deeply lobed, with 3–5 divisions. The flower with often more than five petals which are rather narrow ; the fruit-head about ⅓ inch in diameter, with a slender curved spine to each seed-vessel. 6–12 inches high. Common on the borders of wooded hills, in the spring, from Me., south to S. Car., and west. The first buttercup of the year ; all are fertilized mostly by early bees, flies, and the smaller butterflies, notably *Colias philodice*, but the commoner visitors are the small bees of the genus *Halictus*.

**Swamp
Buttercup**
*Ranunculus
septentrionalis*
**Deep yellow
Late April-July**

This is the next buttercup of the spring, and one confined to swamps and low wet grounds. The flowers are deep yellow and fully 1 inch broad. The hollow stem is generally smooth, but sometimes fine-hairy ; the deep green leaves are divided into three leaflets, each distinctly stemmed, and three-lobed, or only the terminal one stemmed ; the uppermost leaves are long, narrow, and toothless. This buttercup is very variable in both size and foliage, its branches are upright or reclining, and its leaves coarsely cleft and divided. 1–2 feet high, or more. Common in moist rich ground everywhere. Like most of the other buttercups, this one depends mainly upon the beelike flies (*Bombylius*) and the little bees of the family *Andrenidœ* for fertilization.

Swamp Buttercup.   Ranunculus septentrionalis.

Leaf   of
Ranunculus fascicularis.

CROWFOOT FAMILY. *Ranunculaceæ.*

Creeping Buttercup
Ranunculus repens
Deep yellow
May–July

A species of a similar character, the leaves frequently white-spotted or blotched; the deep yellow flowers nearly 1 inch broad, blooming a little later. The seed-vessel tipped with a short stout spine, thus differing from the rather deciduous long straight spine of *R. septentrionalis*. This buttercup creeps or spreads over the ground by runners. Roadsides and waste places or low grounds, generally near the coast, and mainly introduced from Europe, but also indigenous.

Bristly Crowfoot
Ranunculus Pennsylvanicus
Yellow
June–August

Often, and improperly, called a buttercup; the flower has a thimble-shaped, green head formed of the pistils, and insignificant, round yellow petals surround it. It is small, scarcely $\frac{1}{3}$ inch across, and does not in the remotest degree suggest the cup-shape of the buttercup. The stem is remarkably stiff-hairy, and irritating to the touch; it is hollow, coarse, light green, and leafy to the top. Leaves light green, three-divided, with each division three-lobed, cut and slashed like *R. acris*, and hairy above and beneath. 1–2 feet high. Common in wet situations, from Me., south to Ga., and west.

Bulbous Buttercup
Ranunculus bulbosus
Golden or deep yellow
May–July

A small erect plant proceeding from a bulbous base or root, with hairy stem and leaf, and large bright, 1 inch wide, deep or golden yellow flowers, the green sepals of which are strongly reflexed. The leaves are deep green, decoratively cut and slashed, three-divided, each division three-lobed, with only the terminal one stemmed, the lateral ones nearly if not absolutely stemless. 8–16 inches high. Roadsides and fields; abundant in N. Eng., and naturalized from Europe. Müller records the fact that over 60 different species of insects visit these old world-buttercups, i. e., *R. repens*, *R. bulbosus*, and *R. acris*.

Leaf and flower showing reflexed
sepals of Ranunculus bulbosus.

Bristly Crowfoot.   Ranunculus Pennsylvanicus.

CROWFOOT FAMILY. *Ranunculaceæ.*

Tall Buttercup
Ranunculus acris
Golden or deep yellow
May-August

This is the common buttercup of fields and meadows, which has become naturalized from the old country. The stem is hairy, branched and less hairy above, and deep green. The leaves deep green with 3–7 stemless divisions, and these are again correspondingly divided into linear segments; they are cut and slashed in a most decorative and complicated fashion, only the upper ones showing the simple three-parted figure. The flowers, nearly 1 inch broad, are lustrous light golden yellow within, and light yellow without, the 5 broad petals overlapping. The flowers are set on long slender stems, and sometimes continue to bloom until frost. 2–3 feet high. Common everywhere, especially upon moist meadows. The variety named *R. acris*, var. *Steveni* (Lange), is similar except in the shape of its leaf, which has *very broad* instead of linear segments, which impart to the plant a thicker and heavier appearance in the field. This variety is the common form in northern N. Eng. Found at Alstead Centre, and Jefferson, N. H. (M. L. Fernald in *Rhodora*, vol. i, p. 227).

Marsh Marigold
Caltha palustris
Golden yellow
April-May

A thick and hollow-stemmed stocky plant common in marshes in spring, with round or kidney-shaped deep green leaves obscurely blunt-toothed, and brilliant golden yellow flowers resembling buttercups. Often wrongly called cowslips. The flowers are perfect with 5–9 petallike sepals, and numerous stamens; they are honey-bearing, and although the anthers and stigmas mature simultaneously, cross-fertilization is favored by the anthers opening outwardly, and the outermost ones farthest from the stigmas opening first (Müller). The flowers are chiefly fertilized by the beautiful yellow flies belonging to the family *Syrphidæ*. The classical name *Caltha* means cup, and *palus* a marsh—marsh-cup. 8–24 inches high. Common in wet meadows, from Me., south to S. Car., and west.

Ranunculus
acris var. Steveni.

Tall Buttercup.
Ranunculus acris.

CROWFOOT FAMILY. *Ranunculaceæ.*

Goldthread
Coptis trifolia
White
May–July

A tiny woodland plant whose bitter golden yellow threadlike roots contribute to the medicinal stock of the old-fashioned country housewife. The evergreen leaves are lustrous dark green, three-lobed, scalloped, finely toothed, and long-stemmed. The solitary flower terminating a long slender stem has 5–7 white sepals, and has many obscure little club-shaped petals, 15–25 white stamens with golden anthers, and 3–7 pistils on slender stalks. The strange petals terminating the minute cuplike discs are really nectaries intended to minister to thirsty insects. According to C. M. Weed the flower is cross-fertilized mostly by a fungus gnat— a little two-winged fly, and occasionally by a small elongated beetle called *Anaspis flavipennis.* 3–6 inches high. In bogs of woodlands or shady pastures, from Me., south to Md., and west to Minn. The name from the Greek *to cut,* in reference to the cut-leaf.

Columbine
Aquilegia
Canadensis
Scarlet, yellow
April–early
July

A most delicate but hardy plant common on rocky hillsides and the borders of wooded glens. The long-stemmed compound leaves are light olive green, with three-lobed leaflets. The flowers are graded from yellow through scarlet to red at the tip of the spurs. The petals are the 5 tubes culminating in the spurs, and the 5 sepals are the spreading ruddy yellow leaflets grading into a greenish yellow, situated between the tubes. Stamens yellow. Fertilized by moths and butterflies. 1–2 feet high. Common everywhere. Rarely the flowers are altogether golden yellow. The long spurs indicate the adaptation of the flower to long-tongued insects.

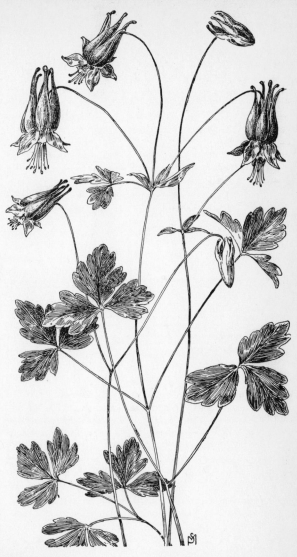

Columbine.   Aquilegia Canadensis.

CROWFOOT FAMILY. *Ranunculaceæ.*

Tall Larkspur
*Delphinium
exaltatum*
Light violet
July-August

A slender and smooth species of larkspur found in the woods from Pennsylvania southward. The deep green leaves have generally five divergent, lance-shaped or wedge-shaped lobes, and the light purple or blue-violet flowers are borne in a slim spike sometimes 10 inches long. 2–6 feet high. In woods, from Allegheny and Huntington Cos., Pa., south to N. Car., and west to Minn. and Neb. The *Delphiniums* are mostly fertilized by the beelike flies, honeybees, and bumblebees.

Field Larkspur
*Delphinium
Consolida*
Lilac to ultra-
marine blue
July-August

A European species, in cultivation and escaped to roadsides and fields, with dissected deep green leaves having very narrow linear lobes, and a scattered flower-spike of showy flowers 1 inch broad, long-spurred, and varying in color from pale magenta, lilac, and purple to ultramarine blue. The commoner species in cultivation is *D. Ajacis*, with larger flower-clusters and with woolly pods ; this has also sparingly escaped. 12–30 inches high. Southern N. J., Pa., and south.

Monkshood
*Aconitum
uncinatum*
Violet-
ultramarine
June-
September

A handsome wild flower, slender-stemmed, weak, and disposed to seek support. The delicate character of the plant is not unlike that of the columbine. The deep green leaves are toothed, have 3–5 lobes, and are rather thick. The purple or violet-ultramarine flowers are composed of 5 sepals, the upper one enlarged, forming the hood, and 2 petals (three more are stamenlike, abortive, and inconspicuous) concealed beneath the hood ; the stamens are numerous. Undoubtedly the flower is largely fertilized by the bumblebee who is its constant visitor ; the stamens ripen before the pistils, and cross-fertilization is thus insured. 2–4 feet high. In woods, southern N. J. and Pa., and south along the Alleghanies to Ga.

Goldthread.   Monkshood.
Coptis trifolia.   Aconitum uncinatum.

CROWFOOT FAMILY. *Ranunculaceæ.*

Black Snakeroot
Cimicifuga racemosa
White
June–July

A tall spreading, slender-stemmed woodland plant, with fuzzy, feathery white flowers borne in a 6–20 inches long, wand-like cluster, having a disagreeable fœtid odor, and compound, sharply toothed, light green leaves. The 4–8 petals are stamenlike, and the stamens are numerous. The flower is assisted in fertilization by the green flesh-flies. Fruit berrylike and purplish. 3–8 feet high. Woods, Me., south to Ga., and west to Minn. and Mo.

Red Baneberry
Actæa spicata var. *rubra*
White
April–June

A bushy woodland plant with compound 3–5 parted leaves, the leaflets toothed and lobed, the lower end-leaflets sometimes again compound. The tiny white, perfect flowers with 4–10 exceedingly narrow petals and numerous stamens; the 4–5 sepals petallike and falling when the flower blooms. Cross-fertilized by the small bees, especially of the species *Halictus.* The stigmas mature before the anthers are open, thus securing cross-fertilization. Fruit a thick cluster of coral red, oval berries borne upon *slender* stems. 1–2 feet high. Woods, from Me., southwest to N. J. and Pa., and west.

White Baneberry
Actæa alba
White
Late April–June

A similar species with the same distribution. The leaflets are more deeply cut, the teeth are sharper, and the lobes are *acute.* The narrow, stamenlike petals are blunt at the tip, and shorter than the stamens. Fruit a china white berry with a conspicuous purple-black eye; the stems are *thick* and fleshy, and usually *red.* Forms with slender-stemmed white berries, and fleshy-stemmed red berries occasionally occur, but these are considered hybrids (Gray's *Manual,* 6th edition). The *Actæas* are not honey flowers and the smaller bees (*Halictus*) visit them for pollen.

Orangeroot
Hydrastis Canadensis
Greenish white
April

A stocky yellow-rooted perennial, sending up in spring a single clear green, round, veiny root-leaf, lobed and toothed, and a hairy stem terminated by two small leaves, from the uppermost one of which springs an insignificant green-white flower scarcely ½ inch broad, with numerous stamens,

Actæa rubra

Actæa alba

Red Baneberry
Actæa spicata var. rubra.

Fruit of
Actæa alba.

about a dozen pistils, and no petals. Visited by the smaller bees and the beelike flies. The fruit a small head of tiny red berries clustered like the lobes of a raspberry. 1 foot high. In woods, southern N. Y., south to Ga., and west to Minn. and Mo.

BARBERRY FAMILY. *Berberidaceæ.*

A family of shrubs and herbs with perfect flowers having one pistil, and as many stamens as petals (except *Podophyllum*) arranged opposite each other. The flowers of the barberry are especially adapted to cross-fertilization; but other members of the family are self-fertilized, or cross-fertilized by the agency of insects, chiefly bees.

Blue Cohosh or Papoose Root
Caulophyllum thalictroides
Greenish, or yellowish
April–May

An early woodland plant common in the west, with generally but one compound leaf (at the top of the long stem) three times parted, the leaflets having 2–3 lobes; a smaller similar leaf accompanies the flower-stalk. The whole plant is covered with a white bloom when young. The simple stem is terminated by a small cluster of yellow-green, or yellowish flowers ½ inch broad, with 6 petallike sepals, and 6 insignificant hood-shaped petals grouped closely about the central pistil. The stigma is receptive before the anthers are ripe, thus assuring cross-fertilization. Frequently visited by the early bumblebees, and bees of the family *Andrenidæ*. The seeds berrylike and blue, in a loose cluster. 1–3 feet high. Rich woodlands from Me., south to S. Car., west to S. Dak. and Neb.

Twinleaf
Jeffersonia diphylla
White
April–May

A little plant when in flower, scarcely 8 inches tall, but attaining double that height later in the season when in fruit. The single white flower, about an inch broad, with 8 oblong flat petals, and half as many early-falling sepals, is a trifle like the bloodroot blossom, but lacks the latter's delicacy and purity of color. The long-stemmed leaf is parted almost completely into two angularly ovate lobes, whitish beneath. Finally (when fruiting) 15–18 inches high. Woods, western N. Y., south to Tenn., and west to Wis.

The fleshy-covered cadet blue seeds
showing groups in pairs
after bursting of the
ovary.

Blue Cohosh.   Caulophyllum thalictroides.

May Apple, or Mandrake
Podophyllum peltatum
White
Late April–May

A common, handsome woodland plant remarkable for its large leaves which frequently measure a foot in diameter ; the *flowerless* stem of the plant bears a leaf with 7–9 lobes, peltate in character ; i. e., supported by the stem in the centre, as an umbrella.

The May Apple has also been called Umbrella Leaf, and, in allusion to its peculiar lemonlike fruit, Wild Lemon. The *flowering* stalks bear two less symmetrical leaves, from between the stems of which droops the ill-smelling but handsome white flower nearly 2 inches broad ; it usually has 6 petals and twice as many stamens ; it is without nectar, but is nevertheless cross-fertilized by the early bees and the bumblebees ; these collect the pollen. Prof. Robertson believes that the plant may be occasionally self-fertilized ; although the anthers do not reach out as far as the stigmas, they sometimes do touch the tip edge of the stigma. Fruit a large, fleshy, edible, lemon-shaped berry. Leaves and root poisonous, and medicinal. The plant is 12–18 inches high, and is common in damp rich woods, from N. Y., west to Minn. and Neb., and south. Not in northern New England.

A plant of the woodlands so common in spring about the neighborhood of Greater New York, seems conspicuously and strangely absent in the vicinity of Boston, where the Skunk Cabbage apparently takes its place. Mrs. Dana remarks that *Podophyllum* " attracts one's attention by the railways," which is perfectly true of southern New York and New Jersey, but it does not apply to New England. The plant is found at Concord, Mass., but it was transplanted there ; in Vermont it is known only at a few stations, in New Hampshire it is rare if not absent, and in Maine, so far as my knowledge goes, it is quite unknown.

May Apple.   Podophyllum peltatum.

POPPY FAMILY. *Papaveraceæ.*

POPPY FAMILY. *Papaveraceæ.*

Herbs with a milky or yellow sap, and regular or ir-regular perfect flowers with 4–12 petals, generally two early-falling sepals, and many stamens. The irregular flowers spurred at the base of the petals. Fertilized mostly by bees. Fruit a dry capsule usually one-celled. Not honey-bearing flowers.

Bloodroot
Sanguinaria
Canadensis
White
April-May

A most beautiful but fragile flower of early spring, 1½ inches broad, with gen-erally 8 (rarely 12) brilliant white petals four of which alternating with the others are a trifle narrow, and impart a four-sided aspect to the full-blown blossom. The petals ex-pand flatly in the morning, and become erect toward late afternoon, and close by evening. The two sepals fall when the flower opens. The golden orange anthers mature after the two-lobed stigma, which is shrivelled when the pollen is ripe ; the outer stamens are somewhat shorter than the inner ones in the advanced flower, and the stigma is prominent in the new flower, so cross-fer-tilization is practically assured. The blossom attracts insects which gather pollen but find no honey, and its chief visitors are honeybees, bumblebees, the smaller bees of the genus *Halictus*, and the beelike flies (*Bombylius*). As the plant breaks through the ground in early April, the leaf is curled into a cylinder which encloses the budding flower ; afterward the blossom pushes upward beyond the leaf. Eventually the light blue-olive green leaf, generally with seven irregular shal-low lobes, is 6–10 inches broad. The dull orange-colored sap is acrid, astringent, and medicinal in quality. Fruit-capsule elliptical-oblong with many light yellow-brown seeds. Plant finally about 10 inches high. Common everywhere on the borders of rich woods shaded road-sides, and copses.

Celandine
poppy
Stylophorum
diphyllum
Golden yellow
April-May

A western woodland species with yellow juice, deeply lobed light green leaves slen-der-stemmed and smooth, and with small four-petaled poppylike golden yellow flowers one inch broad, solitary, or 2–3 in

Bloodroot.
Sanguinaria Canadensis.

Celandine Poppy.
Stylophorum diphyllum.

a terminal cluster. Fertilized mainly by the smaller bees. The ovoid seed-pod hairy. The two sepals falling early. 12–16 inches high. In low damp woods, from western Pa., west to Tenn., Mo., and Wis. Found near St. Libory, St. Clair Co., Ill.

Celandine
Chelidonium majus
Deep yellow
May–August

A common weed naturalized from Europe, and found usually in or about the eastern towns. The leaves are somewhat similar to those of the preceding species, light lustreless green, smooth, and ornamentally small-lobed. The small deep yellow flower (with four petals), ¾ inch broad or less, has a prominent green style, and many yellow stamens. The plant has a strong yellow sap. 1–2 feet high. Common in waste places eastward. Found in Cambridge, Mass., and Plymouth, N. H.

Prickly Poppy
Argemone Mexicana
Yellow
June–September

A yellow poppy with prickly thistlelike leaves, very light green and smooth with a slight whitish bloom, commonly cultivated, and escaped to roadsides and waste places ; a native of Mexico. Flowers usually two inches broad or more, with four bright yellow petals, and numerous golden stamens. This poppy like all others is sought by the honeybee for its pollen ; it does not yield honey. The broad surface of the stigmas of poppies in general being a convenient alighting platform for insects, the flowers are surely adapted to cross-fertilization ; although the anthers ripen in the bud, and are directly over the stigma, Müller is of the opinion that cross-fertilization prevails. Self-fertilization in the case of *Argemone* is even less likely, as the stigmatic surface is small and far less exposed to the overhanging anthers. The fruit-capsule nearly an inch long, and armed with prickles. Rarely the flowers are white. Stem stout, bristly, and 1–2 feet high. Usually found near dwellings and on the neglected borders of old highways, from N. Eng. south, and west to Ohio.

The irregular-flowered group of *Papaveraceæ*, formerly called *Fumariaceæ*, has finely cut compound leaves, and somewhat sack-shaped flowers with spurred petals.

Celandine.
Chelidonium majus.

Prickly Poppy.
Argemone
Mexicana.

POPPY FAMILY. *Papaveraceæ.*

Climbing Fumitory, or Mountain Fringe
Adlumia cirrhosa
White, tinted magenta-pink
June–October

A beautiful and delicate vine climbing and trailing over thickets or shrubbery, with an attenuate, sack-shaped white flower tinted greenish and magenta-pink, or very pale pink, in drooping clusters. The leaves are compound, smooth, prettily subdivided, mostly three-lobed, and the vine climbs by means of their slender stems. The weak and slender stem 8–12 feet long. In moist situations, woods and thickets, from N. Eng., west to Wis. and eastern Kan., and south to N. Car., among the mountains. Named for John Adlum, of Washington, a horticulturist, first interested in the cultivation of grapes in this country.

Dutchman's Breeches
Dicentra Cucullaria
White, yellow-tipped
April–May

This is one of the daintiest wild flowers of the spring, common in southern New York, but rare or entirely absent in north-eastern New England. It occurs frequently in Vermont, but is quite unknown in the uplands of New Hampshire. The plant is characterized by a feathery compound leaf, long-stemmed and proceeding from the root, thin, grayish (almost sage) green in tint, blue and paler beneath; the leaflets are finely slashed and are distributed trifoliately, i. e., in three parts. The flowering stalk also proceeds from the root, and bears 4–8, rarely more, nodding white flowers, of four petals joined in pairs and forming, two of them, a double, two-spurred, somewhat heart-shaped sack, the other two, within the sack, very small, narrow, and protectingly adjusted over the slightly protruding stamens. The spurs are stained with light yellow. The flower is cross-fertilized mostly by the agency of the early bumblebees (*Bombus separatus*, *B. virginicus*, *B. vagans*, and *B. pennsylvanicus*). Prof. Robertson (see *Botanical Gazette*, vol. 14, p. 120) explains in detail the character of the flower and its visiting insects. Honeybees collect only pollen; their tongues are too short to reach the nectar which is secreted in two long processes of the middle stamens; the proboscis of the bumblebee, 8 mm. long, reaches it, that of the honeybee, 6 mm., can not. The honeybee

Dutchman's Breeches.   Dicentra cucullaria.

alights on the flower, forces its head between the inner petals, and gathers only the pollen with its front feet! Such a pendulous position as the flower compels is extremely difficult for insects other than bees to maintain. Butterflies therefore visit the flower with less success than bumblebees. *Pieris rapæ* (Cabbage butterfly, white), *Papilio ajax* (buff and black, crimson spots), and *Danais archippus* (the Monarch, black-and-tan) are common visitors; so are the little long-tongued flies of the tribe *Bombylius* (the beelike flies). Flowering stem 5–9 inches high. In thin woodlands and on rocky slopes from N. Eng., south to N. Car., and west to Neb., S. Dak., and Mo. The name from the Greek, meaning twice-spurred.

Squirrel Corn
Dicentra
Canadensis
White,
magenta-pink
May–June

A similar species with more attenuate flowers, white or greenish white tinted with magenta-pink, 4–8 on the stalk, all very short-stemmed, and narrow at the base, slightly fragrant. 6–12 inches high, the roots bearing many little tubers resembling yellow peas, hence the common name. Rich woodlands, from Me., south along the mountains to Va., and west to Minn., Neb., and Mo.

Dicentra exima is a tall rare species, with less finely cut leaves, large and smooth, and with narrow magenta-pink flowers. Sometimes cultivated. 1–2 feet high. Rocky slopes. Western N. Y., south to Ga. and Tenn., along the mountains.

Pale Corydalis
Corydalis
glauca
Pale pink
May–August

This is another conspicuously delicate wild flower of spring. Its relationship with *Dicentra* is manifested by the pale foliage and the attenuated sacklike blossom; in New England it seems almost to supplant Dutchman's Breeches. The pale or whitish green leaves are compound, and cut into ornamental segments which are generally three-lobed. The pale crimson-pink, or sometimes magenta-pink, slightly curved corolla is half an inch or more long, somewhat round at the top (which is really the bottom), and two-flanged at the bottom or mouth, which is golden yellow. The leaves are scattered alternately on the plant-stem at the branching summit of which are groups of rarely

Pale Corydalis.
Corydalis glauca.

Squirrel Corn.
Dicentra Canadensis.

POPPY FAMILY. *Papaveraceæ.*

more than four flowers. The slender and erect stem whitened with a slight bloom and often stained pinkish, is 8–22 inches high. The seed-pods are erect and slender, 1½ inches long. In rocky situations, from Me., south to N. Car., and west to Minn. Found in the Middlesex Fells, near Boston.

Golden Corydalis
Corydalis aurea
Golden yellow March–May

A golden yellow-flowered species common in the west. The compound pale green leaves are beautifully cut into three-lobed segments, and the bright deep yellow corolla is about ½ an inch long. The seed-pod is beady in outline, slightly curved, and stands at an angle relatively with its neighbors. The slender stem 6–14 inches high. In woodlands from Me., south to Pa., and west to Wis. and Neb.

Fumitory
Fumaria officinalis
Crimson-pink or magenta June–September

A small delicate weed adventive from Europe, found mostly within the seaboard States. The light green leaves are finely cut, and the small crimson-pink or magenta-pink flowers with crimson tips are borne in a dense, long, narrow spike. The reclining stem 6–20 inches long. Waste places and near or in old gardens, from Me. to Fla. Local in the interior. The name from the Latin *fumus*, smoke, in allusion to the smokelike odor of some of the species.

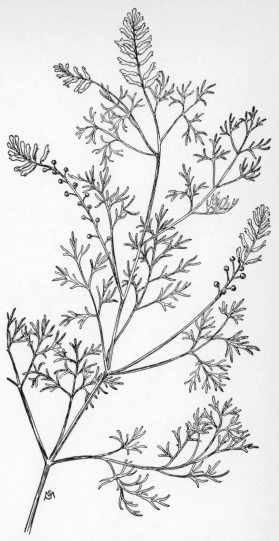

(Sometimes climbing to a height of 4 feet.)

Fumitory   Fumaria officinalis.

MUSTARD FAMILY. *Cruciferæ.*

MUSTARD FAMILY. *Cruciferæ.*

The Latin name of this family, from *Crux*, a cross, arose from the resemblance of the four opposing petals of its flowers to the form of a cross. There are also four deciduous sepals, one pistil, and six stamens, two of which are short; rarely there are less than six. The flowers are generally small and not showy, but they produce honey, and are accordingly frequently visited by the honeybees, the smaller bees, and the brilliantly colored flies of the family *Syrphidæ.*

Toothwort or Crinkleroot
Dentaria diphylla
White
May

A low woodland plant with inconspicuous flowers ⅔ inch wide, having four petals and many yellow stamens. The basal leaves long-stemmed, three-lobed, and toothed, the two upper stem-leaves similar and opposite; all smooth. The flowers borne in a small terminal cluster. The slender seed-pods one inch long. The long root is wrinkled, toothed, and is edible, possessing a pleasant pungent flavor, like watercress. 8–13 inches high. In rich woodlands and damp meadows, from Me., south to S. Car., west to Minn.

Cut-leaved Toothwort
Dentaria laciniata
White or pinkish
April–May

A similar species, but with the leaves deeply cut into narrow lobes, sharply and coarsely toothed; three are borne upon the smooth, or sparingly woolly stem not far below the flower-cluster. The basal leaves are developed after the flowering time. The flowers are often faintly tinged with magenta-pink. Root also peppery. Common everywhere in moist woods or on the borders of thickets.

Spring Cress
Cardamine rhomboidea
White
April–May

A smooth and less conspicuous, slender plant found beside springs, or in wet meadows, with somewhat angularly round root-leaves, and sparingly coarse-toothed, ovate stem-leaves. The flowers, like toothwort, ½ inch broad, succeeded by a long beanlike pod. 6–16 inches high. Common everywhere. The var. *purpurea*, with magenta-purple flowers, has a slightly woolly stem, and blooms a little earlier. Western N. Y., south to Md., and west to Wis. and S. Dak.

Toothwort.   Dentaria diphylla.

MUSTARD FAMILY. *Cruciferæ.*

Small Bitter Cress
Cardamine hirsuta
White
April–June
A bitter-tasting little herb easily distinguished by its exceedingly long thin seed-pods which are an inch long and erect. The tiny flowers with four narrow petals are white, and are frequently visited by the brilliant flies of the family *Syrphidæ.* The little compound leaves mostly at the base of the plant form a rather pretty rosette; the few upper leaflets are exceedingly narrow. 3–12 inches high. Common everywhere in wet places.

Hairy Rock Cress
Arabis hirsuta
Greenish white
May–July
This is a generally hairy little plant (sometimes it is nearly smooth) with a tall slim stem, terminated by a small cluster of tiny white or greenish white flowers beneath which in the later season of its bloom appears a succession of slim seed-pods. The clustered basal leaves are hairy, toothed, and lance-shaped, but blunt at the tip; the stem-leaves clasp the stem, and are widely toothed and small. 12–20 inches high. Common on rocky banks, and in stony pastures from Me., south along the mountains to Ga., and west.

Arabis lævigata
Greenish white
April–May
A perfectly *smooth* species with a slight bloom, taller than the preceding, and with stem-leaves which clasp the stem and are almost pointed either side of it—what is sometimes called a sagittate (arrow-shaped) base. Resembling in other respects the species above described. 1–3 feet high. Similarly distributed but not farther west than Minn.

Carolina Whitlow-grass
Draba Caroliniana
White
March–May
Our native whitlow-grass distinguished at once by its slender or linear seed-pods, which are longer than their stems. The tiny flowers and the pods below them terminate a long smooth stem; the little obtuse-ovate leaves nearly at the base of the plant. An annual of miniature proportions. 1–5 inches high. In sandy and barren fields from eastern Mass., south to Ga., and west to S. Dak., Neb., and Ark.

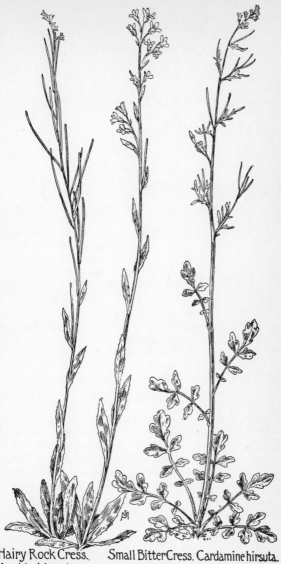

Hairy Rock Cress.
Arabis hirsuta.

Small Bitter Cress. Cardamine hirsuta.
The form often separated as Cardamine Pennsylvanica.

MUSTARD FAMILY. *Cruciferæ.*

Common Whit-low-grass
Draba verna
White
March-May

A species naturalized from Europe, and common throughout our range in barren fields and beside the road. The four white petals are deeply notched; the small hairy lance-shaped and toothed leaves are clus-tered at the base of the flowering-stems. The pods are shorter than their stems, and elliptical. Flower-stems leafless, and smooth above but a trifle hairy below. 1-5 inches high.

Watercress
Nasturtium of-ficinale
White
April-August

A common aquatic plant, much prized for its pungent-tasting young leaves, which are smooth, dark green, or brownish green in spring, and lighter green in summer. The insignificant white flowers terminate the branching stems. Leaves compound with 3-9 roundish leaflets. The scientific name is from *nasus*, nose, and *tortus*, twisted, in reference to its stinging effect upon the nose. Naturalized from Europe. 4-10 inches high. In brooks and small streams everywhere, except in the northernmost parts of our range.

Marsh Water-cress
Nasturtium ter-restre
Yellow
May-August

A yellow-flowered species common everywhere, but naturalized from Europe in the seaboard States; indigenous in the west. The leaves ornamentally cut, of usually seven segments. Pods oblong, about equaling the length of the stems. 1-3 feet high. In wet situations. Found at Lincoln, Neb.

Horseradish
Nasturtium Armoracia
White
June-August

A coarse species well known for the im-mensely strong peppery quality of its large white roots which furnish a favorite spring table relish. The oblong leaves toothed, and roughly veined, the basal ones large. The small white flowers rather conspicuous. Pods nearly round. Escaped from cultivation, into moist ground everywhere; naturalized from Europe. 20-30 inches high.

Whitlow-grass.
Draba verna.

Hedge Mustard.
Sisymbrium officinale.

MUSTARD FAMILY. *Cruciferæ.*

Yellow Rocket or Winter Cress
Barbarea vulgaris
Yellow
April-May

A bright yellow-flowered species with a simple stem terminated by one or more showy spikes of flowers beneath which the long curved seed-pods later appear in a loose cluster. Upper leaves stemless, lower ones cut in usually five divisions, the terminal one very large; all deep shining green. The pretty four-petaled flowers with six stamens four of which are quite prominent, are frequently visited by the early bees and handsome flies of the genus *Syrphidæ*. They yield honey and pollen. 1-2 feet high. In moist places along the road, and in meadows. Me., south to Va., and west. Naturalized from Europe, but indigenous in the west.

Hedge Mustard
Sisymbrium officinale
Light yellow
May-September

A homely straggling weed with tiny light yellow flowers, and light green, smooth leaves, with 3-6 lobes, irregularly blunt-toothed. The generally smooth stem with tall widely spreading, wiry branches, tipped with a few flowers and curiously set with the *close-pressing pods*. 1-3 feet high. In waste places throughout our range. Naturalized from Europe.

Charlock or Field Mustard
Brassica Sinapistrum
Yellow
May-September

A coarse and vexatious weed in cultivated fields and waste places, adventive from the old country, and widely distributed through the northern States. The light yellow flowers over ½ inch broad, in small terminal clusters. The leaves ovate with few if any lobes, indistinctly or sparsely toothed, with short stems or none at all. The seed-pods ⅔-inch long, contracted between the seeds, and lumpy in contour. 1-2 feet high. Me., west to Neb. and S. Dak., and south.

Black Mustard
Brassica nigra
Yellow
June-September

Another common weed in grain fields, and beside the road. A more widely branched plant than the preceding, and with far more deeply lobed leaves; one terminal large division, and generally four lateral ones, all finely toothed. The small *pure* light yellow flowers less than ½ inch broad are frequently

172

Mustard.   Brassica nigra.

visited by the smaller bees, and *Syrphid* flies; the pistil much exceeding the stamens in length, adapts the flower to cross-fertilization. The pod is ½ inch long, four-sided, and lies close to the stem; the seeds are black-brown. 2–5 feet high. Naturalized from Europe, and extending throughout our range.

White Mustard
Brassica alba
Yellow
June–August

A similar but rarer species, more or less hairy, with bristly pods, contracted between the seeds; these are light yellow-brown. The flowers are a little larger. 1–2 feet high. In fields and on roadsides, escaped from gardens; naturalized from Europe. Both of these last species introduced into Neb.

Shepherd's Purse
Capsella Bursa-pastoris
White
April–September

A very common weed on roadsides near dwellings, and on waste ground, with tiny white flowers. The Latin name is literally a *shepherd's little purse*, in allusion to the shape of the tiny seed-pods. The root-leaves are deeply cut, and form a rosette, the stem-leaves are small, lance-shaped, and indistinctly toothed. 8–18 inches high. Naturalized from Europe, and distributed throughout our range.

Wild Pepper-grass
Lepidium Virginicum
White
May–September

A somewhat similar species, but more branched, remarkable for its peppery-tasting seed-pods which cluster thickly about the flowering stems in a cylindrical curving column beneath the few terminating white flowers. Basal leaves obovate (tapering to a stemlike base) with a few small lateral divisions, stem-leaves small and lance-shaped; all toothed. 6–15 inches high. Common on roadsides everywhere.

Peppergrass.
Lepidium Virginicum.

Shepherd's Purse.
Capsella-Bursa-pastoris.

PITCHER PLANT FAMILY. *Sarraceniaceæ.*

PITCHER PLANT FAMILY. *Sarraceniaceœ.*

Swamp plants with pitcherlike leaves, and nodding flowers with 4–5 sepals, five petals, numerous stamens, and one pistil; represented by only one species in the northern United States.

Pitcher Plant
Sarracenia
purpurea
Dull dark red
May–June

A curious and interesting plant found in peat-bogs throughout the north. The strange hollow leaves, keeled on the inner side toward the flower-stem, are usually partly filled with water and the fragments of insects; the latter are apparently drowned, and no doubt contribute to the physical sustenance of the plant; but the raw-meat coloring, the red veining, and the general form of the flower are conducive to the attraction of carrion flies, which are especially fitted for the cross-fertilization of the flower. The style within the blossom is strangely like an umbrella with five ribs, the stigmatic surface on the inside. The folding petals and the flower's drooping position certainly protect the ripening pollen from any disturbance by the elements, but the inquisitive insect finds easy access to it. The general coloring of the whole plant is green with red-purple veining; the sepals are madder purple, and greenish on the inside, the petals are dull pink, and the umbrellalike style green. The outer surface of the pitchers is smooth, but the inner surface is covered with fine bristles pointing downward, which manifestly interfere with the escape of trapped insects. The pitchers are circled about the root in radiating lines, and they measure 4–10 inches in length; the flower-stem is frequently a foot high. The plant is commonly found in the black peat-bogs of wooded hills or in mountain tarns where there is scant sunshine. When the plant is more exposed to the sun its green coloring predominates. It is common north and south, and extends as far west as Minn.

Pitcher Plant.　　Sarracenia purpurea.

SUNDEW FAMILY. *Droseraceæ.*

Bog plants with sticky-hairy leaves which are coated with a fluid designed to attract and retain insects—they are, in fact, carnivorous. The small flowers are perfect, with five petals, and few or many stamens, with the anthers turned outward. Fruit a 1–5-celled capsule. The tiny red filaments of the leaves curl and clasp about a captured insect, and ultimately its juices are absorbed.

Round-leaved Sundew
Drosera rotundifolia
White
July–August

A *very* small plant with long-stemmed round leaves lying close to or upon the ground, both leaf and stem covered with long, fine, red hairs. The red flower-stem is erect and smooth, and bears about four or six small white flowers, which are frequently visited by the fungous gnats and other small woodland insects. The flower-cluster is one-sided, bends over, and the blossoms open one at a time only in the sunshine. The glands of the leaves exude clear drops of fluid, which appear like small dewdrops; hence the popular name, also the Greek δροσερός, meaning dewy. The whole plant is so saturated with color that its sap stains paper a ruddy madder purple. 4–9 inches high. In bogs, from Me., south, and west to the Daks.

Long-leaved Sundew
Drosera intermedia, var. *Americana*

A very similar species, but with elongated blunt-tipped leaves whose stems are long and rather erect. Differing further from the preceding species by the *naked* leaf-stems, the red hairs appearing only upon the little leaves. It is not so common as the other species, but occupies about the same territory.

Slender Sundew
Drosera linearis

A western species with 3-inch long, slender or linear leaves, also with naked, erect stems. The white flowers are few. Shores of Lakes Superior and Huron.

Thread-leaved Sundew
Drosera filiformis
Purple-magenta

The leaves of this larger species are reduced to a mere threadlike shape with no distinct stem; they are glandular, red hairy throughout, the hairs terminated by a red bead or dot. The flowers are fully $\frac{1}{2}$ inch broad, and dull purple - magenta.

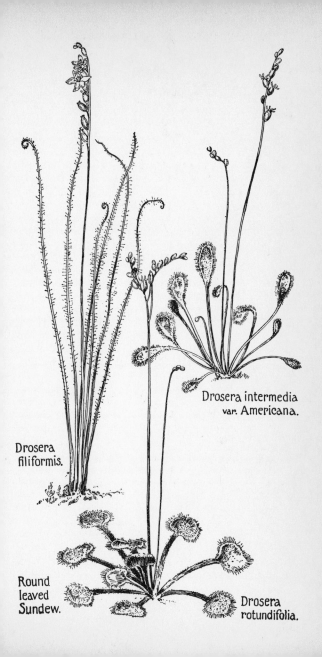

Drosera
filiformis.

Drosera intermedia
var. Americana.

Round
leaved
Sundew.

Drosera
rotundifolia.

There are many in the cluster. 8-18 inches high. In wet sand near the seacoast, from Mass., south. Found in the pine barrens of New Jersey. Nothing is more dainty and beautiful under the magnifying-glass than the spun-glasslike, glandular, ruby hairs of the *Droseras.*

ORPINE FAMILY.   *Crassulaceæ.*

Rather fleshy or succulent herbs, with absolutely symmetrical small flowers ; the petals, sepals, pistils, and stamens equal in number, or the last double in number, differing only in this respect from *Saxifragaceæ.*

Ditch Stonecrop
Penthorum sedoides
Yellow-green
July–September

A familiar weed of ditches and swamps with insignificant greenish yellow, or yellow-green flowers, in slender bending clusters of 2-3 branches, at the top of the erect stem.   The latter is smooth, usually branched, and bears lance-shaped, or elliptical, pointed, light green leaves, finely toothed.   The flower has five sepals, but rarely any petals, ten stamens, and five pistils united below, finally forming a five-angled seed-vessel.   Not fleshy-leaved. 8-20 inches high.   Me., west to S. Dak. and Neb.

Wild Stonecrop
Sedum ternatum
White
April–June

A small species at home on rocky ledges and in stony woodlands.   It has little five-petaled white flowers growing on horizontally spreading branches.   The leaves are small, toothless, fleshy, and rather wedge-shaped ; the lower ones are generally in groups of three.   The flower-cluster is three-spiked and leafy.   3-8 inches high.   The name is from *sedeo*, to sit.

Live-forever or Garden Orpine
Sedum Telephium
Dull garnet red
June–September

A common perennial, with a stout light green stem and *very smooth, fleshy,* dull-toothed leaves, which children are fond of splitting by lateral pressure with the fingers, and forming into green "purses." It is adventive from Europe, and is generally an escape from gardens, establishing itself in fields and on roadsides.   The light green leaves, particularly when young, are covered with a whitish bloom.   The small flowers in thick clusters are opaque crimson.   10-18 inches high.   Common.

Live-forever.   Sedum Telephium.

SAXIFRAGE FAMILY. *Saxifragaceæ.*

SAXIFRAGE FAMILY. *Saxifragaceæ.*

A large family of herbs or shrubs related to the family *Rosaceæ*, but differing from it by having albumen in the seeds, and *opposite* as well as alternate leaves. The flowers are mostly perfect with usually five petals, fertilized by the aid of the smaller bees, and the flies (*Syrphidæ*), or in some instances butterflies.

Early Saxi-
frage
Saxifraga
Virginiensis
White
April–May

A little plant hugging the rocks on dry hillsides and blooming along with the first flowers of spring; the buds are formed early, and appear like little (fine-haired) balls in the centre of the rosettelike clusters of obovate leaves close to the ground. Eventually a cluster expands to a branching downy stem bearing many little white, five-petaled, perfect flowers with ten yellow stamens. The flowers are succeeded by rather odd and pretty madder purple seed-vessels which are two-beaked; often the color is madder brown. Besides some of the earlier bees, the *Antiopa* butterfly (rusty black with a corn color border) and the tortoise-shell butterfly (brown and tan) may be included as among the frequent visitors of the flower; but whether they play any important part in the process of fertilization, it is difficult to say. 4–10 inches high. Me., south to Ga., and west to Minn.

Swamp Saxi-
frage
Saxifraga
Pennsylvanica
Greenish white
May

A much larger plant with less attractive, greenish white flowers with very narrow (linear) petals. The stem is somewhat sticky-hairy and stout. The larger blunt lance-shaped leaves are scarcely toothed, and are narrowed to a rather broad stem. 12–30 inches high. In bogs and on wet banks from Me., south to Va., and west to Minn. and Iowa. The name saxifrage is from *Saxifragus*, meaning a rock or stone breaker! but it is far from evident that the plant's roots, in spreading between the crevices of rocks, succeed in *breaking stone* by vigorous growing ; the name may as well be referred to reputed medicinal virtues of the roots.

Early Saxifrage.   Saxifraga Virginiensis.

SAXIFRAGE FAMILY. *Saxifrageæ.*

False Mitre-wort, Foam-flower, or Coolwort
Tiarella cordifolia
White
Late April– early June

An attractive little plant that decorates the moist woodland floor with its ornamental leaves all through the summer. The feathery spike of fine white flowers with five petals appears conspicuously above the leaves in late spring or early summer ; the ten prominent stamens have orange anthers, and the long pistil in the centre is white. The leaves remotely resemble those of the mountain maple, but they are small, rough hairy over the upper surface, and dark green, sometimes mottled with a brownish tone. The little seed-capsule is characteristically cloven like a tiara, hence the name ; the heart-shaped form of the leaf accounts for the specific *cordifolia*. 6–12 inches high. In rich woods, from Me., south along the mountains to Ga., and west to Minn. Common in the woods of the White Mountains.

Mitrewort or Bishop's Cap
Mitella diphylla
White
April–May

The true mitrewort is very easily distinguished from the false, by several marked differences; half-way up the stem are two opposite leaves nearly if not quite stemless. The flowers instead of being borne on rather long individual stems in a thin feathery cluster, are short-stemmed and distinctly separated; the tiny white blossom has five petals beautifully fringed, which remind one of a highly ornamental snow crystal. This plant is also hairy throughout. The name means *a little mitre*, alluding to the mitre-shape of the seed-pod. 8–16 inches high. Rich woods, Me., south to N. Car., and west to Minn.

Naked Mitre-wort or Bishop's Cap
Mitella nuda
Greenish white
April–June

A much smaller and daintier species distinguished by its naked stem, which is without the two leaflets, and is slightly hairy. The leaves approach a somewhat round form, and the snow-crystallike flowers are greenish white, and few. They have ten yellow stamens. 4–7 inches high. In cool woods and mossy bogs, from N. Eng., south to Pa., and west. The *Mitellas* are common in Vermont, but rare or absent in central New Hampshire.

False   Mitrewort.
Tiarella cordifolia.

Naked Mitrewort.
Mitella nuda.

SAXIFRAGE FAMILY. *Saxifragaceæ.*

Alumroot
Heuchera
Americana
Whitish green
May–July

A stout and tall plant bearing some resemblance to *Mitella nuda* on a large scale; but the flowers are distinctly different; they are borne in a long loose cluster, usually 4–5 on one of the small branching stems, small, bell-shaped, with inconspicuous green petals, very prominent stamens tipped with orange anthers, of which there are but five. The leaves are heart-shaped and scalloped ; the teeth blunt. The stem is more or less hairy, and is 2–3 feet high. Named for Johann Heinrich von Heucher, a German botanist of the early eighteenth century. Rocky woodlands N. Y. and Conn., west to Minn., southwest to Ala. and La.

Golden Saxi-frage
Chrysosplenium
Americanum
Yellow or pur-ple-green
April–June

An insignificant plant of cold bogs or wet places, with a slender low-growing, forking stem, with roundish fine-scalloped generally opposite-growing leaves, and fine yellowish or purplish green flowers with orange anthers, growing close between the points where the leaves join the plant stem. In wet shady places, Me., south along the mountains to Ga., and west to Mich. and Minn. Stems 3–7 inches long. The name means golden spleen, from reputed medicinal qualities.

Grass-of-Par-nassus
Parnassia
Caroliniana
White green-veined
June-September

An interesting perennial herb with single cream white flowers delicately veined with green, about 1 inch broad. A single ovate olive green leaf clasps the flowering stem; the others are long, slender-stemmed and heart-shaped, and spring from the root. The flower has five petals and five straw yellow anthers terminating the fertile stamens and alternating with the petals ; a number (perhaps 15) of abortive stamens encircle the green pistil. The blossom is visited by bees and the smallest butterflies (skippers); chief among the visitors are the larger ones named *Colias philodice* (yellow), and *Pieris rapæ* (white). 8–20 inches high. In swamps and wet meadows, Me., south to Va., west to S. Dak. and Iowa.

Grass-of-Parnassus.　　Parnassia Caroliniana

ROSE FAMILY. *Rosaceæ.*

An extensive family highly esteemed for its luscious fruits, and for its most beautiful flowers, which are dependent in a great measure upon the bees for cross-fertilization. The flowers are extraordinarily rich in pollen and honey; the raspberry yielding the finest flavored honey which is known. The leaves are alternate-growing, and accompanied by stipules, or small leafy formations at the base of the leaf-stalk. The flowers are regular and generally perfect, with usually five sepals and as many petals (seldom more or less), numerous stamens, and one or many pistils. Rarely the petals are absent. The family is very closely allied to *Saxifragaceæ* and *Leguminosæ*. It is mostly composed of trees and shrubs, although the herbaceous members are many.

Meadowsweet
Spiræa salici-folia var. *lati-folia*
Flesh pink
June–August

A common flower on the borders of the road in bloom throughout the early summer. A shrub with light green, nearly smooth, ovate, sharply toothed leaves, and a usually yellowish buff stem of a wiry character, upon which are freely set the alternate leaves. The beautiful flower-spike is pyramidal but blunt and branching, and is closely crowded with flesh pink and white flowers, resembling miniature apple-blossoms, with prominent pink-red stamens. It is frequently visited by the smaller butterflies and the bees, and possesses a slight fragrance. The name is from the Greek, and means *twisting*, alluding to the twist in the pods of some species. 2–4 feet high. Me., south to Ga., and west to Mo. and S. Dak.

Hardhack or Steeplebush
Spiræa tomen-tosa
Deep pink
July–September

A similar species, but readly distinguished by its woolly stem (terra-cotta red) and leaves; the latter are olive green of a dark tone above, and very whitish and woolly beneath. The slender steeple-like flower-spike is crowded with tiny, *deep* rosy pink flowers, smaller than those of the preceding species; the succession of bloom is unfortunately slow, and *downward*, so the top of the

Meadowsweet.
Spiræa salicifo-
lia var. latifolia.

Hardhack.
Spiræa tomentosa.

spike is often in a half-withered condition. 2–4 feet high. In dry or wet ground, same range as the preceding species.

Queen-of-the-Prairie
Spiræa lobata
Deep pink
June–July

A tall western species, also in cultivation, with handsome, fragrant, deep pink, or peach-blossom-colored flowers, and cut-lobed, deep green, smooth, large leaves of sometimes seven divisions. It grows in moist situations or on the prairies. The terminal leaflet is larger than the others. The large compound flower-cluster of perfect fine-petaled flowers, is feathery in character. 2–8 feet high. Western Pa., south to Ga. and Ky., west to Wis. and Iowa. An escape to roadsides in Peacham, Randolph, and Lower Cabot, Vt. (Brainerd, Jones, and Eggleston).

Goat's Beard
Spiræa
Aruncus
Yellowish white
May–July

Another tall and handsome species with a compound flower-spike formed of many little spikes about as large around as one's little finger. The tiny narrow-petaled flowers are yellowish white, and are an exception to the general rule of the family, as they are staminate on one plant and pistillate upon another. The stem is smooth and the deep green leaves are compound, with sometimes eleven small leaflets. The pistillate flower has usually three distinct pistils. 3–6 feet high. In rich woods, N. Y., south to Ga., and west to Mo.

Purple Flowering-Raspberry
Rubus odoratus
Crimson-pink or magenta-pink
June–August

A shrubby roadside species which suffers with a misleading name; the Rose Family is quite incapable of producing a true purple flower. This big-leaved plant exhibits a wild-roselike flower of five broad petals whose color is at first deep crimson-pink, and at last a faded magenta-pink. The large maplelike leaves are 3–5 lobed and a trifle hairy. The stem is covered with short red or brown bristly hairs; the flower-stems are particularly red, as well as the calyx, or flower-envelop. The fruit is insipid and resembles a flat, red raspberry; it is often called Thimble-berry. 3–5 feet high. Common in stony woodlands, beside the shaded road, and in copses. Me.,

Purple Flowering-Raspberry.   Rubus odoratus.

south to Ga., and west to Mich. The name *rubus* is an ancient one for bramble, from *ruber*, red.

Cloudberry, or Mountain Raspberry
Rubus Chamœmorus
White
June–July

One of the interesting relatives of the common raspberry which finds its home among the clouds of high mountain-tops, It is found in the peat bogs of the White Mountains and on the coast of eastern Maine. The cloudberry is another instance of a break in the family rule : the flowers are staminate on one plant and pistillate on another. The solitary white flower is about an inch broad. The plant-stem is herbaceous, not shrubby, and the leaves are rather roundish with 5–9 lobes ; the stem is unbranched and with only 2–3 leaves. The fruit is a pale wine red, or when nearly ripe, amber color, and possesses a delicate flavor ; the lobes are few. 3–10 inches high. Me. to N. Y., north to the Arctic regions.

Dalibarda repens
White
June–September

A delicate woodland plant with a white blossom like that of the wild strawberry, and densely woolly or fine-hairy stems and leaves ; the latter are dark green, heart-shaped, and wavy or scallop-toothed. In form they closely resemble those of the common blue violet. The 1–2 white flowers about $\frac{1}{2}$ inch in diameter are borne on long fuzzy, sometimes ruddy stems ; it is said that they fertilize in the bud before opening. 2–4 inches high. In the northern woods, from Me., south to southern N. J., and west to Ohio and Mich. Found in Langdon Park, Plymouth, N. H.

White Avens
Geum album
White
June–August

A rather tall, fine-hairy plant with angular, branching stem, insignificant five-petaled white flowers, and three-divided leaves, except the simple uppermost ones ; the root-leaves of 3–5 leaflets, all toothed. The flowers succeeded by a burlike densely bristly seed-receptacle. 18–24 inches high. On the borders of woods and shaded roads. Common in the north, but south only to Ga.

Dalibarda repens.

Rough Avens
Geum Virginianum
Cream white
May–July

A bristly hairy-stemmed plant common in low grounds and on the borders of low damp woods, with flowers and leaves similar to those of the preceding species. The stem very stout. The flower has inconspicuous cream white petals which roll backward. Common over the same territory.

Geum strictum
Golden yellow
July–August

A slightly hairy species with compound lower leaves, the leaflets wedge-shaped with round tips, the upper leaves with 3–5 leaflets irregular, oblong, and acute. Flowers golden yellow. Fruit-receptacle downy. Moist meadows Me., south to N. J., west to Kan., Neb., and S. Dak.

Purple Avens
Geum rivale
Brownish purple
July–August

An aquatic or marsh species, with lyre-shaped root-leaves, and irregular compound upper leaves ; the stem-leaves few, and three-lobed. The nodding flowers brownish or rusty purple, with obovate petals terminating with a claw. 2 feet high. Bogs and wet meadows, Me., south to N. J., west to Minn. and Mo.

Long-plumed Avens
Geum triflorum
Dull crimson-red
May–July

An exceedingly pretty and graceful but rare avens, with a decorative, deeply cut leaf, and a ruddy flower-stalk generally bearing three ruddy flowers with scarcely opened acute, erect calyx-lobes. The fruit is daintily plumed with gray feathery hairs, about an inch long. 6–12 inches high. Dry or rocky soil. Me., west to Minn., south to Mo.

Geum radiatum
var. *Peckii*
Yellow
July–early September

This is a dwarf species with smooth stem and showy pure yellow flowers quite an inch broad, which is found on Mt. Washington, and other high peaks in the north. The ornamental roundish leaves are nearly smooth — except the veins. Also on the high mountains of N. Car.

Avens.

Geum triflorum.   Geum radiatum var. Peckii.

Wild Virginia Strawberry
Fragaria Virginiana
White
April–June

Our commonest wild strawberry, at home in the rough dry pasture lands of the north and south. Rather broad, coarsely toothed leaflets, blunt-tipped, and hairy. The flower-stalk not longer than the leaves, and with spreading hairs. The flower has many orange-yellow stamens offset by the five round white petals. The scarlet fruit is ovoid, and the tiny seeds are imbedded in pits over the surface. 3–6 inches high. Common throughout our range; generally in fields. The name from the Latin *fraga*, fragrant.

American Wood Strawberry
Fragaria Americana
White
May–July

A slender species with thin leaflets which are more ovate and less wedge-shaped than those of the other species, and have silk-silvery hairs on the under side. The scarlet fruit is more conical, and the seeds are borne, not in pits, but upon the shining, smooth surface. The sepals are reflexed or turned backward from the fruit. This species is remarkable for its very long, delicate runners. 3–6 inches high. In rocky woodlands and pastures. From N. Eng., N. J., and Pa., west.

Until recently both these very distinct species were included under one title; but the types are easily distinguished apart, even by the leaves, and the fruit is certainly conspicuously different. Of the two species *Fragaria Virginiana* is certainly the commoner, at least in central New Hampshire; both are deserving of the name *Fragaria*, for nothing is more deliciously fragrant than a basketful of the wild berries.

Wild Virginia Strawberry.
Fragaria Virginica.

American
Wood Strawberry.
Fragaria Americana.

**Norway
Cinquefoil**
*Potentilla
Norvegica*
**Yellow
June–
September**

A weedy plant differing from the common cinquefoil by an *extremely* hairy stem and leaf; the latter is composed also of three leaflets instead of five, and it slightly suggests the strawberry leaf. The five not very conspicuous petals are somewhat isolated in the green setting of the flower, which is very leafy in character. There are 15–20 stamens. 12–30 inches high. In dry or waste ground, from Me., south to S. Car., and west. The name is from *potent* for the plant's reputed medicinal powers.

**Rough-fruited
Cinquefoil**
Potentilla recta
**Yellow
June–
September**

A similar stout plant, with a characteristically rough, horned seed-vessel. The five rather narrow leaflets are deep green, very hairy beneath, and slightly so above. The flowers are pure yellow, and ¾ inch broad; the petals are much larger than the lobes of the calyx (flower-envelop), which is the reverse of the case with the Norway cinquefoil. Erect, 1–2 feet high. Adventive from Europe, and in the vicinity of old gardens and waste grounds. Me., south to Va., and west to Mich. Found at Exeter, Penobscot Co., Me.

**Silvery
Cinquefoil**
*Potentilla
argentea*
**Yellow
May–
September**

A small species remarkable for its silvery character. The leaflets are dark green above and silver white beneath. The stem is also covered with the silky white wool, beneath which appears the pale terra-cotta tint of its surface. The five wedge-shaped, narrow leaflets are rolled back at the edge, and quite deeply cut. The pure yellow flowers are rather small, and loosely clustered at the ends of the branches. 5–12 inches long. In dry and sterile fields, or sandy soil, Me., south to N. J., and west to the Daks.

Norway Cinquefoil.　　　　Potentilla Norvegica.

ROSE FAMILY. *Rosaceæ.*

Potentilla frigida
Yellow
June-August

A dwarf Alpine species found on the summits of the White Mountains, rather soft-hairy when young, but smooth later, and with three coarsely toothed leaflets, deep green and somewhat broad. The small yellow flowers are slender-stemmed and generally solitary. 1-3 inches high. Found about the Lake of the Clouds and elsewhere on Mt. Washington. *Poten-*

Potentilla tridentata
White
June-August

tilla tridentata, also found on Mt. Washington and Mt. Wachusett, is less dwarfed, but low-growing. The three leaflets are *coarsely three-toothed* at the tip, smooth and thick. The flowers are white. 1-10 inches high. Coast of Mass., northward, and shores of the upper Great Lakes.

Marsh Five-finger or Purple Cinquefoil
Potentilla palustris.
Magenta-purple.
June-August

This is the only purple-flowered five-finger and it is therefore readily distinguished from the others. The reddish stem is stout, mostly smooth, and a trifle woody at the base. The leaves have from 5-7 leaflets which are blunt-tipped, and sharp-toothed. The rather pretty flowers are magenta-purple within and pale or greenish without, through the influence of the somewhat longer green sepals ; the blossom is nearly one inch broad, and its petals are pointed. 6-20 inches long. In swamps and cold bogs, from Me., south to N. J., and west to Cal.

Shrubby Cinquefoil
Potentilla fruticosa
Yellow
June-September

This is indeed a shrubby species with nearly erect stems, tan brown in color, and quite leafy ; the bark is inclined to peel off in shreds. The leaves are entirely different from those of the other species ; they are toothless, olive yellow-green, with 5-7 lance-shaped leaflets whose edges curve backward. They are silky hairy. The deep yellow flowers, with rounded petals are generally an inch broad. 1-2 feet high. It is a troublesome weed in N. Y., western Vt., Mass., and parts of the west. Swamps and wet places, Me., south to N. J., and west.

Leaf of
Potentilla fruticosa.

Leaf of
Potentilla tridentata.

Purple Cinquefoil.   Potentilla palustris.

ROSE FAMILY. *Rosaceæ*

Silverweed
Potentilla Anserina
Yellow
May–September

The silverweed is decoratively beautiful, and is remarkable for its very silky hairs which cover the under side of the leaves ; the latter are tansylike with about 7–23 sharp-toothed leaflets. The yellow flowers are solitary. Stem 1–3 feet long. In salt marshes and on wet meadows, from Me., south to N. J., and west to Neb. Common on the beaches of Lake Champlain.

Five-finger or Cinquefoil
Potentilla simplex
Yellow
April–August

The commonest of all the five-fingers, often wrongly called wild strawberry, with pure yellow flowers about ½ inch broad. It decorates meadow and pasture, fertile and sterile grounds, and weaves its embroidery over the stony and barren roadside. Its five deep green, shiny, long-stalked leaflets are sharply toothed, firm, and smooth, altogether harder in character than the three strawberry leaflets. The whole plant is generally smooth, but sometimes thinly hairy. Flowers solitary, fertilized mostly by the flies of the genus *Syrphidœ*. Runners 6–20 inches long. Common everywhere in the north. From southern Me., N. H., Vt., and N. Y., west to Minn. The common similar form (or species) is *Potentilla Canadensis*, which is fine-woolly over the stems, and does not creep over the ground so characteristically as *P. simplex*.

Agrimony
Agrimonia Eupatoria
var. *hirsuta*
Yellow
June–August

A most common weed with a glandular-hairy simple stem, and compound leaves with a hairy stalk ; spicy odored when crushed. The usually seven bright green, many - ribbed ovate leaflets coarsely toothed ; the interposed tiny leaflets are ovate and toothed ; there are generally three pairs occupying the spaces between the larger lateral leaflets. The slender spikes of five-petaled yellow flowers with orange anthers are not showy. The seeds are sticky and adhere to one's clothing. 2–4 feet or more high. Common on the borders of woods and in thickets. Me., south to N. Car., and west. Found on the roadside near the Profile House, Franconia Notch, N. H.

Agrimone.
Agrimonia Eupatoria var. hirsuta.

Cinquefoil.
Potentilla simplex.

ROSE FAMILY. *Rosaceæ.*

Smooth Rose
Rosa blanda
Pink
June–July

A comparatively *thornless* wild rose, with usually 5–7 blunt or round-tipped leaflets rather short-stalked, and pale beneath; simply toothed. Rarely there are a few straight slender prickles upon the smooth stem which is usually covered with a slight bloom. The pale crimson-pink flowers are nearly 3 inches broad and are solitary or in small clusters. The fruit is either globular or pear-shaped with persisting sepals. 2–4 feet high. On rocky, moist ground, Newfoundland to Vt. and northern N. J., and west to Ill., S. Dak., and the region of the Great Lakes. *Rosa* is the ancient name of the rose.

Swamp Rose
Rosa Carolina
Pink
June–August

A very bushy species, extremely decorative in character, armed rather sparingly with stout hooked spines. The 5–9 olive green leaflets sharp-toothed, long-stalked, and the stalk bordered with very narrow somewhat toothed stipules (leafy formations); the leaflets either blunt or sharp-tipped. The small clusters of flowers succeeded by showy, globular, red fruit which sometimes sheds its withered sepals. The pale crimson-pink flowers 2–3 inches broad. Largely fertilized by bees. 2–7 feet high. Common in swamps and low ground everywhere. Found at Sankaty Head, Nantucket.

Dwarf Wild Rose
Rosa lucida
Pink
June–July

A low species with generally lustrous green leaves of from .3–7 oval leaflets coarsely and simply toothed; the stipules (compare with species above) are narrow and flaring. A marked characteristic of this rose is the glandular-hairy globose fruit, stem, and lobed sepals; before maturity this condition is quite marked. The spines are wide at the base and rather straight or very slightly curved; the stems are mostly a ruddy madder brown. Flowers a pale or deeper crimson-pink, in small clusters, generally very few together. The commoner rose of N. J. and Pa. 1–5 feet high. In moist situations. Me., south to Ga., and west to Wis.

Spines of Rosa lucida.

Smooth Rose.   Rosa blanda.

ROSE FAMILY. *Rosaceæ.*

Pasture Rose
Rosa humilis

A questionable species so closely connected with *Rosa lucida*, that intergrading types prevent a satisfactory separation of the two. Under the name *Rosa humilis lucida* (*Rosa lucida* of Gray's *Manual*, sixth ed.), the rose of New Jersey, Pennsylvania, and the west is described by Britton and Brown as having thick shining leaves with broad stipules, and numerous flowers. Under *Rosa humilis*, the description embraces a narrow, toothless stipule, usually five leaflets, thin and somewhat shining, few or solitary flowers, a glandular-hairy calyx and stem, and sepals commonly lobed.

Northeastern Rose
Rosa nitida
Pink
June–July

This is a wild rose of the northeast, limited to that section lying between Massachusetts and Newfoundland. It is characterized by a stem *thickly crowded with bristly prickles*, and spines scarcely stouter. The 5–9 leaflets are ovate pointed, shining green, and sharply toothed; the stipules are broad. Flowers pale pink, solitary, or very few in a cluster; the fruit is globular, and the sepals are not lobed. A low species rarely over 20 inches high. On the borders of swamps.

Sweetbrier
Rosa rubiginosa
Pink
June–July

The wild rose or eglantine of the poets, adventive from Europe. It is remarkable for its sweet-scented foliage which is reminiscent of the fragrance of green apples, and for its long, arching stems, which are beautiful with compactly set clusters of pure pink bloom. The very small 5–7 leaflets are *double-toothed*, roundish, deep green above, and lighter colored beneath, where they are resinous, and aromatic when crushed; the leaves are also characteristically glandular-hairy. The somewhat small flowers are pink, or pale creamy pink, and clustered along the main stem upon short stalks. The decidedly recurved spines and the stem are madder brown when old. 4–6 feet high. Common everywhere from Tenn. and Va., northward. Another foreign species, *Rosa canina*, but slightly separated from *Rosa rubiginosa*, has usually simply toothed leaves which are not so odorous. Common in the valley of the Delaware.

Sweetbrier.   Rosa rubiginosa.

PULSE FAMILY. *Leguminosæ.*

PULSE FAMILY. *Leguminosæ.*

A very large family of food-producing plants, with butterflylike flowers, and alternate, usually compound leaves, generally without teeth. The flowers are perfect and are borne singly or in spikes; they are fertilized largely by bees and butterflies.

Wild Indigo
Baptisia tinctoria
Yellow
June–August

A smooth and slender plant with deep gray-green, triple leaves of wedge-shaped leaflets covered with a slight bloom; they are almost stemless. The small pealike blossoms are pure yellow, and terminate the many branches of the upright stem. The flowers are visited by the butterflies and the *Syrphid* flies, but the honeybee, the leaf-cutter bee *Megachile*, and the bees of the genus *Halictus* are probably the most efficient agents of cross-fertilization. The plant grows with a bushy luxuriance in favorable situations, and has a most remarkable habit of turning black upon withering. 18–28 inches high. In dry sandy soil everywhere. Not in central N. H., but common at Nantucket. Found at Pownal, Vt.

Blue False Indigo
Baptisia australis
Light violet
June–July

A beautiful, tall, western species, with pale green smooth stem, light green wedge-shaped, short-stalked triple leaves, and loose flower-clusters, sometimes 10 inches long, of light, dull violet blossoms quite 1 inch long, of a soft, æsthetic hue. The peapodlike fruit is tipped with a spur. Plant 3–6 feet high. On rich alluvial soil, western Pa., south to Ga., and west to Mo. Quite handsome in cultivation.

Rattlebox
Crotalaria sagittalis
Yellow
June–August

The rattlebox, so named because the seeds rattle about in the boxlike, inflated, sepia-black pods, has oval pointed leaves, toothless, and nearly stemless, growing alternately along the bending stem. The yellow flowers are scarcely ½ inch long. The stems and edges of the leaves are soft-hairy. 4–12 inches high. In dry sandy soil everywhere, but not very common.

Baptisia
tinctoria.

1
Blue
False Indigo.
Baptisia australis.

PULSE FAMILY. *Leguminosæ.*

Blue Lupine
Lupinus perennis
Violet
May–June

This is one of our most charming so-called blue wild flowers; but it rings all the changes on violet and purple, and scarcely touches blue. The pealike blossom has violet or deep purple wings and a light violet hood veined with blue-violet. Rarely the sweet-scented flowers are magenta-pink or even white. The horse-chestnutlike leaf has generally eight narrow, light green leaflets. Stem and long-stalked leaves are generally fine-hairy, and frequently show a few touches of purple-red through the green. The flower-spike is quite showy, and pinkish early in the bud. Fertilized by bees. 1–2 feet high. In sandy fields everywhere.

Rabbit=foot or Stone Clover
Trifolium arvense
Gray-pink
August–September

A naturalized species of clover, originally from Europe, remarkable for its oblong fuzzy flower-heads, the corolla of which is green-white and the calyx green with pink tips, all in effect rather gray-pink. The light green triple leaves have narrow, long leaflets with blunt tips. The flowers are sweet-scented. 4–10 inches high. Common in poor soil, old fields, and pastures, everywhere.

Red Clover
Trifolium pratense
Crimson or magenta
May–September

This is our commonest field clover and a special favorite of the bumblebee upon whom it is almost wholly dependent for fertilization. The plant was introduced into Australia some years ago and failed to produce seed the first year through its separation from the American bumblebee. Later when the insect was transported the plants flourished from season to season. The three (rarely 4–5) rather soft, dull bluish green leaflets are conspicuously marked by a whitish or yellow-green triangle. There are two hairy white and green stipules or leafy wings at the base of the leaf-stalk. Stem and leaves are soft-hairy. The somewhat pyramidal globular flower-head ranges through crimson or magenta to paler tints of the same colors, and even white; it yields a plentiful supply of nectar, which is scarcely reached by the short tongues of honeybees; also, the butterflies are not sufficiently heavy to depress the keel of the floret and thus expose

Rabbit-foot Clover.　　Trifolium arvense.

the anthers. The burly bumblebee is therefore the best pollen disseminator of this particular clover. 8–24 inches high. Common in fields and on roadsides, everywhere.

White Clover
Trifolium repens
Cream white
May–October

This is also one of our most common clovers, and a permanent resident of the grassy roadside. It is generally smooth, with roundish or heart-shaped leaflets marked less distinctly with a triangle, and frequently 4-5 leaflets are found on a single stalk. The globular flower-heads are a translucent cream white, and the florets are sometimes more or less tinted with flesh pink. Eventually the florets are reflexed. Fertilized by bees, and rich in honey. It is supposed to be identical with the Shamrock of Ireland, but it is native in the extreme north. 4–10 inches long. Creeping by runners. Common everywhere.

Alsike or Alsatian Clover
Trifolium hybridum
Creamy rose pink
May–October

A species somewhat similar to our white clover, but with a branching, stout, and rather juicy stem. The leaflets are generally obovate but not reverse heart-shaped; i. e., with the lobed tip; the edges are finely toothed, and the surface is not marked with the triangle; a pair of flaring stipules or leafy wings are at the base of the leafstalk. Flower-heads similar to those of white clover but varying from pinkish cream to crimson-pink; the withered florets brownish and turning downward, extremely sweet-scented, and rich in honey. Fertilized mostly by bees. 1–2 feet high. On roadsides, in meadows, and in waste places, from Me. to Idaho, and south to Ga.

Yellow or Hop Clover
Trifolium agrarium
Pale golden yellow
June–September

A small annual species, with a smooth stem and light green, narrow and long leaflets, scarcely suggesting the clover-leaf. The stem is branched and stands nearly upright, or reclines; the leaflets are very finely but rather imperceptibly toothed. The small, dull golden yellow florets bloom from the base of the flower-head upward, and the withered florets, turning downward and becoming brownish, resemble dried hops.

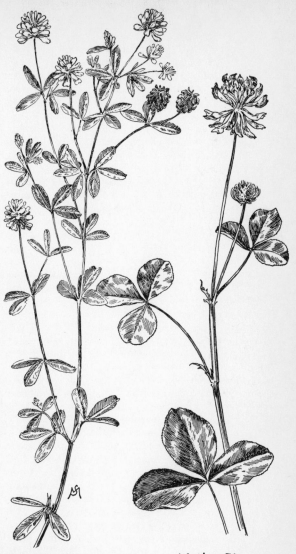

Hop Clover.
Trifolium agrarium.

Alsike Clover.
Trifolium hybridum.

6–15 inches high. Common on roadsides and in sandy fields. Me., south to Va., and west to Iowa.

Low Hop Clover
Trifolium procumbens
Pale golden yellow
June–September

Similar in many respects to the foregoing, but lower, more spreading, and the stems and leaves fine-hairy. The leaflets are shorter and blunt-tipped, the middle one slightly stemmed and the lateral ones stemless. The stipules (leafy formations at the base of the leaf-stalks) are broader than those of the preceding species; they are pointed ovate. The tiny standard of the floret is wide-spread, and not curled up at the edges as in *T. agrarium.* 3–6 inches high. Occasional or common everywhere, especially on roadsides.

Yellow Melilot
Melilotus officinalis
Light golden yellow
June–August

This is sometimes called yellow sweet clover, but its resemblance to clover is in its character rather than its aspect. It is a foreign flower which has established itself in all waste places especially in our seaport towns. The three leaflets are long, blunt-tipped, and toothed. The light golden yellow flowers are strung along in a delicate spike. The stem is smooth and 2–4 feet high. *Melilotus alba* is a similar, taller, white-flowered species. Both common everywhere.

Alfalfa or Lucerne
Medicago sativa
Purple
June–August

A perennial much cultivated for fodder in the west and south; naturalized from Europe. Found in dry fields and sandy wastes in the East. The three leaflets are long and narrow, toothed toward the tip which is obtuse, and furnished with a tiny sharp bristle; each leaflet has a distinct stalk, and that of the middle leaflet is *bent* upward. The purple florets in short clusters. 12–25 inches high. Me., south to Va., and west.

Milk Vetch
Astragalus Canadensis
Greenish cream yellow
July–August

A generally smooth, tall beautiful perennial with a branching stem, and compound leaves of 13–25 or more bluish green, elliptical leaflets set oppositely upon the slender leaf-stem, in general appearance like those of the locust tree. The cream

Alfalfa.
Medicago sativa.

Yellow Melilot.
Melilotus officinalis.

yellow slender blossoms are green-tinged especially at the base, and are thickly set in a dense spike springing from the junction of the leaf-stalk with the plant stem. They are cross-fertilized mostly by the long-tongued bees; the bumblebees, *Bombus separatus*, *B. americanorum*, and *B. pennsylvanicus* are frequent visitors, as are the butterflies,—*Colias philodice*, the clouded sulphur, and *Papilio asterias*, the black swallowtail. The flowers are succeeded by short, broad, leathery, straight, and pointed pods. 1–4 feet high. Along streams and riverbanks, from western New York, and on the shores and islands of Lake Champlain, N. Y. and Vt., south to Ga. and La., and west to Col.

Nonesuch or Black Medick
Medicago lupulina
Yellow
July–September

An annual (adventive from Europe), with a somewhat twisted stem partly lying on the ground, slightly downy or rough ; the three leaflets obovate or wedge-shaped with a bristle tip. The yellow flowers in small, short spikes. About 6 inches high. Pods almost black, kidney-formed, containing but one seed. Common in waste places everywhere.

Tick Trefoil
Desmodium nudiflorum
Pale magenta or lilac
July–August

A common weed which flourishes in dry woods. The generally leafless flower-stem rises from the root, and bears a scattered cluster of very small magenta-pink or lilac flowers, the broad upper petals of which are notched at the apex and turned backward, the lower narrow ones are lilac and white ; the stamens are prominent. The flower is fertilized by honeybees and many other smaller bees, especially those of the genus *Halictus*. The stout, shorter leaf-stalk is terminated by the leaf-clusters, of three ovate, toothless leaflets. The hairy two-jointed pods or seed-vessels stick to one's clothing or are distributed by some similar means of transportation. 18–25 inches high. In woodlands from Me., south, and west to Minn.

Tick Trefoil.   Desmodium nudiflorum.

*Desmodium
acuminatum*
Pale magenta
June–
September

This species has similar flowers, but they are considerably larger and borne on a slender stalk which rises from the plant-stem at the point where the leaf-stalks spring outward. The broad, pointed leaflets are much larger and a trifle hairy. The strange seed-pod like that of the foregoing species is 2–3 jointed. The name is from δεσμός a chain, alluding to the connecting joints of the pod. By means of these joints the pods attach to the furry coats of animals. 1–4 feet high. The same distribution.

*Desmodium
rotundifolium*
**Purple-
magenta**
**July–
September**

The stem of this silky hairy tick trefoil bends or lies near the ground. The leaflets are quite round, comparatively speaking, soft-hairy, and *not* pointed. The flowers are light purple-magenta, and the pod 3–5 jointed, constricted nearly equally at both edges. 2–5 feet long. About the same distribution.

*Desmodium
Dillenii*
Pale magenta
**June–
September**

This species has oblong lance-shaped leaflets, or quite ovate ones, nearly if not quite smooth above, an erect and nearly smooth stem, and branching flower-stalks bearing very small pale magenta flowers. Pod 2–4 jointed, the sections nearly triangular. 2–3 feet high. Not farther south than Va. and Ky., west to Neb.

*Desmodium
paniculatum*
Pale magenta
**July–
September**

A still narrower-leaved species, the deep green leaflets scarcely 2 inches long, and linear lance-shaped, resembling willow leaves. The flower-spikes are rather horizontally branched ; Pale magenta flowers very small. Pod 4–6 jointed. The slender stem 2–3 feet high. Common.

**Canadian Tick
Trefoil**
*Desmodium
Canadense*
**Dull magenta-
pink**
**July–
September**

The most showy species of the genus, with crowded flower-clusters terminating a tall, stout, and hairy stem. The leaves are nearly without stalks, or with short ones, and the three leaflets (longer-stalked) are oblong lance-shaped. The flowers (larger than those of the other species) are nearly ½ inch long, and vary in color from magenta to magenta-pink. Pods 3–5 jointed and quite

Canadian Tick Trefoil.   Desmodium Canadense.

hairy. 2–6 feet high. Common on the borders of copses and on river banks, from Me., south to S. Car., and west to Mo. and Neb.

Trailing Bush Clover
Lespedeza procumbens
Purple=magenta or magenta-pink
August–September

An interesting little plant with a trailing habit, its perpendicular branches rising from a stout horizontal stem. The little leaves are cloverlike. The whole plant woolly hairy. The tiny pealike blossoms magenta-pink or a light purple-magenta. 12–25 inches long. Common in dry soil everywhere.

Lespedeza violacea
Purple
August–September

An upright and tall species with small elliptical leaflets distinctly stalked. Stem sparingly hairy and much branched. The small flowers purple or violet-purple. 1–3 feet high. Common in dry soil, and on the borders of copses everywhere.

Lespedeza reticulata
Purple

An erect species with smooth, dark green, cloverlike leaves, crowding a rather straight, generally smooth stem, which is terminated by the small, crowded, purple flower-cluster ; smaller clusters also spring from the junction of stem with leaf-stalk. The *Lespedezas*, especially this one, are apt to exhibit two kinds of flowers ; those with showy petals, which are sterile, and those petalless and minute, which are abundantly fertile. According to Prof. Robertson, the chief visitors of this flower are the bumblebee *Bombus americanorum*, the leaf-cutting bee (*Megachile*), and the ground bee (*Halictus ;* notably *H. ligatus*). Among the butterflies, *Colias philodice* and *Pamphila cernes* are occasional visitors. 1–3 feet high. Mass. and Mich., south.

Lespedeza polystachya
Yellow-white, spotted

This species has yellow-white flowers purple-spotted, which grow in small dense, bristly, oblong spikes. The stem is silky hairy, and the round-ovate leaflets are slightly separated by the conspicuous stalk of the middle one. 2–4 feet high. Common everywhere on dry hillsides.

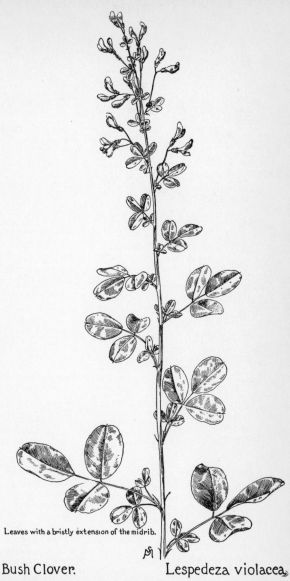

Leaves with a bristly extension of the midrib.

Bush Clover.　　　　　　　Lespedeza violacea

PULSE FAMILY. *Leguminosæ.*

Lespedeza
capitata
White
streaked
The flowers of this species are clustered in small *round* heads terminating a stiff, straight stalk, which is silky hairy. The leaves have three oblong leaflets, and are nearly stemless. The flowers are similar to the foregoing species, or they are white, magenta streaked. Visited by the leaf-cutter bee (*Megachile brevis*) among many others. 2–4 feet high. Same situations everywhere.

Common Vetch
Vicia sativa
Purple
May–August
A climbing annual adventive from Europe where it is cultivated for fodder ; one of the genus is also extensively cultivated in Italy, notably about Naples, and in the vicinity of Pompeii. The flowers, which are purple or even magenta-pink, grow in pairs or singly at the junction of stem with leaf-stalk. The 8–10 leaflets are obtuse oblong, notched at the tip, and the stalk terminates in two twining tendrils. The pod resembles that of the pea, but it is long and slender. Stem 1–3 feet long. N. Eng., south, and west to Minn. and S. Dak.

Cow Vetch
Vicia Cracca
Light violet
June–August
A perennial, and graceful plant climbing by tendrils, and characterized by a fine, downy hairiness. The compound leaf has twenty or more lance-shaped leaflets terminated abruptly by a bristlelike point. The small bean-blossomlike flower is light violet, the upper petal is lined with a deeper violet ; the cluster is sometimes quite four inches long, and is one-sided ; it grows from between the leaf-stalk and the plant-stem. The color of the foliage is rather gray olive green. Fruit like a small pea-pod. Stem 2–3 feet long. Dry soil, on the borders of thickets, and cultivated fields. Me. and N. J., west to Iowa and Minn.

Vicia
Americana
Light violet
Easily distinguished from the foregoing by its generally smooth character and its obtuse elliptical leaflets which are less in number (8–14) and distinctly veined. The light violet flowers are larger, and only 3–9 form the rather loose cluster. 2–3 feet long. In moist soil. Me., south to Va. and Ky., and west to Nev. The *Vicias* are in general cross-fertilized with the assistance of the

Cow Vetch.

Vicia Cracca.

PULSE FAMILY. *Leguminosæ.*

family *Hymenoptera*, the bees; the honeybee is one of the commonest visitors.

Beach Pea
Lathyrus maritimus
Ruddy purple
May–August
A seaside plant, but one common also on the shores of the Great Lakes; its construction and habit similar to those of *Vicia*. There are 6–12 oval leaflets, bristle-tipped, and a ruddy purple flower-cluster of 5–12 bean-blossom-shaped florets; the cluster is somewhat long-hemispherical in outline. At the base of the compound leaves are a pair of conspicuous arrow-head-shaped stipules, or leaflets. The pod is veiny and about 2 inches long. The stout stem is angled and 1–2 feet high. Sandy soil Me., south to N. J., and west to Oregon.

Lathyrus palustris
This is a slender marsh-loving plant with an angled and winged stem, narrow lance-shaped stipules (leafy formations at the base of the compound leaves), and with 2–4 pairs of lance-shaped leaflets. The loose and ruddy purple spare flower-cluster (of 2–6 flowers about $\frac{1}{2}$ inch long) is as long as the compound leaf. The narrow, veiny pod is about 2 inches long. Stem 1–3 feet long. In wet situations, from Me., Mass., N. J., and N. Y., west to the Pacific coast.

Ground Nut
Apios tuberosa
Maroon and pale brown-lilac
August–September
A climbing vine reaching a height of about four or five feet. The root is tuberous and edible. The compound leaf is composed of 3–7 toothless, ovate-pointed leaflets, smooth and light green. The æsthetic flower-cluster is maroon and pale brown-lilac in color with a texture of velvet; the bean-blossomlike florets are cloyingly sweet, and suggest English violets with a slight and strange horse-chestnut odor. They are fertilized mostly by the various bees, including the honeybee. The name is from ἄπιον, a pear, alluding to the pear-shape of the tubers. The plant is exceedingly beautiful and worthy of cultivation. On low, damp ground, from Me., south, and west to S. Dak., Neb., and Kan. Found in Campton, N. H.

Ground Nut.   Apios tuberosa.

PULSE FAMILY. *Leguminosæ.*

Wild Bean
Phaseolus perennis
Red-purple
July–September

Another perennial climber, distinguished by its leaf of three leaflets pointed at the tip and rounded at the base. The plant is very fine-hairy and considerably branched. The flower-cluster is thin and about 4–8 inches long ; the red-purple blossoms are scarcely over $\frac{1}{3}$ inch long. The pods are stalked, drooping, and a trifle curved. Stem 5–12 feet long. In thickets Me., south, and west to Minn. and Neb.

Strophostyles angulosa
Greenish white or purple
July–September

A similar, but annual species, with a low-twining stem about 6–8 feet long, the leaflets sometimes bluntly lobed and sometimes entire. The 3–10 greenish white or red-purple flowers about $\frac{1}{2}$ an inch long, in a loose cluster. The slender linear pod is fine-hairy and about 3 inches long or less. Stem branching at the base and about 4–8 feet long. Sandy river-banks, and meadow borders, Mass., south, and west along the Great Lakes to Minn., and southwest to Kan.

Wild or Hog Peanut
Amphicarpœa monoica
Magenta-lilac
August–September

A dainty vine with delicate light green leaves formed of three smooth, angularly ovate-pointed leaflets, and bearing two kinds of fruit. The perfect lilac or magenta-lilac narrow blossoms are in small drooping clusters ; these are succeeded by many small pods about an inch long holding generally three mottled beans. The other fruitful blossom is at the base or root of the plant in rudimentary form with but few free stamens ; it is succeeded by a pear-shaped pod containing one large seed—hence the name wild peanut. The name of the plant means *both* and *fruit*, in reference to the two kinds of fruit. The pod of the upper blossom is curved and broad at the tip, it matures about the middle of September. The slender stem twines about the roadside shrubbery, and is from 2–7 feet long. Common everywhere in moist ground from Me., to S. Dak., Neb., and La. Found in Campton, N. H.

Wild Bean.
Phaseolus perennis.

Hog Peanut.
Amphicarpæa monoica.

Wild Senna
Cassia
Marilandica
**Golden yel-
low, brown-
tipped**
July–August

A showy and decorative plant with compound leaves of 12–20 broad lance-shaped leaflets of a rather yellow-green tone. They are smooth and somewhat sensitive to the touch. The flower-clusters are loosely constructed. The light golden yellow flowers of five slightly unequal petals are accented in color by the prominent chocolate brown of the anthers; the stamens are very unequal in length. 3–8 feet high. In swamps and alluvial soil from Me., south, and west to Minn., Neb. Kan., and La.

Partridge Pea
Cassia
Chamæcrista
Yellow
**July–Septem-
ber**

An erect annual species with large showy yellow flowers, 1¼ inches across, in groups of 2–4 at the bases of the sensitive leaves; often the five petals are purple-spotted at the base. The 20–30 leaflets, less than an inch long, are blunt lance-shaped and pointed with a tiny bristle. The slender pod about 2 inches long is slightly hairy. 1–2 feet high. In dry or sandy fields, everywhere. But not in Me., N. H., or Vt., or if in Me., very rare.

**Wild Sensitive
Plant**
Cassia
nictitans

A similar species, but tall, and with very small and inconspicuous yellow flowers. The 12–40 tiny leaflets scarcely ⅔ inch long. The flowers in groups of 2–3 at the bases of the leaves. 6–12 feet high. Me., south to Ga., and west to Ill., Kan., and Tex. Not in N. H., and if in Me. exceedingly rare, for only one record exists.

Partridge Pea.　　　Cassia Chamæcrista.

GERANIUM FAMILY. *Geraniaceæ.*

A small family of plants with symmetrical and perfect flowers of mostly five parts, viz. : five petals, five sepals (usually distinct), and five stamens or twice that number. Fruit a capsule. Cross-fertilized by bees, butterflies, and the beelike flies.

Wild Geranium or Cranesbill
Geranium maculatum
Magenta-pink
May-July

A delicate wild flower pale or deep magenta-pink, or quite light purple ; sometimes the ten anthers are a delicate peacock blue. The deeply cut, five-lobed leaf is rough-hairy ; the stem and the unfolded flower-envelop (the bud) are also remarkably hairy. The blossoms are cross-fertilized mostly by the agency of honeybees, and the smaller bees of the genus *Halictus*—particularly *Halictus coriaceus*, and the *Syrphid* flies. The flower is, perhaps, quite incapable of self-fertilization in the absence of insects, as the pollen is ripe and the anthers fall away before the stigma is receptive. The leaves with their brown or white spots are the occasion of the specific title, *maculatum*. 1-2 feet high. In woodlands and wooded roadsides, from Me., south to Ga., and west. Found in Campton, N. H.

Herb Robert
Geranium Robertianum
Magenta
May-September

A rather handsome and decorative species adventive from Europe, distinguished for its generally *ruddy* stems and strong odor when bruised. The ornamental leaves with 3-5 divisions are deep green sometimes modified with the ruddy tinge of the plant. The flowers are deep or pale magenta, and are succeeded by long-beaked seed-vessels. 10-18 inches high. On the borders of rocky woods, from Me., south to N. J., and west to Mo.

Geranium Bicknellii

A somewhat similar species, but distinguished by its almost skeleton-lobed leaf and remarkable seed-vessel the persistent style of which splits upward *from the base* and bears the seed at the tip. The flowers are pale magenta, and are

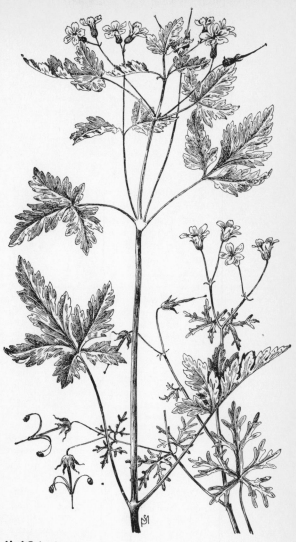

Herb Robert.
Geranium Robertianum.

Geranium Bicknellii.

generally borne in pairs. 8–16 inches high. Me. to southern N. Y., and northwest to western Ontario, Canada.

Geranium Carolinianum
Pale magenta
May-August
Another similar species but one more commonly distributed through the South. The leaves are deeply cut and narrowly lobed, and the pale magenta flowers are borne in compact clusters. The beak to the seed-vessel is nearly an inch long, and is short-pointed in contradistinction to that of the foregoing species, which is long-pointed. The curved sections of the beak are also shorter. The stem is fuzzy and 8–15 inches high. In poor soil from Me., south to Mex., and west. This geranium as well as the others is more or less dependent upon the small bees (*Halictus*), and the *Syrphid* flies for cross-fertilization. The flower has ten perfect stamens, however, and the inner circle of their anthers is so near the stigma that self-pollinization may easily occur ; that is the expressed opinion of Professor Robertson.

False Mermaid
Floerkea pro-serpinacoides
White
April-June
A slender and weak-stemmed little plant, with small compound leaves of from 3–5 leaflets sometimes thrice cleft. The tiny white flowers with three petals are borne singly on long and slender stems proceeding from the base of the leaves. The flower is succeeded by 1–3 fleshy spherical seed receptacles which are set snugly within the remaining three sepals. 6–15 inches high. In swampy land, and on river-banks, from Me., southwest to Pa., and westward.

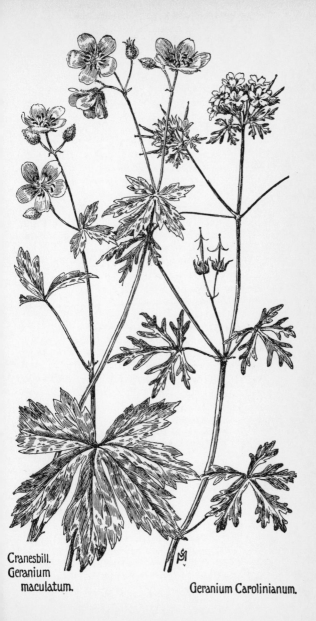

Cranesbill.
Geranium
maculatum.

Geranium Carolinianum.

SORREL FAMILY. *Oxalidaceæ.*

A small family of low herbs in our range, with trifoliate leaves and perfect, regular flowers of five parts ; the ten stamens united at the base. Fruit a five-celled capsule. Juice sour and watery. Cross-fertilized by the smaller bees and the beelike flies.

Wood Sorrel
Oxalis
Acetosella
White pink-veined
May–July

One of the most dainty of all woodland plants, common in cool, damp situations. The leaf composed of three light green heart-shaped leaflets which droop and fold together after nightfall. The frail flowers nearly an inch broad, with five notched petals, are borne singly on delicate long stems, and are either pinkish white, striped with crimson lines, the color deepening toward the centre of the blossom, or white with crimson-pink lines. Fertilized by the smaller bees (*Halictus*), and the *Syrphid* flies. Cleistogamic flowers (a kind fertilized in the bud without opening) are also borne on small curved stems at the base of the plant. A stemless perennial about 3–4 inches high, growing from a creeping scaly-toothed root. Common in thin, damp woods from Me. to the mountains of N. Car., and west on the north shore of Lake Superior. Found at Profile Lake, Franconia Notch, N. H. A native of the old world, and a most interesting flower frequently introduced in the paintings of Fra Angelico and Sandro Botticelli.

Violet Wood Sorrel
Oxalis violacea
Pale magenta
May–June

Another most dainty woodland species common in the South, and cultivated as a house plant in the North. The leaves are similar to those of the preceding species. The flowers are variable, sometimes white, but generally light magenta (the rose purple of Dr. Gray) ; they are *never* violet. The long flower-stalks bear 3–6 or more blossoms, in contradistinction to *O. Acetosella* which bears but one flower on a stalk. It is frequented by the same class of insects which visit the last. 4–8 inches high. Rocky ground and thin woods, from Me., south, and west to the Rockies. Also among the Andes, South America.

Wood Sorrel.   Oxalis Acetosella.

**Yellow Wood
Sorrel or
Lady's Sorrel**
Oxalis cymosa
**Yellow
May–Septem-
ber**

One of the commonest yellow sorrels of the north ; not a woodland plant but familiar by every roadside and in every field and garden. The light green stem erect, rather smooth, or sparingly hairy (viewed under the glass) ; the leaves of three heart-shaped leaflets (smaller than those of the last species), long-stemmed and somewhat drooping ; without small leafy formations at the junction of leaf-stem and plant-stem. The rather deep lemon yellow flowers scarcely ½ inch broad, with five long ovate petals and ten yellow stamens alternately long and short ; the heart of the blossom is green. There are 2–6 flowers on a somewhat horizontally spreading, branched stem, which are succeeded by hairy seed-pods ½ inch long set at scarcely a wide angle with their stalks. Visited by the smaller bees, and *Syrphid* flies, and also occasionally by the tiny butterflies (*Hesperia*). 3–12 inches high, with a weak stem but strong root. The *O. corniculata*, var. *stricta*, of the sixth ed. of Gray's *Manual*.

**Yellow Wood
Sorrel or
Lady's Sorrel**
Oxalis stricta
**May–Septem-
ber**

A far less common species, an annual or perennial, sustaining itself by far-reaching running roots. Generally less upright than the last. With leafy formations at the bases of the leaf-stalks. Pods elongated, and erect, often set at a sharp angle with their stalks. In other respects very similar to the foregoing species, but rare ; near Burlington, Vt. (T. E. Hazen).

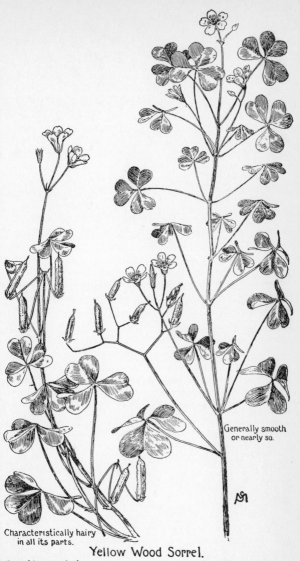

Generally smooth
or nearly so.

Characteristically hairy
in all its parts.

Yellow Wood Sorrel.

Oxalis stricta.   Oxalis cymosa.

FLAX FAMILY. *Linaceæ.*

A small family mostly composed of not very tall herbs, slender and frail flowered, but remarkable for having furnished the world with linen from time immemorial. The perfect, symmetrical flowers (of the genus *Linum*) have five petals, sepals, styles, and stamens ; the petals before expansion are rolled-up. The fruit is usually in a capsule. Mostly fertilized by the smaller bees and bee-like flies.

Wild Yellow Flax
Linum Virginianum
Yellow
June-August

A smooth perennial, with small yellow flowers terminating slender branches ; the five tiny yellow petals scarcely give the flower a width of $\frac{1}{3}$ inch. The small leaves are lance-shaped, thin, and one-ribbed. The sepals are ovate and pointed. 1-2 feet high. Dry woodlands, and shady places, throughout the north, and south to Ga.

Linum sulcatum

A somewhat similar species, but an annual with a usually simple stem and alternate leaves ; the stem corrugated, at least above, the sharp, lance-shaped leaves three-ribbed, and the yellow flowers a full half-inch broad. 1-2 feet high. In dry soil from E. Mass., west to the Great Lakes, through the mountains south to Ga., and southwest to Tex. Rare along the seacoast.

Common Flax
Linum usitatissimum
Light blue-violet
June-September

A rather delicate-appearing and pretty annual adventive from Europe or escaped from cultivation ; it has been under cultivation since prehistoric times for its linen fibre and its seed oil. The stem erect, branching, and ridged, the alternate leaves lance-shaped, sharp, and three-ribbed. The delicate blue-violet flowers, $\frac{3}{4}$ inch broad, with five slightly overlapping petals, are fertilized mostly by the honeybee. 9-20 inches high. Along roadsides, by railways, in cultivated fields, and in waste places.

Common Flax.   Linum usitatissimum.

MILKWORT FAMILY. *Polygalaceæ*

Mostly herbs with generally alternate leaves, and perfect but irregular flowers with five sepals, the two lateral ones petallike, large, and colored ; the others small. The three petals are connected with each other in a tubelike form ; the lower one is often crested at the tip. The generally eight stamens are more or less united into one or two sets and in part coherent with the lower petal, but free above. Stigma curved and broad ; the anthers generally cup-shaped and opening by a slit or hole at the apex. Cross-fertilization effected by the agency of bees and the beelike flies.

Fringed Milkwort or Flowering Wintergreen
Polygala paucifolia
Magenta or white
May–July

An exceedingly dainty, low perennial rising from prostrate stems and roots sometimes a foot long. The few broad, ovate, bright green leaves are crowded at the summit of the stems, the lower ones reduced to the size of a mere scale. The leaves live through the winter and turn a bronze red. The flowers, nearly $\frac{7}{8}$ inch long, are generally magenta or crimson-magenta, and rarely white. The three petals are united in a tube, the lowest one terminating in a pouch containing the pistil and anthers, and furnished at the end with a fringe or beard. This last serves as a landing platform for bees who will naturally depress the pouch by their weight ; the rigid pistil and stamens, however, refusing to bend with the pouch are forced out through a slit at the top of the latter and come in direct contact with the under parts of the insect visitor. Thus cross-fertilization is in a large measure secured by the pollen-daubed bee brushing against the exposed stigma of the next flower visited. The honeybee and the ground bees of the genus *Halictus* and *Andrenidæ* are the commonest visitors. The little plant often bears cleistogamous subterranean flowers on tiny branchlets. Erect stem 3–6 inches high. Common in damp, rich woods, from Me., south to Ga., and west to Ill. and Minn. Found at Holderness, N. H. ; white specimens near Bangor, Me.

Seneca Snakeroot.   Polygala Senega.

MILKWORT FAMILY. *Polygalaceæ.*

Milkwort
*Polygala
polygama*
**Dull crimson
June–July**

The tiny æsthetic, dull crimson flowers of this species are borne in delicate long clusters at the tips of the leafy stems. The leaves are light dull green, lance-shaped, and crowded on the slender stem, toothless, and rather blunt, with a bristlelike tip. Rarely the flowers are nearly white ; the eight stamens are more or less conspicuous. The plant also bears cleistogamous flowers on subterranean horizontal branches, and these are numerous enough to justify the specific title, *polygama.* 5–15 inches high. Dry sandy soil common everywhere, but locally abundant only.

**Seneca
Snakeroot**
*Polygala
Senega*
**White or
greenish white
May–June**

A much less showy species with white or greenish white flowers and fewer lance-shaped leaves, the lowest ones very small and scalelike. The small terminal flower-cluster dense. It bears no cleistogamous blossoms. Stem 6–12 inches high, simple or slightly branched. In rocky woodlands, from western New Eng., south to N. Car., among the mountains, and west to Minn. and Mo.

*Polygala
sanguinea*
**Magenta
June–
September**

A branching and leafy species with globular or oblong, compact flower-clusters of deep or pale magenta blossoms ; rarely they are white. It is the calyx which contributes the ruddy magenta to the flower ; the yellowish petals are hidden within. The stem is slightly angled. The little leaves are similar to those of *P. polygama.* 6–12 inches high. In moist and sandy fields and roadsides, New Eng., south to S. Car., and west to Minn., Ark., and La.

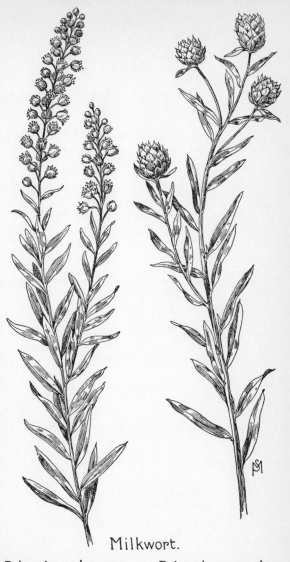

Milkwort.

Polygala polygama.   Polygala sanguinea.

MILKWORT FAMILY. *Polygalaceæ*

Cross-leaved Milkwort
Polygala cruciata
Dull magenta-pink
July–September

An attractive species whose leaves are generally arranged in clusters of four — hence the specific title, *cruciata*. Stem square or almost winged at the angles, widely branched, and smooth. The delicate dull magenta flowers in heads like clover bloom, with the florets crowded. 3–13 inches high. Margins of swamps, or low ground, from Me., south, and west to Minn. and La.

Short-leaved Milkwort
Polygala brevifolia
Dull magenta-pink
June–September

A species very similar to the last, but with a slenderer stem and shorter leaves more sparingly distributed. The flower-spikes much smaller and the flowers stemmed. 3–10 inches high. A coastwise *Polygala*, common on the borders of brackish swamps, from R. I., Long Island, N. J., and Del., south.

Whorled Milkwort
Polygala verticillata
Magenta-tinged or whitish
June–September

A slender and smooth species with usually many branches, and with long slender lance-shaped leaves tipped with a slight bristle, arranged in circles of 4–5, or scattered singly among the branches. The greenish white or magenta-tinged flowers are compactly clustered in conic spikes, nearly an inch long. The little florets are distinctly stemmed. All the *Polygalas* are assisted in the process of fertilization by the bees and some of the smaller butterflies, notably *Colias philodice*, yellow. 6–12 inches high. Common everywhere in fields or on roadsides. The var. *ambigua* is nearly the same in structure, but is taller, slenderer, and only the lower leaves are in circles ; the others are alternate. The flower-spikes are very long and loose, some of the lower flowers being isolated ; the blossoms are a trifle larger, and mostly a pale magenta. In dry soil, N. Y., N. J., and Pa., south to Ga., and southwest to Tenn. and La.

Cross-leaved Milkwort.　　Polygala cruciata.

SPURGE FAMILY. *Euphorbiaceæ.*

Plants with usually a milky and acrid juice, bearing staminate and pistillate flowers on one plant or exclusively either kind on one plant, so there shall be staminate ones, and pistillate ones, hence they are largely dependent upon insects for fertilization. The flowers are irregularly or imperfectly constructed, i. e., in some instances without petals, and in others polypetalous or even monopetalous. Fruit generally a three-lobed capsule. Represented in the northern countries by the genus *Euphorbia*, but largely a tropical family.

Seaside Spurge
Euphorbia polygonifolia
Whitish green
July–September

A prostrate, spreading weed common in the sand of the seashore ; stem branched and smooth. Flowers inconspicuous and usually solitary at the bases of the small linear oblong leaves. Seed-capsule round-ovoid, and ash gray-colored. Branches 3–7 inches long. Along the Atlantic coast from R. I., south, and on the shores of the Great Lakes.

Milk Purslane or Spotted Spurge
Euphorbia maculata
Whitish or ruddy
June–September

A prostrate weed common throughout North America, in open places and on roadsides. Stems usually dark red, hairy and spreading radiately like common pusley ; leaves toothed, red-blotched, and dark green in color, oblong and obtuse, about 1 inch long. The whitish or ruddy inconspicuous flowers growing at the bases of the leaves. Branches 3–12 inches long. Common everywhere.

Euphorbia Preslii
Whitish or ruddy
May–September

A smooth or slightly hairy annual, the oblique and three-ribbed leaves of which are red-spotted and margined ; similar to those of the preceding species. The stem branched and nearly upright. The insignificant flowers whitish or ruddy, and obovoid in shape. 8–20 inches high. Common everywhere in fields, by roadsides, and on the borders of thickets.

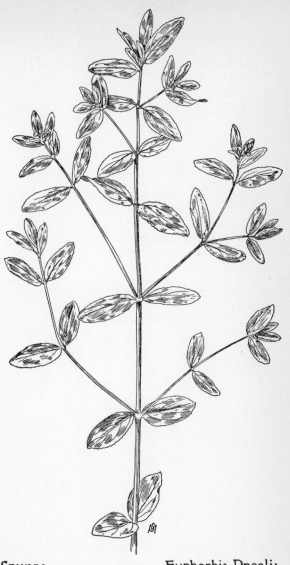

Spurge.   Euphorbia Preslii.

SPURGE FAMILY. *Euphorbiaceæ.*

White Margined Spurge, or Snow on the Mountain
Euphorbia marginata
White
May–September

A very handsome species cultivated for its ornamental white-margined leaves surrounding the rather insignificant flowers. An annual with bright green foliage, the leaves ovate-pointed, toothless and stalkless. Stem stout 2–3 feet high. In dry soil, Ohio and Minn. west to Col. Also an escape from gardens in the east.

Sun Spurge
Euphorbia Helioscopia
Greenish and tan
June–September

An annual species naturalized from Europe, with a smooth, erect, stout stem, often branched from the base. Leaves obovate and finely toothed. The insignificant flowers terminating the branchlets, of an indeterminate color, generally green and tan. 8–12 inches high. Common in waste places from N. Y. to Ohio, and along the Great Lakes.

Cypress Spurge
Euphorbia Cyparissias
Greenish and tan
June–September

A perennial spreading by horizontal rootstocks, and an escape from gardens to roadsides and waste places in the eastern States. Leaves bright light green, linear and almost filiform. The stems thickly clustered and very leafy, terminated by a large flower-cluster flat dome-shaped. The insignificant flowers indeterminate in color, but generally greenish dull yellow, or tan, or russet red ; they are rather ornamental, with crescent-shaped glands. The plant is milky juiced, like all the *Euphorbias*, and it has become naturalized from Europe. It is poisonous if eaten in any quantity. Fertilized by bees and butterflies. 5–12 inches high. Common everywhere in the east. Found in Campton, N. H., near an old graveyard.

Cypress Spurge.   Snow on the Mountain.
Euphorbia Cyparissias.   Euphorbia marginata.

CASHEW FAMILY. *Anacardiaceæ.*

Trees or shrubs with alternate compound leaves, and small regular, generally polygamous flowers, i. e. pistillate, staminate, and perfect flowers on the same plant or on different plants; the flowers of five parts in general. Fruit a berry. Cross-fertilized by bees, the beelike flies, and butterflies. The juice of some species is intensely poisonous.

Dwarf Sumac
Rhus copallina
Green-white
July-August
A shrub with fine-hairy branches, and compound dark green leaves of 9–21 ovate lance-shaped shining leaflets, toothless, or with few obscure teeth; the stem is wing-margined between the leaflets. The green-white flowers are polygamous, and collected in a cone-like terminal cluster, succeeded by the maroon-red hairy fruit. 1–7 feet high; sometimes a tree 25 feet high. Common on rocky hillsides from Me., south, and west to Minn., Neb., Mo., and Tex.

Staghorn
Sumac
Rhus typhina
June
A similar and very common shrub in thickets among the hills, with golden brown twigs densely covered with velvety hairs, and leaves of 11–31 lance-shaped, sharply toothed leaflets, dark green above and whitish, fine-hairy beneath; turning a brilliant scarlet in the early fall. The leaf-stem not winged. The polygamous green-white or whitish green flowers similar to the preceding; the fruit very densely covered with maroon-red hairs. Dry, rocky soil, especially among the mountains, from Me., south, and west to Minn. and Mo. The wood is a dull greenish yellow handsomely grained; the bark is used for tanning leather.

Smooth
Sumac
Rhus glabra
A similar smooth-stemmed shrub with leaves of 11–31 toothed leaflets, dark green above and whitish beneath; the stem not winged. The flowers and fruit similar to those of the preceding species. 2–12 feet high, sometimes 18 feet high. About the same distribution as the above.

Dwarf Sumac.   Rhus copallina.

CASHEW FAMILY. *Anacardiaceæ.*

Poison Sumac An exceedingly poisonous shrub with
Rhus venenata compound, smooth, lighter green leaves,
Whitish green green on both sides, of 7–13 thin obovate
June but pointed leaflets *without teeth*. More
frequently found in swampy land, and irritatingly
poisonous to the touch. The flowers are whitish green
and are borne in loose clusters at the angles of the
leaves ; they are also polygamous. Fruit a green-gray
berry in slim clusters. 6–15 feet high, or sometimes 24
feet high. In wet, low grounds, from Me., south, and
west to Minn. and Mo.

Poison Ivy A vine with a shrubby character in its
Rhus more southern range, but pushing its way
toxicodendron with rapidly running rootlets in the colder
Whitish green northern region. A noxious poison, in-
May-June deed, producing a painful, burning erup-
tion of the skin, if the latter comes in contact with any
part of the plant ever so lightly ; some persons are far
more susceptible to the poison than others, but it has
been demonstrated that it acts only by *contact*. An
excellent remedy to use until a physician can be con-
sulted, is the well-known Extract of Witch-hazel
("Pond's Extract") applied by saturating cloths and
wrapping them about the inflamed parts. The triple
leaf of Poison Ivy should never be mistaken for that of
the Virginia Creeper, which has five leaflets strongly
toothed. The leaflets of the poisonous plant are smooth,
but not shining, light green, toothless, and generally
ovate-pointed without lobes ; but sometimes the larger
leaves are shallowly notched or sinuous at the edge.
The flowers are whitish green, and with the fruit are
similar to those of the preceding species. Climbing high
on the trunks of trees, on stone walls, in thickets, or
running over low ground, or meadows ; sometimes
bushy, erect, with gray stems 2–3 inches thick, and 1–4
feet high. Me., south, and west to S. Dak., Utah, Ark.,
and Tex. Common in the Pemigewasset Valley, N. H.

Poison Sumac.
Rhus venenata.

Poison Ivy.
Rhus toxicodendron.

STAFF-TREE FAMILY. *Celastraceæ.*

Shrubs with simple opposite or alternate leaves, and small regular, generally perfect flowers with 4–5 petals and as many stamens inserted on a disc set at the base of the ovary (or sometimes merged into it) and at the bottom of the calyx. Fruit a pod with 2–5 cells. Insect visitors commonly bees.

Climbing Bittersweet
Waxwork
Celastrus scandens
Greenish white
June

A twining, shrubby vine common on old stone walls and roadside thickets, and sometimes climbing trees to a height of twenty or more feet. The light green leaves are smooth and ovate or ovate-oblong, finely toothed, and acute at the tip; they grow alternately and somewhat in ranks owing to the twisting of the stem. The tiny flowers are greenish white, and grouped in a loose, spikelike terminal cluster; the five minute petals are finely toothed along the edge, and the five stamens are inserted on a cup-shaped disc, in the manner explained above. The flowers are succeeded in September by the beautiful orange fruit, a globular berry in loose clusters, but properly speaking a capsule whose orange shell divides into three parts, bends backward, and exposes the pulpy scarlet envelop of the seed within. The fruit is charmingly decorative, and if it is picked and placed in a 'warm room before the shells open, it will expand and remain in a perfect condition thoughout the winter. Climbing 6–25 feet. Along roadsides, streams, etc., from Me., south to N. Car., among the mountains, and west to the Daks., Kan., Oklahoma, and N. Mex. Rare in the White Mountain region of N. H.

Bittersweet.
Celastrus scandens.

JEWEL-WEED FAMILY. *Balsaminaceæ.*

Juicy-stemmed herbs with smooth simple-toothed leaves and irregular perfect flowers whose sepals and petals are not clearly distinguished as such, the spurred sack being one of the three sepals; the other two are lateral and small. Petals five, or three with two of them two-cleft into dissimilar lobes. The five stamens are short. Admirably adapted to fertilization by long-tongued insects, such as bumblebees.

Pale Touch-me-not or Jewel-weed
Impatiens aurea
Pale yellow
July–September

A common, translucent-stemmed plant of wet and shady situations in the north, especially on mountainsides. The sack of the pale yellow, sparingly brown-spotted honey-bearing flower is obtuse and rather short—in fact, somewhat bell-shaped, or as broad as it is long. The spur is scarcely ⅓ the length of the sack. It is a more robust and a lighter green species than the next. Undoubtedly it is assisted in the process of fertilization by the bumblebee and the honeybee. Throughout the north, and south as far as Ga., but by no means as common as *I. biflora.*

Spotted Touch-me-not
Impatiens biflora
Gold yellow variable
July–September

The commoner one of the two species, usually ruddy stemmed; very variable in color, with smaller flowers, sometimes deeply freckled with red-brown over a deep gold-colored ground, and at other times pale buff yellow scarcely spotted. The sack is deep, longer than it is broad, and terminates with an incurved spur nearly one half or fully one third of its length. In Professor Robertson's opinion it is especially adapted to the long bill of the hummingbird, but it is also visited by the honeybee, bumblebee, and the bees known as *Melissodes bimaculata* and *Halictus confusus*, as well as the butterfly *Papilio troilus.* The flower develops its stamens first, and afterward its pistil, so cross-fertilization is almost an assured thing. 2–5 feet high. Me., south, and west to Mo. Found in Campton, N. H.

Jewelweed.   Impatiens biflora.

BUCKTHORN FAMILY. *Rhamnaceæ.*

BUCKTHORN FAMILY. *Rhamnaceœ.*

Shrubs or small trees, often thorny, with simple, mostly alternate leaves, and small regular, perfect or polygamous flowers. There are 4–5 petals to the rather inconspicuous flowers, or, in some cases, none at all. The fruit a berry, or a capsule. Visited by bees and flies.

**Common
Buckthorn**
*Rhamnus
cathartica*
**Whitish green
May–June**

A shrub commonly cultivated for hedges as its twigs are often armed with formidable thorns. A native of Europe and Asia, and an escape from cultivation in this country, particularly in New England and New York. The smooth deep green leaves are ovate and finely toothed ; they grow alternately. The flowers are clustered at the angles of the leaves, and are an inconspicuous white-green : they are staminate and pistillate on different plants, and scarcely measure a tenth of an inch across. The flower is succeeded by a black berry the juice of which is powerfully medicinal. 6–16 feet high. In dry soil along roadsides and near dwellings, from Me., west to N. Y.

*Rhamnus
alnifolia*

A native species with thornless branches, leaves similar to those of the foreign species, and greenish flowers without petals, staminate and pistillate on different plants. There are five stamens and calyx lobes. In swamps, from Me. to N. J., Pa., Neb., and in Cal.

**New Jersey
Tea**
*Ceanothus
Americanus*
**Cream white
May–July**

A shrubby species with a coarse, woody brown-green or bronzy stem, and dull green ovate-pointed leaves, sharply but finely toothed, very fine-hairy, and conspicuously three-ribbed ; the stems short, and ruddy. The tiny cream white flowers are set in small blunt cone-shaped clusters on long stems from the leaf angles. There are five slender petals and as many stamens. The rather pretty plumy flower-cluster is lightly odorous. In Revolutionary times the American soldiers brewed an indifferent-flavored tea from the dried leaves. Stems 1–4 feet high ; root reddish. In dry open woodlands, from Me., south, and west to Minn. and Mo.

New Jersey Tea.   Ceanothus Americanus.

VINE FAMILY. *Vitaceæ.*

VINE FAMILY. *Vitaceæ.*

Climbing shrubs mostly with tendrils, and with a profusion of sap. The joints rather thick and the bark generally shredded. The flowers are regular and perfect or polygamous — some plants with perfect, others with staminate flowers. Petals 4-5, stamens the same. Fruit a berry, or *grape*. Commonly visited by bees and the beelike flies.

Northern Fox Grape
Vitis Labrusca
Greenish
May-June

The familiar wild grape of the north bearing *large* black grapes with a bluish bloom, tough skin, and a sweet and musky flavor, $\frac{2}{3}$ inch in diameter. The tendrils are forked, the bark shreddy, the young twigs and leaves very woolly and rust-tinged. The large light green leaves, opposite a tendril or flower-cluster, are slightly toothed, entire, or deeply lobed, and rusty-woolly beneath. The fertile greenish flowers are in a compact cluster ; the grapes, in scant numbers, ripen in September and October. This species is a parent of the Isabella, Catawba, and Concord grapes. Thickets, from Chesterville, Me., south to Ga., in the mountains, and west to Minn. Common at Saddle River, N. J.

River Grape
Vitis vulpina

A species with smooth greenish branches, and smooth, shining, light green leaves ; the tendrils in irregular occurrence. The leaves sharply three-lobed (sometimes more lobes) and sharply toothed. The blue-bloomed black grapes are less than $\frac{1}{2}$ inch in diameter, and rather sweet ; they ripen from July to September. Banks of rivers or near water, from Me., south to Md., and west to Minn., S. Dak., and Ark. In the east the grapes are sour and ripen late.

Virginia Creeper
Ampelopsis quinquefolia
Whitish green
July

A familiar creeping or trailing vine extensively cultivated, common in its wild state on low, rich ground. It climbs by means of disc-bearing tendrils, and aërial rootlets. The deep green leaves are compound, with 5-7 (generally with five) lance-shaped, sharply toothed leaflets, much curved, troughed, and conspicuously veined. The insignificant yellow-green or whitish green flowers are perfect or

Northern Fox Grape.   Vitis Labrusca.

MALLOW FAMILY. *Malvaceæ.*

polygamous (staminate, pistillate, and perfect flowers occur on the same plant), and are borne in a rather broad cluster ; they are succeeded by the beautiful, small cadet blue berries early in October ; both leaf- and berry-stalks are deep red. The leaves turn a brilliant deep red in autumn. In thin woods and thickets, from Me., south, and west to the Daks. and Tex. Not infrequently it is mistaken for poison ivy (*Rhus toxicodendron*), a needless error, as the latter bears *three* never five leaflets.

MALLOW FAMILY. *Malvaceæ.*

Herbs or shrubs with alternate, more or less cut or divided leaves. The flowers perfect, regular, and rolled-up in the bud ; rarely the staminate flowers are on one plant, and the pistillate on another, thus necessitating cross-fertilization ; or rarely there are all three kinds of flowers, showing a stage of development. There are generally five sepals and five petals ; the stamens are indefinite in number. The fruit generally a capsule. Fertilization assisted by bees and butterflies.

Marsh Mallow
Althaea officinalis
Pale crimson-pink
August–September

An erect perennial plant with branching stem and velvety-downy, generally three-lobed leaves. They are light green, ovate, toothed, and stout-stemmed. The holly-hocklike flowers, an inch or more broad, pale crimson-pink and veined ; the stamens monadelphous, that is, collected in one column or tube around the central pistil, which is characteristic of the family. Flowers borne in small terminal clusters or at the leaf-angles. The thick root mucilaginous and officinal; it is commonly used in confectionery. 2–4 feet high. In salt marshes on the coasts of Mass., N. Y., and N. J. Naturalized from Europe.

Round-leaved Mallow, or Cheeses
Malva rotundifolia
White

An exceedingly common weed, annual or biennial, creeping over the ground, with ornamental, dark green, round leaves, having usually five shallow scalloped-shaped lobes, irregularly toothed ; the stalks very long. Flowers clustered in

Common Mallow.   Malva rotundifolia.

MALLOW FAMILY. *Malvaceæ.*

magenta-veined
June–October
the leaf-angles, white or pale pinkish magenta, magenta-veined; in shape like a miniature hollyhock, but the five petals notched. Stems 4–10 inches long. Common in waste places and as a garden weed everywhere. The name is from the Greek, and refers to the soft character of the leaves (albeit they are hard!); the popular name, Cheeses, refers to the round, cheeselike form of the seed-receptacle. Naturalized from Europe.

High Mallow
Malva sylvestris
Light magenta or pinkish
June–September
A common biennial with an erect branching stem, slightly fine-hairy or sometimes smooth. The leaves lighter green, rather long-stalked, toothed, and angularly five-lobed or occasionally seven-lobed. The flowers with the same family resemblance to the hollyhock, magenta-pink, or light magenta, the petals with about four deeper veins; the clusters (few-flowered) at the leaf-angles. 18–30 inches high. A delicate-flowered plant common on roadsides and in waste places everywhere. Adventive from Europe.

Musk Mallow
Malva Moschata
White or magenta-pink
June–September
A very similar but perennial species, with the leaf division deeply slashed or cut. The medium green leaves with very narrow divisions and short stalks. The white or very pale magenta-pink flowers nearly two inches broad, flat, and borne in terminal clusters; they are also veined. The leaves have a delicate odor of musk when crushed. 1–2 feet high. Common in the same situations as the above species, with the same distribution; from Europe.

Purple Poppy-mallow
Callirrhœ involucrata
Magenta
May–August
A distinctly western flower, occasionally escaped from cultivation in the east, a perennial bearing large showy, purple-crimson or magenta flowers slightly resembling the *Malvas*. The leaves slashed like those of the preceding species, but not so deeply; the lobes more obtuse. The stem hairy, and the flowers borne singly with long stalks. 1–2 feet high. In dry ground, from Minn., Neb., and Utah, south.

Musk Mallow.

Malva moschata.

MALLOW FAMILY. *Malvaceæ.*

Swamp Rose-mallow
Hibiscus Moscheutos
Pale pink or white
August–September

A tall perennial with stout shrublike stems and large showy flowers. The leaves olive green, bright above and densely white woolly beneath ; ovate pointed and indistinctly toothed, with long stalks ; the lower leaves three-lobed. Flowers 4–6 inches across, with five broad petals conspicuously veined, pale crimson-pink or white, with or without a crimson base. The flowers are borne singly or in scant clusters ; they show a strong family resemblance to the hollyhock. 4–6 feet high. The most frequent visitors of the genus *Hibiscus* are the honeybees and bumblebees. In marshes near the coast, and in brackish water near saline springs in the interior, from eastern Mass., south, and west to Ill. and Mo., especially near the shores of lakes.

Halberd-leaved Rose-mallow
Hibiscus militaris
Flesh pink color

A similar but smooth species with the same period of bloom. The upper leaves often halberd-shaped, i. e., like an arrowhead with conspicuous flanges, the lower also halberd-shaped or plainly three-lobed. The flowers flesh pink, sometimes with a dark magenta centre ; 2–3 inches broad. Stem 2–5 feet high. On the banks of rivers and small streams from Pa., south, and west to Minn. and Neb.

Bladder Ketmia
Hibiscus Trionum
Sulphur yellow

A species adventive from southern Europe, with a singular and beautiful inflated calyx, resembling spun glass, five-angled, roundish, and hairy. An annual often escaping from gardens, with handsome, large pure yellow, or sulphur-colored flowers, with a black-purplish centre, that quickly fade ; hence called Flower-of-an-hour. The leaves deeply cut, with 3–7 lobes. 1–2 feet high. Near dwellings from New Eng., south, and west to Neb.

Hibiscus coccineus
Red-scarlet

A handsome southern species, with large, deep red-scarlet flowers over six inches broad, and deeply cleft leaves. Common in cultivation. 4–7 feet high. In deep marshes near the coast from S. Car., south.

Sabbatia.   Sabbatia chloroides.

Arrowhead.   Sagittaria latifolia.

Large Flowering Trillium.   Trillium grandiflorum.

Day Lily.   Hemerocallis fulva.

Hooker's Orchis.   Habenaria Hookeriana.

Large Purple-Fringed Orchis.   Habenaria fimbriata.

Showy Lady's Slipper.   Cypripedium spectabile.

Bouncing Bet.   Saponaria officinalis.

Evening Lychnis.   Lychnis alba.

Marsh Marigold.   Caltha palustris.

Wild Swamp Rose.   Rosa Carolina.

Fringed Polygala.   Polygala paucifolia.

Bird-foot Violet.   Viola pedata.

Shinleaf.   Pyrola elliptica.

Fringed Gentian.   Gentiana crinita.

Oswego Tea.   Monarda didyma.

Monkey Flower.   Mimulus ringens.

Twin Flower.   Linnæa borealis.

Early Golden-rod.   Solidago juncea.

New England Aster.   Aster Novæ Angliæ.

Robin's Plantain.   Erigeron bellidifolius.

Elecampane.   Inula Helenium.

Cone-flower.   Rudbeckia hirta.

Common Thistle.   Cirsium lanceolatum.

Swamp Rose-mallow.　　　Hibiscus Moscheutos.

ST. JOHN'S-WORT FAMILY. *Hypericaceæ.*

A small family of shrubs and herbs, with opposite, toothless leaves generally stemless, and dotted with blackish spots. The flowers perfect, with five (or four) parts, and often with numerous stamens. Fruit a capsule.

St.Peter's=wort
Ascyrum stans
Yellow
July–August

A plant familiar in the pine barrens of New Jersey, with oval, stemless, thickish leaves and four-petaled lemon yellow flowers, closely resembling the next species. The stem conspicuously two-edged. 1–2 feet high. In sandy soil, Long Island, N. Y., N. J., and Pa., south.

St. Andrew's Cross
Ascyrum Crux-Andreæ
Yellow
July–September

A low, branching, smooth plant with small deep green leaves, oblong or narrowly obovate, stemless and thin, growing oppositely. The lemon yellow flowers with four petals arranged in pairs in the form of an ✕, in a final cluster, or at the leaf-angles ; petals numerous ; flower ¾ inch broad. 5–10 inches high. Sandy soil, Nantucket, Mass., south, west to Neb., and Tex.

Great St. John's=wort
Hypericum Ascyron
Deep yellow
July–August

An erect and showy perennial with tall branching stem, the branches four-angled. Leaves ovate-oblong, pointed, stemless and slightly clasping the plant-stem. The flowers large and showy, 1–2 inches broad, deep lemon yellow, with five narrow petals; stamens numerous. 2–6 feet high. River-banks and meadows, Vt. to Conn., N. J., Pa., Iowa, and Minn.

Shrubby St. John's=wort
Hypericum prolificum
Golden yellow
July–August

A shrubby species with stout, branching stem, the branchlets two-edged, and leafy. Leaves deep green, lighter beneath, linear-oblong, and very short-stemmed ; several smaller leaflets at the junction of leaf with the stem. Flower-clusters thick, loose, and flat. The flowers golden yellow, with numerous deep golden yellow stamens. 1–3 feet high. In sandy soil N. J., south to Ga., and west to Minn.

Hypericum adpressum

A simple-stemmed species blooming in the same season and with similar golden yellow flowers. The deep green leaves (rather closely set upon the plant-stem) oblong or lance-

268

St. Andrew's Cross.　　Ascyrum hypericoides.
Ascyrum Crux-Andreæ. Linnæus.

shaped. The flowers in small terminal clusters, with deep golden yellow stamens. 1-2 feet high. In low ground, Nantucket, Mass., to N. J. and Pa., south to Ga. and La., and west to Mo. and Ark.

Hypericum ellipticum
Lighter gold yellow

A common St. John's-wort blooming in the same season, with a simple, slightly four-angled stem. Leaves dull light green, thin, elliptical (often perfectly so) or oval, obtuse, and stemless, sometimes narrowed at the base. Flowers pale gold yellow, about ½ inch broad ; stamens numerous and golden yellow. The pointed pods succeeding the flowers are pale terra-cotta color. 8-20 inches high. In wet places and along streams from Me., south to Conn., northern N. J., and Pa., west to Minn.

Hypericum virgatum
Bright ochre yellow
July–September

A slender-stemmed species generally branched above, the stem somewhat four-angled. Leaves oblong lance-shaped, acute, and stemless. Flowers numerous, deep bright ochre yellow, coppery in tone ; stamens numerous, blossom same size as the preceding. 1-2½ feet high. In low grounds, pine barrens of central N. J., Del., south, and west to Ill.

Common St. John's-wort
Hypericum perforatum
Deep golden yellow
July–September

This is, generally speaking, the commonest species. A perennial naturalized from Europe, and a native of Asia. Stem simple or much-branched. Leaves dusky green, stemless, *small*, elliptical, or oblong-linear, more or less brown-dotted. Flowers shiny, deep golden yellow, with numerous stamens ; the clusters terminal, on several branchlets. 1-2 feet high. Common everywhere.

Spotted St. John's-wort
Hypericum maculatum

A species with the same season of bloom, remarkable for its spottiness ; its stem slender and round, often tinged with dull red. The leaves ovate pointed, or oblong, thickly dotted with sepia brown, stemless or nearly so, and often flushed with a ruddy color. The golden yellow flowers marked with thin blackish lines, more conspicuous upon the back of the petal than on its face. 1-3 feet high. In moist places and damp thickets from Me., south, and west to Minn. and Tex.

St. John's-wort.

Hypericum ellipticum. Hypericum perforatum.

ST. JOHN'S=WORT FAMILY. *Hypericaceæ.*

Hypericum mutilum
Pale golden orange
July–September

An annual, and an extremely *small-flowered* species, diffusely branched, the branchlets four-angled, and slender. The leaves light dull green, oblong or ovate, blunt-pointed, and stemless. Flowers scarcely $\frac{1}{5}$ inch broad, pale golden orange, or light orange yellow, with only 5–12 stamens. 6–24 inches high. In meadows and low grounds everywhere.

Hypericum Canadense
Deep golden yellow

A very similar species, but with *linear* leaves and *tiny* deep golden yellow flowers about $\frac{1}{5}$ inch broad, withering early in the day. The leaves light dull green and obscurely three-veined, the two side veins scarcely visible. The branches wiry, angular, and erect. The budlike, tiny pods succeeding the flowers are conspicuously ruddy, and exceed in length the five-lobed green calyx. In moist sandy soil, Me., south to Ga. and Ky., and west to Minn. and S. Dak. Found in Campton, N. H.

Orange=grass or Pine=weed
Hypericum nudicaule
Deep golden yellow
June–September

Also an annual, with an entirely different aspect from that of the two preceding species, although it is tiny-flowered. The stem erect, diffusely branched, and *apparently leafless;* the branches like slender wires, and the leaves minute and scalelike, leaning closely to the branchlets. Flowers deep golden yellow, nearly stemless, and open only in the sunlight. 5–10 inches high. In sandy soil from Me., south, and west to Minn., Mo., and Tex. Found near Brattleboro, Vt.

Marsh St. John's=wort
Hypericum Virginicum
Pinkish flesh-color
July–September

A perennial with an erect stem and stemless, close-set, light green, ovate leaves, sepia dotted, and with a slight bloom beneath. The stem, together with the leaves, late in the season (September) is more or less pinkish or crimson-stained, and the seed-vessels are magenta. The flowers are pinkish flesh-color, with orange glands separating the three groups of golden yellow stamens. Flowers in small terminal clusters. 1–2 feet high. In marshes, from Me., south, and west to Neb.

Drawn life size.

Hypericum Canadense.

Marsh St. John's-wort.
Hypericum Virginicum.

ROCK-ROSE FAMILY. *Cistaceæ.*

Small shrubs or herbs with regular flowers, the five green sepals of unequal size, the two outer smaller ones resembling bracts, or small leaflets. Petals 3–5. But one style or none at all. Seed-receptacles (on slender stalks) opening at the top. Visited by butterflies and honeybees in particular.

Frostweed
Helianthemum Canadense
Yellow
June–August

A perennial, remarkable for the fact that ice-crystals form about the cracked bark of the root in late autumn. Lance-oblong dull green leaves hoary with fine hairs on the under side. With two kinds of flowers, the early ones solitary, one inch broad, with showy yellow petals which are more or less crumpled in the bud, which fade early and fall away; these early blossoms have innumerable stamens. The later ones have few, and are small and clustered at the bases of the leaves. Pods of the larger flower ¼ inch long; of the smaller one, not larger than a pin head. Low. In sandy soil from Me., south, and west to Minn. The name from the Greek words *sun* and *flower;* the flowers open only once in sunshine.

Hudsonia tomentosa
Yellow
May–June

A bushy little shrub with tiny awl-shaped, scalelike leaves, oval or longer, downy, and set close to the plant-stem. The small yellow flowers crowded along the upper branches; they open only in sunshine. The stem 5–10 inches high, hoary with down. Sandy shores Me. to Md., and along the Great Lakes to Minn. Also on the sandy beaches of Lake Champlain, Burlington and Apple Tree Bays.

Pinweed
Lechea minor
Greenish or magenta-tinted
June–September

An insignificant, fine-hairy, perennial herb, with tiny linear leaves, larger on the upper parts of the plant, and very small near the base. The three tiny, greenish (or magenta-tinted), narrow petals remain within the green sepals after fading. The pod nearly globose, and appearing like a pin head. The upright smooth (when old) stem 10–18 inches high. Common in dry, sterile ground.

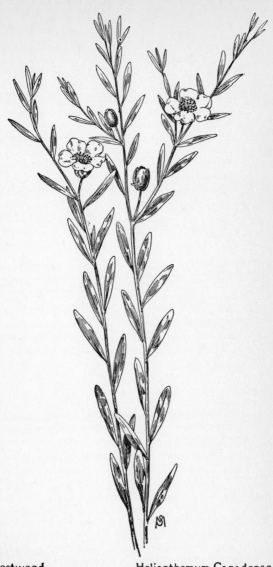

Frostweed.   Helianthemum Canadense.

VIOLET FAMILY. *Violaceæ.*

VIOLET FAMILY. *Violaceæ.*

A small family of generally low herbs with perfect, but rather irregular flowers of five petals, the lowest of which is spurred. There are five perfect stamens whose anthers turn inward and lie touching each other around the pistil. It is a family of nectar-yielding flowers commonly visited by many species of bees and a few butterflies, and cross-fertilization is effected by their assistance and by structural contrivances. The name is Latin.

Bird=foot Violet
Viola pedata
Light violet etc.
April–June

A beautiful violet, very common in the southeast part of Massachusetts, including the Island of Nantucket. The plant is generally smooth and tufted; the leaves, dull pale green, are cut into 3–5 segments, three of which are again cut and toothed, so that the average leaf possesses nine distinct points, or more. The pale blue-violet or lilac flowers, larger than those of any other species, are often an inch long. In the var. *bicolor* the two upper petals are deep purple; this form is found from Mass. to Md. and Ill.; it is common in the latter State. But the most familiar tint of the common Bird-foot Violet is blue-violet, more or less dilute, and never *blue*. Rarely there are white flowers. The lower, spurred petal is grooved, and partly white veined with violet; the throat of the flower is obstructed with the orange anthers and the style, which bar the way to the nectar in the spur. The useful visitors which effect cross-fertilization are naturally long-tongued insects; among them are the ever-present yellow butterfly (*Colias philodice*), and the bumblebees, *Bombus virginicus*, and *B. pennsylvanicus*. 4–10 inches high. In dry sandy fields. Me., south, and west to Minn., S. Dak., and Mo. Found in the Middlesex Fells, Mass.

Viola palmata
April–May

A very common species, generally smooth, but sometimes fine-hairy, with heart-shaped or longer, deep green leaves, deeply lobed or cut especially on the sides. Flowers smaller, and bright light violet, or rarely white. Dry ground, mostly woodlands, from Me., south to Ga., and west to Minn., Neb., and Ark.

Viola palmata.

VIOLET FAMILY. *Violaceæ.*

Common Violet
Viola palmata
var. *cuculata*
Light purple
etc.
April–June
The commonest violet of all, familiar on roadsides and in fields. The leaves deep green, heart-shaped, scallop-toothed, and somewhat coiled, especially when young. Both stem and leaf are smooth. The flower varies in color from light purple to pale violet; rarely it is white purple-veined; the three lower petals are white at the base, and two of these—the lateral ones—are beautifully fringed or bearded at the throat of the flower. The leaf-stalks are usually a little longer than the flower-stalks. 3–7 inches high. In low grounds everywhere, especially in marshes where the flower-stalks exceed those of the leaves, and the flowers are much larger. This species is cross-fertilized mostly by bumblebees, the insect touching the stigma first.

Arrow-leaved Violet
Viola sagittata
Light violet
April–May
A very small species with deep green, arrow-shaped leaves with blunt points, and scallop-teeth, but the upper part of the leaves sometimes plain-edged. A slight grayish bloom often characterizes the foliage when it is seen *en masse*. The small flower is light violet or deeper violet; its lateral petals are bearded, as are also the upper ones; the lower petal is veined, and its spur is short. 2–8 inches high. In wet meadows or dry borders from Me., south to Ga., and west to Minn., Neb., and Tex. It bears late cleistogamous flowers.

Viola Selkirkii
Selkirk's Violet is a rather uncommon, small, woodland species generally found among the hills. The stalks are erect and smooth, the leaves dark green and heart-shaped, deeply lobed at the base. The flowers are pale violet and beardless, with deep spurs. Moist soil, from Me. to Vt., Mass., and Pa., and westward to Minn. Also in Europe and Asia.

Marsh Violet
Viola palustris
Light lilac
May–July
A small smooth species whose flower-stalks generally exceed those of the leaves, which are broad heart-shaped and indistinctly scalloped. Sometimes the leaves are kidney-shaped. The small flowers are light violet or lilac, with purple veins; the petals are

Arrow-leaved Violet.   Blue Violet.
Viola sagittata.   Viola palmata var. cuculata.

nearly, if not quite, without beards. 3–6 inches high. In marshes and wet soil in the alpine region of the mountains of New England, and north; also in the Rockies. A native of Europe. Found on Mt. Washington and Mt. Moosilauke, N. H.

Sweet White Violet
Viola blanda
White
April–May

A small species with olive green, round heart-shaped leaves slightly scalloped, and *sweet-scented* white flowers, very small, with purple-veined petals, bearded, and *not* broadly expanded; fertilized mostly by the honeybees, and the bees of the genus *Halictus.* 3–5 inches high. In swamps, wet meadows, moist woodlands, and often in dry situations, from Me., south to Ga., and local westward. The var. *renifolia* is slightly soft-hairy, the leaves are round kidney-formed, and the flower-petals are usually beardless. From Me., Vt., and Mass., to western N. Y. and Minn.

Lance-leaved Violet
Viola lanceolata
White
April–June

A smooth, remarkably narrow-leaved species, the leaves lance-shaped or even linear lance-shaped, indistinctly scalloped, and generally blunt. The flowers white, veined with dull purple, and the petals beardless; they are slightly fragrant. Cross-fertilized by the aid of the small bees of the genus *Halictus* and *Andrena.* 2–5 inches high. Common in moist ground and on river-banks from Me., south, and west to Minn. It bears cleistogamous flowers.

Round-leaved Violet
Viola rotundifolia
Pale golden yellow
April–May

A very early and rather inconspicuous violet, most frequently found on woodland floors and rocky hillsides. The stalks are smooth, or very slightly fine-hairy, and 2–4 inches high, generally the flower-stalks exceed those of the leaves. The smooth deep green leaves are round or long heart-shaped, indistinctly scalloped, and small in the flowering season; but by midsummer they lie flat upon the ground and attain a diameter of 2–4 inches. The small flowers are pale golden yellow, the lateral petals are bearded and veined with madder purple; the lower petal is also strongly veined and has a short spur. In cool and somewhat damp, or even dry, situations

Sweet White Violet.
Viola blanda.

Lance-leaved Violet.
Viola lanceolata.

from Me., south in the mountains of N. Car., and west to Minn. Found in Campton, N. H.

Downy Yellow Violet
Viola pubescens
Pale golden yellow
April–May

This is a rather tall and forking species lacking the lowly habit of the common violet. The light green stem is fine-hairy above, though usually smooth below. The leaves are deep green, broad heart-shaped, slightly scallop-toothed, and somewhat soft-hairy to the touch. The small flowers are pale golden yellow, veined with madder purple; the lower petal, conspicuously veined, is short (set horizontally), with a two-scalloped tip and a short spur. The flowers grow singly on thin stalks from the fork of two leaf-stalks. The anthers and the style obstruct the throat of the flower, and the side petals, heavily bearded, compel the entering insect to brush against the stigma and finally against the anthers in the effort to obtain nectar. The commonest visitors are the small bees of the genus *Halictus* and *Andrena*, and the bee-fly *Bombylius fratellus;* the yellow butterfly, *Colias philodice*, is an occasional caller. 6–17 inches high. In woodlands from Me., south to Ga., and west to S. Dak. and Iowa. The var. *scabriuscula* is not so tall, the stems are slender, it is only slightly fine-hairy, and the leaves are generally acute at the apex, and distinctly scallop-toothed. 4–12 inches high. In moist thickets or woodlands from Me., south to Ga., and Tex., and west to Neb.

Canada Violet
Viola Canadensis
Pale violet, white
May–July

A smooth sweet-scented species with a tall, leafy stem resembling that of the foregoing. The heart-shaped, deep green leaves, broader or longer, with a slightly toothed edge, on long stalks, growing alternately. The flowers springing from the forking leaf-stalks are lighter or deeper violet on the outside of the petals and nearly white on the inside, with the throat yellow-tinted; the three lower petals are purple-veined, the side petals bearded, and the middle petal is acutely tipped. Rarely the flowers are altogether white. 5–15 inches high, occasionally more. In hilly woods from Me., south to S. Car. and Tenn., among the mountains, west to Neb., S. Dak., and in the Rockies.

Downy Yellow Violet.   Viola pubescens.

Pale Violet
Viola striata
White or pale lavender
April–May

A handsome, somewhat western species, with smooth, straight stems, and deep dull green, heart-shaped leaves, finely scallop-toothed, and more or less curled at the base when young, the tips acute. The moderately large flowers white, cream-colored, or very pale lavender, the lateral petals bearded, the lower one thickly striped with purple veins, and broad. The flower-stalk exceedingly long. The stigma of the flower projects far beyond the anthers, so self-fertilization is impracticable ; among the most frequent visitors (according to Prof. Robertson) are the bees of the genus *Andrena*, and the small bees, *Osmia albiventris* and *Halictus coriaceus. Colias philodice*, the butterfly who "puts a finger in everyone's pie," is also an occasional visitor. 6–16 inches high. In moist woods and fields from western New Eng., to Minn., and Mo., and south along the Alleghanies to Ga.

Dog Violet
Viola canina
var. *Muhlenbergii*
Light purple
April–June

A low creeping violet ; the light green stems with many toothed stipules (leafy formations at the angles of the stems), and small round heart-shaped yellow-green leaves, obscurely scalloped, and slightly pointed at the tip. The pale purple or violet flowers are small, with the side petals slightly bearded, and the lower petal purple-veined and long-spurred. Rarely the flowers are white. 2-6 inches high. Visited by the small bees of the genus *Halictus.* Common in wet woodlands and along shady roadsides, from Me., south to N. Car. and Tenn., and west to Minn. *Viola canina* var. *puberula* is characteristically fine-hairy, the leaves are ovate and small, and the stipules are deeply toothed. It bears cleistogamous flowers. In sandy soil from Me. and Vt., westward to Mich. and S. Dak.

Pale Violet.   Viola striata.

LOOSESTRIFE FAMILY. *Lythraceæ.*

Herbs or shrubs in our range, with four-sided branches and generally toothless, opposite leaves and perfect flowers, though these are occasionally in two or even three forms, i. e., with long filaments (the stem part of the stamen minus the anther) and a short style, or vice versa. Petals 4–7. Stamens 4–14, sometimes the petals are absent. Cross-fertilization effected in a number of instances through the agency of bees and butterflies.

Hyssop Loosestrife
Lythrum Hyssopifolia
Pale purple magenta
July– September

A smooth branching annual, with pale green stem and leaves, the latter alternate and lance-shaped, with stemless base, at which there are frequently little narrow leaflets, growing upon a separate stem of their own, which, lengthening, forms lateral, leafy branches above. The pale purplish magenta flowers usually have six petals and the same number of stamens, or less ; they grow singly in the angles of the leaves. 6–15 inches high. In salt marshes from Me. to N. J., also (according to Britton and Brown) in Cal., and along the coast of South America.

Lythrum lineare

A similar, paler flowered species with linear leaves growing oppositely ; the tiny flowers grow in two forms, explained under the family description above. A perennial 2–3 feet high. Salt marshes from N. J., south along the coast to Fla. and Tex.

Lythrum alatum

A tall slim species with much darker leafage and a smooth, much-branched, and angled stem. The leaves alternate (the lowest opposite), lance-shaped, pointed at the tip, and broader at the base. The flowers deep purple-magenta, ¼ inch or more broad, and dimorphous, that is, in two forms, as explained above ; the stamens very long in some blossoms. 1–3 feet high. In low moist ground, from Mass. (East Lexington, and Boston), Vt. (Charlotte), south to Ky., and west to Minn., S. Dak., Col., and Ark.

Loosestrife.   Lythrum alatum.

LOOSESTRIFE FAMILY. *Lythraceæ.*

Purple or Spiked Loosestrife
Lythrum salicaria
Purple-magenta, light
June–August

A most beautiful species naturalized from Europe and called by the English, Long Purples, Spiked Willow-herb, etc. An erect, smooth, or slightly hairy slender perennial, generally much-branched. The medium green leaves lance-shaped with a heart-shaped base, growing oppositely or in circles of three, and stemless. The long-petaled, purple-magenta (light or deep) flowers, growing in circles, with 8–12 stamens, longer and shorter; the flowers, in fact, trimorphous, that is, developing *three* relative lengths of stamens and style. Unquestionably dependent upon insects for cross-fertilization; the honeybee, the bumblebee, and many of the butterflies are common visitors; *Colias philodice* is frequently among the number. 20–35 inches high. In wet meadows, and on the borders of swamps, from Me., Vt., and Mass., south to Del., and in eastern N. Y. Mrs. Dana says: "It may be seen in the perfection of its beauty along the marshy shores of the Hudson, and in the swamps of the Wallkill Valley." It is also abundant near Bedford, Mass., and in Worcester Co., Mass. It responds readily to cultivation.

Swamp Loosestrife
Decodon verticillatus
Magenta

A somewhat shrubby plant, nearly smooth, with reclining or recurved stems of 4–6 sides, and lance-shaped leaves nearly stemless, opposite-growing, or mostly in threes; the uppermost with clusters of small, bell-shaped magenta-flowers, growing from their bases. Flowers with five wedge-lance-shaped petals half an inch long. Stamens 10, five short and five long. 2–8 feet long. Swampy places. N. Eng. south and west to Minn. and La.

Clammy Cuphea
Cuphea viscosissima
Magenta-pink
June–September

A cold and clammy, hairy, branching, homely annual, with ovate-lance-shaped dull green leaves, and small magenta-pink flowers with ovate petals on short claws. Stem branching, 1–2 feet high. Dry sandy fields from R. I. south to Ga. and west to Kan. and La.

Swamp Loosestrife   Decodon verticillatus.

MEADOW-BEAUTY FAMILY. *Melastomaceæ.*

Herbs (in our range) with opposite leaves of 3–7 veins, and perfect, regular flowers having four petals, and as many calyx-lobes ; there are either four or eight prominent stamens; in our species the anthers open by a pore in the apex. The stigma being far in advance of the anthers, the flower is cross-fertilized, and mostly through the agency of butterflies and bees. The seed are in a four-celled capsule.

Meadow-beauty or Deer-grass.
Rhexia Virginica
Magenta
July–August

A stout-stemmed perennial, sometimes branched (the stem rather square), with smooth, light green, three-ribbed leaves, sharp-toothed, ovate pointed or narrower, and stemless. The flowers with four broad magenta or purple-magenta petals ; the golden anthers large. There are eight stamens slightly varying in length ; the pistil reaching beyond them secures the cross-fertilization of the flower ; the honeybee and *Colias philodice* (the omnipresent yellow butterfly) are the only visitors I have happened to observe. 10–18 inches high. In sandy marshes, from Me. south, and local west to Ill. and Mo.

Rhexia aristosa

A similar species, with square stem and narrow, small, linear leaves. The large magenta flowers with rounded petals are furnished with a tiny awnlike point. · In sandy swamps, and the pine barrens of New Jersey, south to S. Car., local.

Rhexia Mariana

A slender, round-stemmed species, rather hairy, and with short-stemmed linear-oblong, toothed leaves, three-ribbed, and acute. The flowers are light magenta and similar to those of *Rhexia Virginica*. In sandy swamps, and in the pine barrens of New Jersey, south and southwest to Tex. The name, from the Greek ῥῆξις, means a break or crevice, alluding to the situation of the plant.

Meadow Beauty.   Rhexia Virginica.

EVENING PRIMROSE FAMILY. *Onagraceæ.*

EVENING PRIMROSE FAMILY. *Onagraceæ.*

Herbs, or sometimes shrubs. The perfect flowers commonly with four petals and four sepals (rarely 2–6), and with as many or twice as many stamens; the stigma with 2–4 lobes. Fertilized by moths, butterflies, and bees.

Seedbox
Ludwigia alternifolia
Yellow
June–September

A nearly smooth herb with many branches, and lance-shaped, toothless, opposite-growing leaves which taper to a point at either end. The solitary light yellow, four-petaled flowers, about ⅔ inch broad, with sepals nearly as long as the petals. The seed-capsule is four-sided and wing-margined, rounded at the base; the seeds eventually become loose and rattle about when the plant is shaken. 2–3 feet high. Common in swamps, from Mass., to northern N. Y., south, and west to Mich. and Kan.

Ludwigia polycarpa
Green
July–September

A less showy species with very narrow lance-shaped leaves, and tiny inconspicuous, stemless flowers whose rudimentary petals are pale green. The flowers grow at the junction of leaf-stem with plant-stem. The four-sided, top-shaped seed-capsule is furnished at the base with linear or awl-shaped leaflets. 1–3 feet high. In swamps from Mass. southwest to Ky., and west to Minn. and E. Kan.

Water Purslane
Ludwigia palustris
Pale reddish
June–September

A common uninteresting aquatic species found in swamps and ditches. The tiny inconspicuous flowers without petals, or, when the plant grows out of water, with very small ruddy ones. The lance-shaped, opposite-growing, slender-stemmed leaves (with the flowers growing at their bases) an inch long or less. The elongated capsule indistinctly four-sided. Stems 4–12 inches long, creeping or floating. Shallow marshes, and muddy ditches everywhere. Named for C. G. Ludwig, a German botanist.

Fireweed.

Epilobium angustifolium.

Hairy Willow Herb.
Epilobium hirsutum.

EVENING PRIMROSE FAMILY. *Onagraceæ.*

Fireweed, or Great Willow Herb
Epilobium angustifolium
Light magenta
July–August

A tall perennial herb with ruddy stem and dark olive green, lance-shaped, white-ribbed leaves without teeth or nearly so, resembling those of the willow. The light magenta or rarely white flowers in a terminal showy spike with four broad and conspicuous petals, eight stamens, and a prominent pistil. The slender velvety, purple-tinged pods, gracefully curved, open lengthwise and liberate a mass of silky down in late August and September, which gives the plant a wild and dishevelled appearance. 4–7 feet high. Common on newly cleared woodland, especially where the ground has been burned over. From Me., south to N. Car., and west to S. Dak. and Tex.

Hairy Willow Herb
Epilobium hirsutum
Magenta
July–August

A foreign perennial species which has become naturalized about towns near the coast. The deep yellow-green leaves oblong lance-shaped, finely toothed and stemless. The four-petaled magenta flowers, $\frac{7}{8}$ inch broad, in a short terminal cluster, or between leaf-stem and plant-stem. There are eight stamens. Seed-pod long and slender, the seed wafted by means of a long tuft of silky hairs at the tip. 3–4 feet high, densely soft-hairy, stout and branching.

Epilobium palustre
Lilac
July–August

A small uncommon species. The stem angled or marked with hairy lines, sparsely finely hairy throughout. The broad linear, obtuse leaves erect or ascending, and stemless, with curled-back margins. The seed-capsules extremely long and with scarcely apparent slender stems. 6–12 inches high. Flowers the same as in the next species. White Mountains, N. H., and Pa., west to Minn. Found on Mt. Washington.

Epilobium lineare
Lilac
July–August

A very slender swamp species, with small linear or narrow lance-shaped light green leaves with a short but distinct stem, and *tiny* lilac or pale magenta flowers, scarcely $\frac{1}{4}$ inch broad. The whole plant minutely hairy together with the capsule. More branched than the next species. 1–2 feet high. In bogs from Me., southwest to Pa., and west to S. Dak.

Epilobium lineare.   Epilobium coloratum.

Epilobium
strictum
Lilac
July-August

A similar species with densely soft white hairy stem, leaves, and seed-pod. The leaves broader and less acute than those of the last species, with short stems or none at all. The veins distinct. Flowers like those of the previous species. 1–3 feet high. In bogs from Me., south to Va., and west to Minn.

Epilobium
coloratum
Lilac
July-August

A very common species in the north, with a minutely hairy branching stem, often ruddy, and lanceolate leaves, distinctly but not conspicuously toothed, short-stemmed, and yellow-green in color, often ruddy-tinged. The tiny flowers pale lilac, and sometimes nodding; in fact, all these small-flowered *Epilobiums* after being plucked show nodding blossoms. Seed-pod green, exceedingly long and slender, the seeds dark brown, the hairy plume, at first pale, finally cinnamon brown. 1–3 feet high. In wet situations everywhere.

Epilobium
adenocaulon
Lilac
July-August

Differs from the foregoing species in having erect flowers (though they may nod at first), broader, blunter, and less toothed leaves with shorter stems, and lighter colored seeds with a slight prolongation at the top. 1–3 feet high. In wet situations throughout the north; not south of Pa. The silky plumes of the seeds of these few last small-flowered species described may become grayish white as in *E. adenocaulon;* but at first they are *absolutely white.* At best the *Epilobiums* are a difficult *genus* to separate distinctly, and are not a little puzzling to the botanist.

Common
Evening
Primrose
Œnothera
biennis
Pure yellow
July- August

A very familar biennial, and nocturnal species, with light green leaves more or less lance-shaped, sometimes broad, slightly resembling those of the fireweed, slightly toothed or toothless. Large showy pure yellow flowers, lemon-scented, with eight prominent and spreading stamens;

Evening Primrose.   Œnothera biennis.

the golden pollen is loosely connected by cobwebby threads, and is transported from flower to flower mostly by moths ; the Isabella tiger-moth (*Pyrrharctic isabella*) is chief among the number. The blossoms are also frequented by the honeybee and bumblebee ; they usually open just before sundown, and fade in the strong sunlight of the following day ; the sudden opening of the flower in the twilight hour is interesting and remarkable. The soft-hairy plant-stem, leafy throughout, is 1–6 feet high. Roadsides and fields everywhere east of the Rocky Mountains. The flower of var. *grandiflora*, from the southwest, is very large ; the corolla is 3–4 inches in diameter. It is commonly cultivated. The var. *cruciata* has remarkably narrow petals linear and acute ; Mass., Vt., and N. Y.

Oakes's Evening Primrose
Œnothera Oakesiana
Pure yellow
July–August

An annual, slenderer than the foregoing species, and not hairy but covered with a slight close woolliness. The calyx-tips not conspicuously close together. Dry situations Mass. and N. Y., west to Neb.

Œnothera sinuata
Pure yellow
May–July

A lower slightly fine-hairy species with oblong or lance-shaped leaves wavy-toothed or often deep-cleft like those of the dandelion ; the small light yellow flowers borne at the bases of the leaves turn pinkish in fading. About 1 foot high. In sandy soil, from N. J. south, and west to S. Dak., Kan., and Tex. Also in Vt. according to Britton and Brown, but not recorded by Brainerd, Jones, and Eggleston, in *Flora of Vermont.*

Sundrops
Œnothera pumila
Pure yellow
May–July

A small slightly hairy biennial, with diurnal, rather small pure yellow flowers, borne in a loose spike or at the bases of the leaves, the latter light dull green, toothless and obtuse, lance-shaped but broader nearer the tip. 10–20 inches high. In dry sunny fields, from Me. to N. J., and west to Minn. and Kan.

Sundrops.
Œnothera *fruiticosa*   Œnothera pumila.

Sundrops
Œnothera
fruticosa
Pure yellow
May–July
A similar diurnal species with flowers $\frac{1}{2}$–1 inch broad, borne in a loose spike or at the bases of the leaves; the latter are oblong or lance-shaped and very slightly toothed. Cross-fertilized by butterflies and bees, especially those of the genus *Andrena*, and the brilliant little flies of the genus *Syrphidæ*. The stigma extends far beyond the anthers, so self-fertilization is impossible except with the agency of insects. The seed-pods strongly ribbed and winged. Very variable, 1–3 feet high. Common in fields and on roadsides everywhere. The var. *linearis* is slender, has very narrow, linear-lance-shaped leaves, and the less ribbed seed-pods taper into the slender stalk. From Conn. south, and west to Mo. Blooming from June to September.

Enchanter's
Nightshade
Circœa
Lutetiana
White
July–August
An inconspicuous perennial of damp and shady woodlands, with opposite thin, frail deep green leaves, ovate pointed, remotely toothed, and long-stemmed. The tiny white flowers have two petals so deeply cleft that they appear as four; they are borne at the tip of a long slender stem, which is set about with the little green burlike, white-haired, nearly round seed-pods. Fertilized by the beelike fly (*Bombylius*), the brilliant green *Syrphid* fly, and the mining bee (*Andrena*). Plant-stem very smooth and swollen at the joints. Common in cool and moist woodlands everywhere. Named for the enchantress Circe. This and the next species are often found close together in Campton, N. H.

Circœa
alpina
White
July–August
A smaller species, the stem of which is watery and translucent, ruddy and smooth. The thin and delicate heart-shaped leaves are shiny, coarsely blunt-toothed, and distinctly different from those of the preceding species. Tiny leaflets, or bracts, are set immediately beneath the flowers. The burlike buds are club-shaped. 3–8 inches high. Common only in the north and among the mountains.

Enchanter's
Nightshade.
Circæa Lutetiana.   Circæa alpina.

GINSENG FAMILY. *Araliaceæ.*

Generally herbs in our range, with compound, mostly alternate leaves and tiny five-petaled flowers in crowded clusters; stamens five, alternate with the petals; the flowers perfect or more or less polygamous; staminate and pistillate flowers occurring on the same plant. Fruit a cluster of berries, which with the root, bark, etc., are slightly aromatic. Visited by numerous woodland insects as well as the bees of the genus *Halictus*, and occasionally by butterflies.

Spikenard
Aralia racemosa
Green-white
July-August

A tall, branching, smooth woodland herb, with a round, blackish stem, and large compound leaves of generally 15–21 ovate leaflets, heart-shaped at the base, finely double-toothed, and deep green with brownish stems. The greenish white flowers are arranged in small round clusters which in the aggregate form a large, terminal, pointed spike, or perhaps several smaller spikes from the base of the leaves. Visited by the bees of the genus *Halictus*, and the beelike flies (*Syrphidæ*). Fruit a round dull brown-crimson berry (in compact clusters) sometimes, when over-ripe dull brown-purple. The large roots are esteemed for their spicy and aromatic flavor. 3–5 feet high. Rich woodlands from Me., south through the mountains to Ga., and west to Minn., S. Dak., and Mo.

Bristly Sarsaparilla or Wild Elder
Aralia hispida
Dull white
June-early July

A characteristically fine-hairy plant, with similar leaves generally hairy on the veins beneath and irregularly double-toothed; they are perhaps longer and more pointed than those of *Aralia racemosa*, and rounded at the base. The tiny dull white flowers are arranged in somewhat hemispherical clusters, several of which crown the summit of the stem. The fruit is somewhat oblate-spheroidal in shape and dull brown-crimson when ripe. 12–34 inches high. In rocky woods, from Me., south to N. C., through the mountains, and west to Minn. and Ill. Found in Campton, N. H.

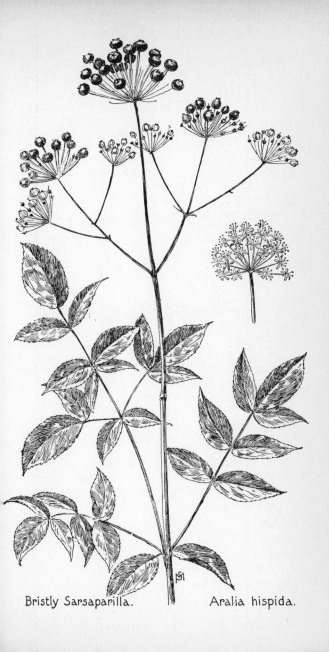

Bristly Sarsaparilla.   Aralia hispida.

GINSENG FAMILY. *Araliaceæ.*

Wild Sar-saparilla
Aralia nudicaulis
Green-white
May–June

A so-called stemless *Aralia*, whose true plant-stem scarcely rises above ground, the leaf-stem and flower-stem apparently separating near the root. There is a single long-stalked leaf rising 7–12 inches above the ground, with three branching divisions of leaflets ; there are about five ovate, finely toothed, light green leaflets on each division. The flower-stalk is leafless and bears 3–7 rather flat hemispherical clusters of greenish white flowers whose tiny petals are strongly reflexed ; the five greenish stamens are conspicuous. The fruit is a round purple-black berry in clusters. Common in moist woodlands, from Me., south along the mountains to N. C., and west to Minn., S. Dak., and Mo. The aromatic roots are used as a substitute for the true Sarsaparilla (*Smilax officinalis*), of South America.

Ginseng
Panax quinquefolium
Pale green-yellow
July–August

The roots of Ginseng which, in the estimation of the Chinese, are possessed of some potent medicinal virtue, are so much in demand for export that through the assiduity of collectors the plant has become rare. The large deep green leaf has five thin, obovate, acute-pointed leaflets, sharply and irregularly toothed ; in arrangement it slightly resembles the horse-chestnut leaf. The plant-stem is smooth and green, and the compound leaves are borne three in a circle. The yellowish green flowers (the staminate lily-of-the-valley-scented) are crowded into a single hemispherical cluster ; they are polygamous. The fruit is a deep ruby red berry, in a scant cluster. The name is a corruption of the Chinese Jin-chen, meaning manlike (from the two-legged appearance of the root). The plant is small—8–15 inches high. Rare in rich cold woods. Me., N. H., and Vt. to Conn., west to Minn. and Neb.

Dwarf Ginseng
Panax tri-folium
Dull white
May–June

A tiny species with a *spherical* root, generally three compound leaves composed of about three toothed, ovate leaflets, and dull white flowers, staminate and pistillate, on the same plant, borne in a single cluster. Fruit yellow. 4–8 inches high. Me., south to Ga., in the mountains, and west to Minn. and Iowa.

Ginseng.
Panax quinquefolium.

PARSLEY FAMILY. *Umbelliferæ.*

Herbs with hollow stems, generally deeply cut compound leaves, and tiny flowers in mostly broad flat-topped clusters, perfect (often polygamous), having five petals, as many stamens, and two styles. In some flowers the styles protrude from the yet undeveloped blossom, and the stigmas are touched by the visiting insect long before the anthers are mature, thus securing cross-fertilization. Commonly visited by countless insects, including the honeybee, the bumblebee, and many butterflies, chief among which are the Black Swallowtails. The many species are not easily distinguished apart, as the flowers are very similar ; in general, minute characteristics of the seed show the radical differences best. Strong-scented plants remarkable for their aromatic oil.

Wild Carrot or Queen Anne's Lace or Bird's Nest
Daucus Carota
Dull white
July– September

One of our commonest weeds, naturalized from Europe, and familiar by every wayside near a dwelling. A coarse and hairy-stemmed biennial with exceedingly fine-cut leaves, yellowish green, and rough to the touch; they are thoroughly decorative. The dull white flowers, in extremely flat-topped clusters, are gracefully disposed in a radiating pattern as fine as lace ; in the centre of the cluster is frequently found a single tiny deep purple floret. Visited by innumerable insects, flies, butterflies, bees, and moths, most of which are attracted by the peculiarly strong odor. The aged flower-cluster curls up and resembles a bird's nest, from which circumstance the plant derives that name. 2–3 feet high. In waste places and fields everywhere ; it is often a most troublesome weed. A near relative of the garden carrot.

Hemlock Parsley
Conioselinum Canadense
Dull white
August– September

A smooth, perennial species somewhat similar in appearance to wild carrot, but with a slender-branched flower-cluster composed of far less showy dull white flowers. The leaves similar, the lower long-stemmed, the upper quite stemless. The fruit or seed is smooth, flat, and prominently five-ribbed, the two side ribs exceedingly

Wild Carrot   Daucus Carota.

---

broad. 2–4 feet high. In cool swamps among the hills, from Me. and Vt., southwest through the mountains to N. Car., west to Minn. and Mo.

Cowbane
Tiedemannia
rigida
Dull white
August–
September

A tall and slender species, poisonous to taste, and with large tuberiferous roots. The leaves are deep green, and altogether different in form from those of the preceding species; they are long-stemmed and composed of 3–9 lance-shaped or broader, remotely toothed leaflets, more or less variable in shape. The tiny dull white flowers are in slender clusters. The seed is flat-sided, broad, and the ribs are not sharp or prominent; the side ribs are broad. Another denizen of the swamps; from N. Y., south, and west to Minn. and Mo. Named for Prof. Tiedemann, of Heidelberg.

Cow Parsnip
Heracleum
lanatum
Dull white
June–July

A common very tall perennial with a stout, hollow, ridged stem, sometimes stained lightly with dull brown-red. The leaves are dark green, compound—in three divisions, toothed and deeply lobed, rather soft-hairy beneath, and with a leafy formation at the junction of the leaf-stem and plant-stem. The insignificant dull white flowers, in large flat clusters, have five petals, each of which is deeply notched and of unequal proportions. The seed is very broad, flat, and generally oval. 4–8 feet high. Wet ground, shady borders of moist thickets, from Me., south to N. Car., and west to S. Dak. and Mo. Named for Hercules.

Wild Parsnip
Pastinaca
sativa
Light gold
yellow
June–
September

A common biennial familiar on waysides and the borders of fields, with a tough, strongly grooved, smooth stem, and with dull deep green, compound leaves composed of many, toothed, thin, ovate divisions. The dull (in effect greenish) light gold yellow flowers are gathered in small clusters set on slender stems, and form a broad, flat-topped cluster. The stem, 2–5 feet high, is extremely strong and difficult if not impossible to break. Seeds flat and thin. Common. Naturalized from Europe.

Wild Parsnip.   Pastinaca sativa.

PARSLEY FAMILY. *Umbelliferæ.*

Meadow Parsnip
Thaspium aureum
Golden yellow
June-August

Sometimes called Golden Alexanders. A western species not very distant from *Zizia aurea*. It has medium green lance-shaped or ovate, toothed leaflets, three of which *generally* compose a leaf; the root-leaves are single, mostly distinctly heart-shaped, the others simply rounded at the base. The golden yellow flowers are gathered in sparse flat-topped clusters. The seed is equally angled with deep flanges or ribs and is distinctly different in this respect from the flat seeds of *Pastinaca sativa;* they mature in *early autumn.* 15–36 inches high. Found on the borders of thickets, and woodland roads, from Ohio, west to Mo., southwest to Tenn., and west to Ill. The var. *atropurpureum* bears deep dull purple flowers, and is confined to the same range. *T. barbinode* is a similar species with stem- and leaf-joints and flowering stems more or less fine-hairy. Leaves with 3–6 leaflets. Flowers light gold yellow. Seed with seven prominent wings. Beside streams, commonest in the Mississippi Valley ; N. Y., west to Minn., and south.

Water Parsnip
Sium cicutæfolium
Dull white
July–September

A stout and branching species often growing in shallow water. The compound leaves deep green, with 7–15 linear or lance-shaped leaflets sharply toothed ; the finely cut lower leaves generally submerged. The dull white flowers are in a flat dome-shaped cluster. The seeds are prominently ribbed, and the leaves are variable in form. 2–6 feet high. Throughout the country.

Berula angustifolia

A similar but smaller aquatic species 6–34 inches high, with 7–19 leaflets, more or less lobed, and a dome-shaped cluster of white flowers. From N. Y. to Ill. and Neb. Also in the Rockies and the far west.

Early Meadow Parsnip
Zizia aurea
Light gold yellow
May–June

A very common smooth perennial, found on shaded roadsides or meadow borders. The medium light green leaves are doubly compound ; generally three divisions (or leaflets, properly speaking) of 3–7 leaflets, all narrow, pointed, and sharply toothed,

Early Meadow Parsnip.   Zizia aurea.

but varying to broader types. The stem is often branched. The tiny dull light gold yellow flowers have prominent stamens, and are collected in many small clusters, each widely separated from the other, but all forming a thin radiating cluster. Visited commonly by many flies, small butterflies, and but few bees. Seeds slightly ribbed. 16–34 inches high. Everywhere. Me. to S. Dak.

Caraway
Carum carui
Dull white
June–July

A common weed in the north, naturalized from Europe. Biennial or perennial; the lower basal leaves long-stemmed, the upper stemless; all finely cut, and ornamental; deep olive gray-green; the flowers grouped like those of wild carrot, but far less showy, dull white or gray-white, in scattered thin groups like *Zizia*. The seed is oblong, slightly curved, plainly ribbed, exceedingly aromatic, and is much used as a spice in cakes, and also in confectionery. The flowers are frequently visited by various flies and bees, the yellow butterfly *Colias philodice*, and also the white cabbage butterfly *Pieris rapæ*. 1–2 feet high. Local from Me., west to Pa., Minn., S. Dak., and Col. Found in Campton, N. H.

Water Hem-
lock or Spot-
ted Cowbane
Cicuta
maculata
Dull white
June–August

An erect, slender, usually much-branched and smooth perennial herb, very poisonous to the taste. The stem marked with dull magenta lines. The leaves deep green, smooth, often tinged ruddy, with coarse sharp teeth, and conspicuously veined, the lower ones nearly a foot long. The 9–21 leaflets lance-shaped or broader. The inconspicuous dull white flowers in a thin, flat, somewhat straggling cluster; they are polygamous. The seed ovate, flat on one side, or nearly so, and inconspicuously ribbed on the other. 3–6 feet high. Visited by numberless bees, wasps, and butterflies. Wet meadows and borders of swamps, from Me., south and west to S. Dak.

Poison
Hemlock
Conium
maculatum
Dull white
June–July

A similar much-branched herb, from which is obtained a virulent poison, used in medicine. It bears the name of the Hemlock employed by the ancient Greeks in putting to death their condemned political prisoners, philosophers, and crimi-

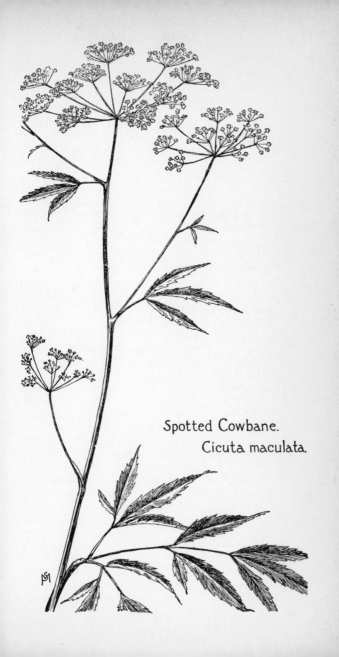

Spotted Cowbane.
Cicuta maculata.

nals. Socrates died by this means. The dark green leaves are deeply dissected and toothed ; the leaf-stems are sheathed at the base, and the dull white flower-clusters are slender-branched. The ovate seeds are flat and irregularly ribbed. The stem is also spotted or marked with ruddy color like that of *Cicuta.* 2–5 feet high. In waste places, Me. and Vt., south to Del., west to Minn. and Iowa ; also in Cal. Naturalized from Europe.

Sweet Cicely
Osmorrhiza
brevistylis
Dull white
May–June

The round, slightly silky hairy stem (especially when young) of this familiar perennial herb is dull green often much stained with dull madder purple—a brownish purple. The compound leaf is cut and toothed similar to that of Poison Hemlock; when young it is distinguished by its fine-hairiness ; later that characteristic is less evident ; it is mostly three-divided, appears fernlike, deep green, and thin. The lower leaves are large, sometimes considerably over a foot long. The stems of the dull white flower-clusters are slender and few, consequently there is no appearance of an aggregate flat-topped cluster such as generally distinguishes the family *Umbelliferæ.* The flowers are staminate and perfect, the latter maturing the anthers first ; cross-fertilized by many flies and bees. The tiny blossom has five cloven white petals and a very short style, scarcely $\frac{1}{24}$ inch long, which distinguishes it from the next species. 16–34 inches high. In moist rich woodlands, from Me., south through the mountains to N. Car., west to Minn. and Neb. The large aromatic roots are anise-flavored and edible, but the similar general appearance of the Poison Hemlock often leads to dangerous if not fatal results.

Osmorrhiza
longistylis

This is so similar to the preceding that the differences are not obvious to the casual observer. The leaves and stem are either very slightly hairy or smooth. The style under the magnifying glass shows a greatly superior length; it is fully $\frac{1}{12}$ inch long or more. The seeds of both species are nearly alike, linear, compressed, and bristly on the ribs. The roots of *O. longistylis* are more spicy than those of *O. brevistylis.* Me., south to Ala., and west to the Dakotas.

Seed-vessel of
Osmorrhiza longistylis
showing the long double style.

Sweet Cicely.   Osmorrhiza brevistylis.

PARSLEY FAMILY. *Umbelliferæ.*

Water Pennywort
Hydrocotyle Americana
Dull white
June–August

A small, creeping marsh plant, with a weak, pale green, smooth stem, which frequently takes root at the joints, and a round-heart-shaped, light green leaf, thin, smooth, and shining, the edge doubly scalloped, and the stem about an inch long. The tiny white flowers, 1–5 in a cluster, are inconspicuous and grow at the angles of the leaves. In wet places, Me., south to Pa., and N. Car., west to Minn. and Mo.

Sanicle or Black Snakeroot
Sanicula Marylandica
Greenish yellow
May–July

The green stem is smooth, light green, slightly grooved, and hollow like most of the members of the Parsley Family. The leaves are deep green of a bluish tone, smooth, toothed, and palm-shaped, that is with radiating lance-shaped leaflets, arranged like those of the horse-chestnut; of the five leaflets the lower two are deeply cleft; the upper leaves are in three divisions and stemless. The tiny pale greenish yellow flowers are in very small clusters; the five petals of each floret are curiously incurved toward the centre of the flower, and beneath them are the five stamens securely restrained from accomplishing the process of self-fertilization; later the petals unfold; the flowers are both staminate and perfect, intermixed. In the few *perfect* flowers the two mature styles protrude beyond the petals, and the visiting insect must brush against them, generally after having visited some staminate flower. Cross-fertilization now completed, the styles curve backward so that the withering stigmas are safely out of the way of the maturing stamens, which are not released from the enfolding petals until the anthers begin to shed their pollen. The long stamens of the sterile flowers mature early, and are a conspicuous factor in the green-yellow coloring of the flower-clusters. The fruit, a tiny ovoid bur with many hooked bristles, often retains the recurved slender styles. Visited by the *Syrphid* flies, the bees, and a few butterflies. 18–38 inches high. In rich woodlands. Me., south to Ga., west to Minn. and Kan.

Water Pennywort.   Hydrocotyle Americana.

DOGWOOD FAMILY. *Cornaceœ.*

Shrubs or trees, with opposite or alternate toothless leaves, and generally perfect flowers—sometimes they are diœcious; that is, the two kinds of flowers grow on separate plants; or polygamous, that is, perfect, staminate and pistillate flowers growing on the same plant or different plants. The genus *Cornus, within our range*, which is represented here by two species, has perfect flowers. Cross-fertilization is effected mostly by bees and the beelike flies.

Dwarf Cornel
Bunchberry
Cornus
Canadensis
Greenish white
May–July

An exceedingly dainty little plant common on wooded hilltops, and remarkable for its brilliant scarlet berries which grow in small, close clusters. The leaves are light yellow-green, broadly ovate pointed, toothless, and deeply marked by about 5–7 nearly parallel, curving ribs; they are set in circles. The flowers are greenish and tiny, closely grouped in the centre of four large slightly green-white bracts, or leaflets, having the semblance of petals, and imparting to the whole the appearance of a single blossom about an inch broad. The flowers are succeeded in late August by a compact bunch of exceedingly beautiful but insipid scarlet berries, of the purest and most vivid hue. The commonest visitors are the bees of the genera *Andrena* and *Halictus*, together with many woodland flies — bee-flies, and the familiar "bluebottle." 3–8 inches high. In cool, damp, mossy woods; frequently found on summits over 4000 feet high, among the Adirondacks and the White Mountains. From Me., south to N. J., and west to Ind., Minn., Col., and Cal.

Flowering
Dogwood
Cornus florida
Greenish white
April–June

A tall shrub and often a tree, whose familiar flowers, appearing just before or with the ovate deeper green leaves, have four similar broad green-white or rarely pinkish bracts, ribbed, and notched on the blunt tips. Fruit ovoid and scarlet, in small groups. 7–40 feet high. Vt., Mass., south to Ky. and Fla., and west to Mo. and Tex. Name from *cornu*, a horn, in allusion to the hardness of the wood.

Flowering Dogwood.
Cornus florida.

Bunchberry.
Cornus Canadensis.

PYROLA FAMILY. *Pyrolaceæ.*

PYROLA FAMILY. *Pyrolaceæ.*

Formerly classed as a suborder under the Heath Family. Generally evergreen perennials with perfect, nearly regular flowers, the corolla very deeply five-parted, or five-petaled ; twice as many stamens as the divisions of the corolla ; the style short, and the stigma five-lobed. Fruit a capsule.   Visited by numerous flies and bees, as well as smaller butterflies.

Pipsissewa
Prince's Pine
Chimaphila
umbellata
Flesh or
cream color
June–July

A familiar and beautiful evergreen plant of the deep woods, generally found under pines, spruces, or hemlocks.   The dark green leaves are thick and shining, sharply toothed along the upper half of the edge and indistinctly toothed on the lower half; they are blunt or abruptly dull-pointed at the apex, wedge-shaped at the base, short-stemmed, and arranged in circles about the buff-brown plant-stem. The flowers are dainty pale pinkish or waxy cream color ; the corolla has five blunt lobes which turn backward as the flower matures, and at the base, next to the dome-shaped green ovary, is a circle of pale magenta ; the ten short stamens have five double madder purple anthers ; the style is remarkably short—scarcely noticeable, and the gummy stigma is nearly flat and five-scalloped.   The flowers are delicately scented. Mostly fertilized through the agency of the bees of the genera *Halictus* and *Andrena*, and the numerous small flies common in woodlands ; the stigma is very sticky and broad. Seed-pod a globular brown capsule. 6–12 inches high. In dry woods, from Me., south to Ga., west to Cal.

Spotted
Wintergreen
Chimaphila
maculata

A very similar species remarkable for its green-white-marked leaves. The leaves instead of being broad and blunt near the tip like those of *C. umbellata*, taper gradually to a point ; they are remotely toothed, dark green, and strongly marked with white-green in the region of the ribs. They are about two inches long. 3–9 inches high. Somewhat common in N. Y., and in the White Mountains, extending westward only as far as Minn. The name, from χεῖμα, winter, and φιλέω, to love.

1
Pipsissewa.
Chimaphila
umbellata.

1

Chimaphila
maculata

2

PYROLA FAMILY. *Pyrolaceæ.*

One-flowered Pyrola
Moneses grandiflora
Ivory white June-August

A very small plant, bearing a single blossom, somewhat like that of the common Shinleaf. The leaves are thin, deep green, shining, round or nearly so, with rather fine indistinct teeth, and flat-stalked. The five petals of the cream-colored or ivory white flower are a bit pointed; the ten white stamens have two-pointed dull yellow anthers, and the long green pistil bends downward; not far below the flower on the stem is a tiny bract or minute leaflet. 2–5 inches high. In pine woods usually near brooks. From Me., south to R. I. and Pa., and west to Mich. and Ore. Also in the Rocky Mountains. South to Col.

Small Pyrola
Pyrola secunda
Greenish white June-July

A northern woodland plant with ovate pointed deep green leaves, rather round-toothed, and long-stemmed; the leaves circled near the base of the plant-stem. The leaf-stalks are also somewhat flat and troughed. The flower-stalk is tall, bracted or remotely set with minute leaflets, and bears a one-sided row of small greenish white flowers which finally assume a drooping position; the corolla is bell-shaped and five-lobed; the pistil is extremely prominent. The slender flower-stalk is often bent sideways. 3–9 inches high. In woodlands, from Me., south to Pa., and west to Minn. Found on the slopes of the White and Adirondack Mountains. The var. *pumila* is a tiny form 2–4 inches high, with rounded leaves, and but 3–8 flowers. Vt. (Bristol, Sutton, Newark, and Fairhaven), Me., and N. H., but not common, and west to Mich., on the shores of Lake Superior. Blooms from July–August.

Pyrola
chlorantha
Greenish white June-July

This is a small-leaved species with dainty drooping flowers, and a stem of very moderate height without bracts or minute leaflets, or at least possessing but one. The leaves are dull olive green, obscurely scalloped-edged, rather round, and thicker than those of the common *Pyrola* (Shinleaf). The nodding, greenish white flowers have obtuse, elliptical, convergent petals. They

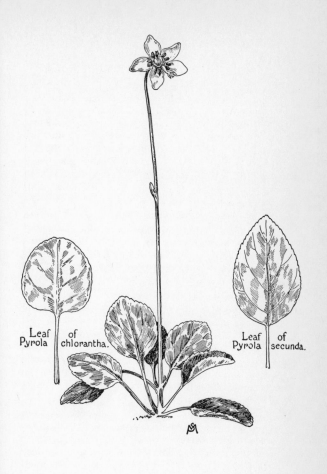

Leaf of Pyrola chlorantha.

Leaf of Pyrola secunda.

One-flowered Pyrola   Moneses grandiflora.

PYROLA FAMILY. *Pyrolaceæ.*

are slightly fragrant. 4–9 inches high. But 3–9 flowers. Woods, Me., south to Md., west to Minn., and Col.

Shinleaf
Pyrola elliptica
Greenish white
June–July
Perhaps the commonest of all the Pyrolas, rather taller than *P. chlorantha*, with evergreen, dark olive green, elliptical, thin, and obscurely shallow-toothed leaves, the stalks somewhat flat or troughed; they exceed their stalks in length. The greenish white waxy flowers nod; they are very fragrant; the five petals are thin and obovate, and form a protective cup about the pale ochre yellow anthers; the pistil is extremely long, bends downward and then curves upward, exposing the tiny five-lobed stigma to the visiting insect which is most likely to alight upon the invitingly exposed pistil. The flowers form a loose cluster, each on a ruddy pedicel (stemlet), and are borne on an upright stalk generally ruddy at the base, and having a tiny leaflet or bract half-way up. Commonly visited by the beelike flies (*Syrphidæ*), and the bees of the genera *Halictus* and *Andrena*. 5–10 inches high. Rich woods, from Me., south to Md., and west to S. Dak. and Ill. The name is from *Pyrus* or *Pirum*, a pear, in allusion to the shape of the leaf.

Round-leaved Pyrola
Pyrola rotundifolia
White
June–July
A similar but much taller species, with nearly round or very broad oval leaves, thick, very indistinctly toothed or toothless, and a deep shining green; the stems usually longer than the leaves, and narrowly margined; they are evergreen. The white waxy flowers are like those described above, but the roundish obovate petals spread open much more; they are also very sweet-scented. 8–18 inches high. In dry or damp sandy woodlands, from Me., south to Ga., and west to Minn., S. Dak., and Ohio.

Pyrola asarifolia
This similar species has pale crimson or magenta flowers, and very round heart-shaped leaves, rather wide, shining, and thick. The southern limit, northern N. Y. and New Eng. But both species are more frequently found northward.

Pyrola asarifolia.

PYROLA FAMILY. *Pyrolaceæ.*

Indian Pipe
Monotropa
uniflora
White or
pinkish
July–August

A familiar clammy, white, parasitic plant, deriving its nourishment from roots and decayed vegetation, generally found in the vicinity of rotting trees. The stem is thick, translucent white, and without leaves, except for the scaly bracts which take their place. The white or delicately pink-salmon-tinted flower has five, or sometimes four, oblong petals, and the 10–12 stamens are pale tan color. The flower is in a nodding position, and is usually solitary, although rarely two may be found on one stem ; the latter is often pink-tinged and springs with several others from a mat of entangled fibrous rootlets. The enlarged ovary finally assumes an erect position, becoming a pale tawny salmon color ; it is usually ten-grooved and five-celled, and forms a large, fleshy, ovoid seed-vessel. The plant is at home in the dim-lit fastnesses of the forest, and it quickly withers and blackens after being gathered and exposed to sunlight. 3–9 inches high. Nearly throughout the country.

False Beech-
drops or
Pine-sap
Monotropa
Hypopitys
Tawny
reddish, etc.
June–
September

A somewhat similar parasitic plant found most frequently over the roots of oaks and pines. The stems are in clusters, and are slightly downy ; they are whitish, pale tan color, or reddish, with many bracts. The small bracts are thin, papery, yellowish red, and they turn black when withering. The small vase-shaped flowers are light crimson-red more or less touched with yellow ; the tips of the flower are quite yellowish. The cluster of 3–10, or rarely more, drooping flowers is slightly fragrant. The fleshy vase-shaped seed-vessels become erect. 4–12 inches high. In dry woods from Me., south, and west to Ore. and Ariz. The generic name is from the Greek, and means turned one-sided, in allusion to the one-sided drooping method of flower-growth.

Indian Pipe.
Monotropa uniflora.

False Beech-drops.
Monotropa Hypopitys.

HEATH FAMILY. *Ericaceæ.*

Mostly shrubs and a few perennial herbs with simple leaves and generally regular, perfect flowers, the corolla of 4–5 lobes or petals, and as many or twice as many stamens. Fruit a capsule or berry. Cross-fertilized by various bees, by the beelike flies, butterflies, and moths. To this family belong the blueberries, huckleberries, and cranberries.

Creeping Snowberry
Chiogenes serpyllifolia
White
May–June

The daintiest member of the Heath Family, with (often terra-cotta-colored) roughish stems creeping closely over rocky and mossy ground. The stiff dark olive evergreen leaves are tiny, broad, ovate pointed, and sparsely covered with brownish hairs beneath ; the margin of the leaves rolled backward. The tiny white flowers are bell-shaped with four rounded lobes. They grow at the angles of the leaves and assume a nodding position. The berry is shining china white, ovate, and about ¼ inch long. Both leaf and berry possess a wintergreen flavor. Branches 3–11 inches long. In cool damp woods and peat bogs, frequent on hill-tops, from Me., south to N. Car., and west to Minn. Found in Campton, N. H. The name (Greek) means "snow-offspring" ; it is appropriately dainty.

Bearberry
Arctostaphylos Uva-ursi
White or pink-white
May–June

Also a trailing, hillside plant of a shrubby nature, with more cr less ruddy, hairy-rough branches. The toothless leaves are thick, dark evergreen, round-blunt at the tip, narrowed at the base, and finely veined. The white or rarely pinkish white flowers are bell-shaped or vase-shaped, and are borne in terminal clusters. The style extends far beyond the anthers, and is touched first by the tongue of the visiting insect. The berry is an opaque red ; it is dry and insipid. In dry rocky soil, from Me., south to N. J., west to Minn., S. Dak., and Col. The name is from ἄρκτος, a bear, and σταφυλή, a berry ; the specific title is mere Latin repetition—*Uva*, a bunch or cluster of fruit, and *Ursus*, a bear.

Creeping Snowberry.
Chiogenes serpyllifolia

Bearberry.
Arctostaphylos Uva-ursi.

HEATH FAMILY. *Ericaceæ.*

Trailing Arbutus
Epigœa repens
White and pink
April–May

The Mayflower of New England, common on the borders of rocky woods and hillsides, and blooming beside the remnants of snow-drifts in early spring. It is common in the vicinity of evergreen woodlands. The light brown stems are shrubby and tough, creeping close to the cold earth under decayed leaves and grasses; they are rough-hairy. The old dull light olive green leaves are more or less rusty-spotted; the sides spread angularly from the central depressed rib. The new leaves develop in June. The surface is rough and netted with fine veins; beneath it is rough-hairy and much lighter in color. The sweet-scented, white or delicately pink-tinted flowers are five-lobed, tubular, and possess a frosty sheen; they are in general trimorphous, that is, the stamens and styles are of three relative and reciprocal lengths; but commonly the flowers are dimorphous—confined to staminate and pistillate forms. The staminate blossoms contribute a touch of light yellow to the delicate surrounding of pure pink and white. The commonest visitors are the early queen bumblebees, *Bombus pennsylvanicus*, *Bombus terricola*, and *Bombus bifarius*. The flower is nectar bearing. Branches 6–12 inches long. Me., south to Fla., and west to Minn.

Wintergreen or Checkerberry
Gaultheria procumbens
White
July–August

The familiar Boxberry of the Middle States, common in wildernesses and all evergreen woodlands. The broad, ovate, evergreen leaf is stiff, thick, and shiny dark green, with few small teeth or toothless, and very nearly stemless. The younger leaves are yellow-green; all are clustered at the top of the buff-brown or ruddy stem. The white, waxy flowers are vase-shaped and nodding; they grow from the angles of the leaves. The dry but exceedingly aromatic berry is pure red (a deep cherry color), often $\frac{1}{3}$ inch in diameter, and is formed of the calyx which becomes fleshy, surrounds the seed-capsule, and has all

1
Trailing Arbutus.
Epigæa repens.

2
Checkerberry
Gaultheria procumbens.

HEATH FAMILY. *Ericaceæ.*

---

the appearance of a true fruit. 2–5 inches high. From Me., south, and west to Mich. The same aromatic essential oil exists in sweet birch as in this wintergreen.

Mountain Laurel
Kalmia latifolia
White, pinkish
May-June

A stout and tall shrub in its southern range, often forming impenetrable thickets. The stem and branches are irregular and angular in growth; the leaves are evergreen, shiny dark green, elliptical, firm, and toothless. The young leaves are a yellower green. The beautiful flowers are borne in large, dome-shaped clusters; they are exceedingly conventional and ornamental in form, bowl-shaped with five lobes, waxy white, pinkish-tinged in maturity, and pure pink in the corrugated, cone-shaped bud. There are ten depressions or pockets in the sides of the corolla in which the tips of the anthers are securely held, their filaments forming a series of arching spokes from the centre of the flower which is stained with a tiny crimson star; the style is prominent and pale green. The insect visitor, commonly a moth, often a bee, struggling and pushing its way to the heart of the flower, releases the stamens and these spring backward, showering pollen over the fuzzy body of the intruder. The pollen of *Kalmia* is more or less connected by webby threads, and its adhesive character is peculiarly adapted to the purpose of cross-fertilization; the next blossom visited by the insect probably has a receptive stigma about which the pollen strings become quickly entangled. The flower-stalks are hairy-sticky, thus preventing pilferers, such as ants, who would be useless as fertilizing agents, from entering the blossoms. The seed-capsule is somewhat globular but five-lobed, and at first assumes a dull red hue. 3–6 feet high, and in its southern range often attaining a height of 20–35 feet. In woodlands, preferring sandy soil or rocky slopes, from Me., south, and west to Tenn. and Ohio. Named for Peter Kalm, a German botanist, who visited this country in the middle of the eighteenth century.

Mountain Laurel   Kalmia latifolia.

Sheep-laurel or Lambkill *Kalmia angustifolia* **Crimson-pink June–July** A shrub of lesser proportions, and small, narrow, drooping leaves, elliptical or lance-shaped, evergreen, and dull olive green often rusty-spotted, lighter green beneath. The flower is crimson-pink, small, but otherwise like that of Mountain Laurel, except that the filaments and all other parts are more or less pink-tinged. The stem is terminated by the newer leaves which stand nearly upright; beneath these is the encircling flower-cluster; below, the leaves droop. The foliage is poisonous to cattle. 8–36 inches high. Common in swamps. Me., south to Ga., west to Wis.

Pale Laurel *Kalmia glauca* **Crimson-pink or lilac** A similar and even smaller species, blooming about the same time, distinguished by its two-edged branches which seem to grow in sections set at right angles with one another. The narrow, evergreen leaves grow oppositely or are set in groups of three; the edges are rolled back rather strongly; they are conspicuously *white-green* beneath. The crimson-pink or often light lilac flowers, $\frac{1}{2}$ inch broad, terminate the stem. 6–20 inches high, confined to cold peat bogs and hillside swamps, from Me., south to northern N. J., and west to Mich.

White Swamp Honeysuckle *Rhododendron viscosum* **White June–July** The wild Rhododendrons are also shrubs which bear characteristically showy flowers. This species has a much branched stem, and obovate or blunt lance-shaped, yellow-green leaves, with a few scattered hairs above. The twigs are hairy, and the stem almost bare of leaves. The flowers (expanding later than the leaves) are pure white or pink-tinged, with the outside surface covered with ruddy, sticky hairs; they are very fragrant; the stamens are prominent, the anthers yellow; the pinkish pistil is longer than the stamens. Visited most frequently by bees, butterflies, and moths, and protected from creeping insects by the sticky-hairy outer surface of the corolla-tube. 3–7 feet high. In swamps from Me., south, west to Ohio and Ark; generally near the coast. The var. *glaucum* has much lighter colored leaves rather whitish beneath, and sometimes hairy. Me. to Va. The name (Greek) means rose-tree.

Pale Laurel   Kalmia glauca.

HEATH FAMILY. *Ericaceæ.*

Pinxter Flower or Wild Honeysuckle
Rhododendron nudiflorum
Pale or deep pink
April–May

A more leafy shrub with branching stem, characterized by its extremely golden yellow-green foliage. The ovate leaf tapers and is pointed at both ends, the edge and surface are very slightly hairy. The delicate and beautiful flowers are pale or deep crimson-pink with the base of the tube a trifle stronger ; the broader corolla lobes do not curve back conspicuously ; the stamens and pistil, all exceedingly prominent, are light crimson. The flowers are delicately fragrant, grow in small terminal clusters expanding before or with the leaves, and when fading the corollas slide down the pistils, depend from them a while, and finally drop. The most frequent visitors are the honeybees and moths. 2–6 feet high. In swamps or in shady places, from Me., south, and west to Ill.

Flame Azalea
Rhododendron calendulaceum
Orange-yellow and reddish
May–June

A most beautiful and showy species, entirely southern, but commonly cultivated. The leaves are hairy and generally obovate, sometimes with only a few scattered hairs above. The flower, expanding with or before the leaves, has five broad lobes scarcely if at all backward curved ; it is nearly flame color or orange-yellow more or less suffused with pink, has very little or no fragrance, and the outer surface of the tube is slightly fine-hairy and sticky. The ruddy stamens prominent. 4–12 feet high. In dry woodlands, southern N. Y. and Pa., in the mountains, to Ga.

Rhodora
Rhododendron Rhodora
Light magenta
May

A familiar flower of New England and one famous in the verses of the poet Emerson. The leaves are slightly hairy, light green, oval or oblong, and rather obtuse ; the color deeper above and paler beneath. The flowers are narrow-lobed, light magenta, and formed somewhat like the honeysuckle, with the upper lip slightly three-lobed, and the lower in two nearly separate sections ; they grow in thin clusters terminally, and precede the unfolding of the leaves or else expand with them. 1–3 feet high. Wet hillsides and cool bogs. Me., N. Y., N. J., and eastern Pa., in the mountains.

Pinxter Flower.   Rhododendron nudiflorum.

HEATH FAMILY. *Ericaceæ.*

Great Laurel
Rhododendron maximum
Pink spotted orange
June–July

A tall shrub, or often a tree, with showy clusters of pink-white flowers spotted with gold orange, and greenish at the base, the five lobes of the corolla, broad, blunt, and substantially even in shape. The leaves shiny dark green, 4–9 inches long, ever-green, leathery, drooping in the winter season, and spreading in summer. They are oblong, toothless, slightly rolled under at the edge, and dark beneath. The flower-stems are sticky-hairy, thus preventing the pilfering of creeping insects ; the flowers are mostly visited by bees, but the honey they produce is said to be poisonous. 5–35 feet high. Damp woods, rare from Me. to Ohio, plentiful from Pa. to Ga.; abundant through-out the Alleghany region, where, on the mountain sides, it forms impenetrable thickets.

Rhododendron Catawbiense
Light purple or lilac
May–June

A species similar in many respects to the foregoing, but generally not more than 5 feet high. The leaves are broadly ob-long or oval, the tips with an abrupt very small point, pale green beneath. The large flowers are light purple or lilac. This species is hybridized with other less hardy ones, notably the *R. arboreum* of the Himalayas, and from these proceed most of the Rhododendrons familiar in ornamental grounds. 3–6, or rarely 18 feet high. In the higher Alleghanies from Va. to Ga.

Lapland Rose-bay
Rhododendron Lapponicum
Light purple
July–August

A dwarf species confined to the summits of high mountains in the north. The olive green leaves are small, oval or elliptical, and grouped in clusters on the otherwise bare stem. They are covered, together with the branches, with minute rusty scales. The flowers have a five-lobed corolla which is bell-shaped and light purple, dotted. There are 5–10 stamens. A prostrate branching plant that hugs the rocky slopes of the mountain. 2–12 inches high. Sum-mits of the White Mountains, N. H., and the Adiron-dacks, N. Y. Found at the head of Tuckerman's Ravine, Mt. Washington, N. H.

Great Laurel.   Rhododendron maximum.

DIAPENSIA FAMILY. *Diapensiaceæ*.

DIAPENSIA FAMILY. *Diapensiaceæ*.

Low perennial herbs, or tufted shrubs of a mosslike character, very closely related to the *Ericaceæ*—the attachment of the stamens to the corolla being the principal difference,—with five-parted tiny flowers whose style is tipped with a three-lobed stigma. Fruit a capsule.

Pyxie or Flowering Moss
Pyxidanthera barbulata
White or pink
April–May

An interesting and pretty mosslike little plant common on the pine barrens of New Jersey. The linear or lance-shaped leaves, scarcely ⅓ inch long, are medium green, sharp at the tip, and hairy at the base when young ; they are crowded toward the ends of the branches. The white or pale pink flowers are small, with five blunt lobes between which are curiously fixed the five conspicuous stamens ; they are numerous, and apparently stemless. Branches prostrate and creeping. 6–10 inches long. In sandy soil, dry pine barrens. From N. J., south to N. Car. Found at Lakewood, N. J. The name is from two Greek words, box and anther, referring to the anthers which open as if by a lid.

PRIMROSE FAMILY. *Primulaceæ*.

Herbs with leaves variously arranged, and with perfect, regular flowers. The corolla (usually five-cleft) is tubular, funnel-formed, or salver-formed. Stamens as many as there are lobes to the corolla and fixed opposite to them, but the corolla lacking in the genus named *Glaux*. Seeds in a one-celled and several-valved capsule.

Featherfoil
Hottonia inflata
White
June–August

A peculiar aquatic plant of a somewhat spongy nature, common in shallow stagnant water. Its strange appearance is due to the cluster of inflated primary flower-stalks which are about ½ inch thick, constricted at the joints, and almost leafless. The leaves are cut into threadlike divisions, and are beneath the water, densely distributed on the floating and rooting stems. The insignificant whitish flower, ¼ inch long, has a corolla much shorter than the calyx. The seed-capsule is globular. Stems sometimes 18 inches long. Shallow ponds and ditches, from Mass., to central N.Y., and south. Named for Peter Hotton, botanist.

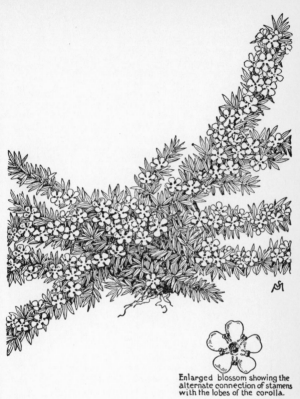

Enlarged blossom showing the
alternate connection of stamens
with the lobes of the corolla.

Pyxie Moss.   Pyxidanthera barbulata.

PRIMROSE FAMILY. *Primulaceæ.*

American Cowslip or Shooting Star
Dodecatheon Meadia
Light magenta
April–May

A handsome wild flower, frequently cultivated, but confined in its natural state to the country west of Pennsylvania. The blunt lance-shaped deep green leaves proceed from the root ; they are generally toothless or nearly so, and their stems are long and margined. The tall primary flower-stalk is topped by a small cluster of delicate pendulous light magenta, pink-magenta, or white flowers, the five long corolla-divisions of which are strongly turned backward. The exposed stamens are close-clustered—grouped in a conelike figure ; the anthers are long, thin, and golden yellow ; the base of each is thickened and marked with magenta-purple. The flower is cross-fertilized by bees. According to Professor Robertson, a visiting bee to reach the nectar must force its tongue between the anther-tips and come more or less in contact with the mature stigma ; the anthers at this period are still immature. Among the visitors are the bumblebee *Bombus americanorum*, the bees of the family *Andrenidæ*, and the clouded sulphur butterfly *Colias philodice.* 8–20 inches high. Moist hillsides, cliffs, open woods, or prairies, from Penn. to S. Dak., south to Ga. and Tex. Name from the Greek, meaning twelve gods.

Dwarf Canadian Primrose
Primula Mistassinica
Pale magenta-pink
June–July

A delicate little plant found only in the northern part of our range, bearing a family resemblance to the yellow English Primrose. The light green leaves are blunt lance-shaped, tapering to a distinct stem, thin, green on both sides, rarely with a slightly mealy appearance beneath, and shallow-toothed. The pale magenta-pink or lighter pink corolla is five-lobed, bluntly scallop-tipped, and stained with yellow in the centre (sometimes the yellow is absent). The few flowers are clustered at the top of the long slender stalk. This species is apt to intergrade with *Primula farinosa*, a taller one, with leaves white-mealy beneath (at least when young), and flowers with a more cuniform lobe, borne in thicker clusters. Confined to moist situations ; Me., central N. Y., and Canada.

Star Flower
Trientalis Americana.

Shooting Star.
Dodecatheon Meadia.

PRIMROSE FAMILY. *Primulaceæ.*

Star Flower
Trientalis Americana
White
May-June

A delicate and interesting little woodland plant with a long horizontally creeping root which sends upward an almost bare or few-scaled thin stem terminating in a circle of sharp-pointed, lance-shaped, light green leaves, thin, shiny, and tapering to both ends. There are 5-9 leaves in the circle, from the centre of which proceed two threadlike stalks, each bearing a fragile, white, star-shaped flower with 6-7 pointed divisions. The stamens are long and delicate, with tiny golden anthers, which mature later than the stigma. Cross-fertilization effected mostly through the agency of the beelike flies (*Bombylius*). 3-7 inches high, or rarely more. In moist thin woods, from Me., west to Minn., and south to southern N. J. and the mountains of Va. Common in the thin woodlands of the White Mountains.

Fringed Loosestrife
Steironema ciliatum
Yellow
June-July

A rather handsome perennial commonly found in low moist situations, particularly on river flats. The smooth light green leaves are ovate or ovate lance-shaped and sharply pointed; on the upper edge of the stem is a fringe of erect hairs—hence the specific term, *ciliatum*. The leaves are in pairs which are set at right angles with each other. The pretty light golden yellow flowers, not far from a pure yellow tone, are five-lobed, the divisions oval and finished with an abrupt sharp point (called mucronate); these tips are somewhat twisted or puckered; about the centre of the corolla is a terra-cotta-colored ring; within this are five straw-colored stamens alternating with five abortive ones; in the centre is the pale green pistil. The smooth, erect stem 18-22 inches high or more. Common in low ground and on the borders of thickets from Me. west to British Columbia, south to Ga., Ala., and to Ariz.

Steironema lanceolatum
Yellow
June-July

A narrow-leaved species smaller and slenderer in every respect. The leaves are lance-shaped and linear, indistinctly stemmed and smooth; the lower ones are much shorter and broader, and the stems are distinct and long. The flowers are similar to those of *S. ciliatum*, but smaller—a little over ½ inch broad. 8-20

Steironema ciliatum.

inches high. Moist ground from Me., west to Minn., and south. The *Steironemas* are cross-fertilized, according to Prof. Robertson, by bees ; in Connecticut by *Macropis ciliata* and *Macropis patellata*, and in Illinois by *Macropis steironematis*. The name is from two Greek words, sterile and thread, in allusion to the abortive stamens.

**Four=leaved
Loosestrife**
*Lysimachia
quadrifolia*
**Yellow
June–July**

A delicate and pretty species common on all low lands, especially sandy river banks. The light green leaves are pointed lance-shaped or broader, and are arranged in a circle of generally four, but sometimes three and six. From the bases of these leaves project slender long stems, each bearing a single star-shaped light golden yellow flower, prettily dotted around the centre with terra-cotta red, which sometimes extends in faint streaks all over the corolla lobes. The stamens and pistil project in a cone-shaped cluster ; the stigma is advanced so far beyond the anthers that self-fertilization rarely if ever occurs. The *Lysimachias* are visited by the bees of the genus *Macropis*, by bumblebees, and by honeybees evidently for the purpose of collecting pollen. Stem smooth or very minutely hairy (under a glass), straight and round, 12–30 inches high, simple or rarely branched. Sandy soil or often moist ground, Me., west to Minn., south to Ga.

*Lysimachia
stricta*
**Yellow
June–August**

Along with preceding species bloom the slender spirelike clusters of the simple-stemmed *Lysimachia stricta*, whose flowers are not appreciably different, though recorded by Dr. Gray and others as having slenderer corolla-divisions. This variation, however, is not so apparent ; but at the base of the divisions the red spots are double in *L. stricta*, while they are single in *L. quadrifolia*. The slender *flower-spike* is distinctly characteristic of *L. stricta ;* it forms an aggregation of misty yellow color (when a large colony of the plants is seen) which is never present with the other species. Often little elongated bulblets appear at the bases of the leaves. Leaves lance-shaped and sharp-pointed at either end ; in both species apt to be sepia-dotted. Stem 8–20 inches high. Moist and sandy soil. Me., west to Minn., south to Ga.

Loosestrife.
Lysimachia stricta.   Lysimachia quadrifolia.

Lysimachia producta
Light golden yellow
June–August

A species closely allied to *L. stricta.* The smooth stem is simple or very slightly branched, the lance-shaped light green leaves, pale green beneath, grow oppositely or in circles of 3–5, and the terminal flower-spike, loosely flowered, is sometimes 18 inches long. The corolla-divisions are dotted and striped with dark red, ovate-oblong and rounded at the tips. From this last fact it would seem as though the plant could not easily be confused with either *L. stricta* or *L. quadrifolia*, for the flowers of both these species are decidedly pointed star-shaped. In low damp ground on the borders of thickets, from Me. and Mass., west to Mich. (Vide *Rhodora*, vol. i., pp. 131–134. M. L. Fernald on "Ambiguous Loosestrifes.")

Moneywort or Myrtle
Lysimachia nummularia
Light golden yellow
July– September

An extremely beautiful trailing vine with a creeping, not climbing, habit, which has become naturalized from Europe. It takes kindly to cultivation, and is particularly decorative when planted in rustic baskets in which it best displays the graceful pendulous character of its stems. The leaves are dark green, shining, small, almost round, and short-stemmed. One rather large light golden yellow flower, with five ovate divisions to the corolla, grows from the junction of the leaf-stalk and plant-stem; it is not spotted with terra-cotta like the other members of this genus. Stems 6–20 inches long. In moist ground near dwellings, mostly an escape from gardens; Eastern States. In many places it is reported as a troublesome weed. Found in Campton, N. H., and Amherst, Mass.

Glaux maritima
Purple-white
June

A low, fleshy seaside plant with oblong, toothless, and stemless light green leaves, from the bases of which grow the solitary dull purple-white or pinkish flowers *without a true corolla*, but with a five-scalloped calyx. The seaside from N. J. and Cape Cod north.

Moneywort.
Lysimachia nummularia.

Glaux maritima.

PLUMBAGO OR LEADWORT. *Plumbaginaceæ.*

Pimpernel
Anagallis
arvensis
Red, pur-
ple, etc.
June-August
A low spreading annual; the common Poor Man's Weather-glass of England, which has become naturalized in this country. The small solitary flowers are a variety of colors, scarlet, purple, white, etc. The corolla has five broad divisions but hardly any tube. The leaves are ovate, stemless, and toothless, and grow oppositely in pairs, or in circles. Stem 6 inches long. Waste sandy places, Eastern States, generally near the coast. The flowers open only in sunshine, and close at 4 o'clock.

PLUMBAGO OR LEADWORT FAMILY.

Plumbaginaceæ.

Perennial herbs with small, perfect, regular flowers of five parts—i. e., five-lobed corolla, five stamens, and five styles; the flower-tube funnel-formed and plaited; the ovary one-celled and bearing a solitary seed. Seaside plants.

Sea Lavender
or Marsh
Rosemary
Statice
Limonium
var.*Caroliniana*
Lavender
July-
September
A seaside plant with a slender much-branched stem growing from a thick woody root very astringent in character, the branches rather erect. The leaves, also starting from the root, are blunt lance-shaped or obovate, long-stemmed, toothless or nearly so, and tipped with a bristly point; the mid-rib is prominent. The branches bear many solitary, or 2-3 (in a group) tiny lavender flowers with a curious tooth between each of the five tiny lobes; the lobes of the calyx are also very acute. The character of the plant is branchy and naked-stemmed, with flowers so insignificant that the delicate lavender color is much eclipsed by the rather light subdued green. 1-2 feet high. In salt marshes from Me., south. Found in Nantucket, Mass.

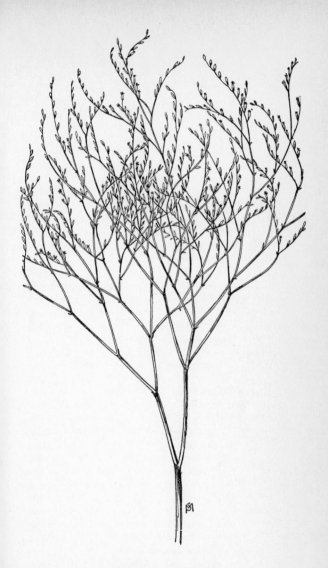

Marsh Rosemary.
Statice limonium var. Caroliniana.

GENTIAN FAMILY. *Gentianaceæ.*

Smooth herbs with generally opposite leaves, toothless and stemless; *Menyanthes* and *Limnanthemum* are two exceptions to this rule. Flowers regular and perfect, the corolla with 4–12 lobes; alternating with these are a corresponding number of stamens. Fertilized mostly by the bees and the beelike flies.

Lesser Centaury
Erythræa Centaurium
Light magenta
June–September

An erect and smooth annual naturalized from Europe, with several short branches above, and elliptical or oblong light green leaves, somewhat acute ; the uppermost rather linear. The small tubular light magenta flowers five-lobed and very nearly stemless. They are numerously borne at the summits of the branches. 6–12 inches high. Waste places and the shores of the Great Lakes, from Quebec to Illinois. The name *Erythræa* is from the Greek, meaning red. The flowers are weak in color, and the plants are really more delicate than beautiful.

Erythræa ramosissima
Magenta-pink
June–September

A small species from Europe similar in many respects to the foregoing, but the stem very much branched, the leaves oval or long-ovate, the larger lower ones blunt, the upper small and acute. The flowers are magenta-pink, and, with few exceptions, distinctly stemmed. The tube of the corolla is nearly twice as long as the five lobes of the calyx. 3–8 inches high. Waste places or fields, wet or shady, from southern N. Y. to east Pa. and Md.

Spiked Century
Erythræa spicata
Magenta-pink
June–September

An erect and smooth annual naturalized from the old country, with small, blunt, oblong, light green leaves ; the upper ones rather acute, and all more or less close to the generally forking stem. The very small magenta-pink, or crimson-magenta flowers tubular and five-lobed, stemless and also close to the plant-stem, the tube of the corolla a little longer than the calyx-lobes. 6–16 inches high. Shores of Nantucket, Mass., and Portsmouth, N. H.

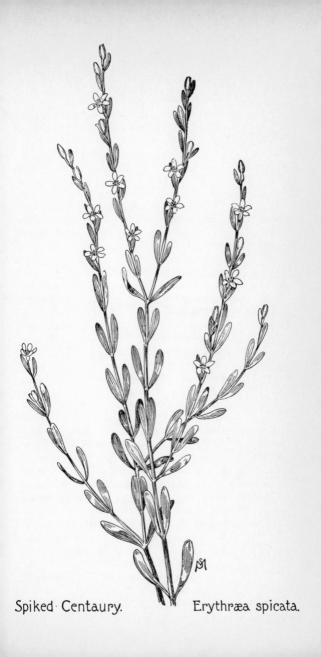

Spiked Centaury.   Erythræa spicata.

Lance-leaved Sabbatia
Sabbatia lanceolata
White
June-September

A not very uncommon wild flower in the swamps of the pine barrens of New Jersey, with white, starlike, five-lobed flowers, nearly an inch broad, which in fading turn yellowish, and ovate or lance-shaped light green leaves with 3-5 ribs. The plant-stem slender, somewhat four-sided, branched above, or sometimes simple. The branches are borne relatively opposite. The flowers are numerous. 1-3 feet high. Pine barrens N. J., to Fla.

Rose Pink
Sabbatia angularis
White or Pink
July-August

The stem of this species is decidedly and sharply four-sided, it is also rather thick and much branched. The light green leaves are five-ribbed, ovate, acute at the tip, and somewhat clasping at the base. The delicately fragrant flowers are an inch or more broad, pale crimson-pink or sometimes white, and marked in the centre with a yellow-green star (a characteristic of many of the *Sabbatias*). The style is cleft at the tip—i. e., two stigmas. The calyx-lobes are about one third as long as the corolla. 2-3 feet high. Fertile ground, N. Y. and Pa., west to Mich., and south.

Sea Pink
Sabbatia stellaris
Pink
July-August

A pretty species common on salt meadows, with crimson-pink flowers as large as or larger than a nickel. The light green leaves oblong lance-shaped or linear, the uppermost small and bractlike. The numerous flowers are borne solitary at the ends of the branches; the linear calyx-lobes almost equal (the rule is flexible) in length the lobes of the pale crimson-pink or white corolla. More than half the style is two-cleft, the stamens are golden yellow, and the centre of the flower is green-yellow edged with ochre or sometimes red. 6-20 inches. Along the coast from Me. to Fla. Closely allied to the next into which it appears to pass.

Sabbatia gracilis
Pink

Like the preceding. The stem exceedingly slender and much branched. The leaves linear or linear lance-shaped, the uppermost almost threadlike. The exceedingly narrow lobes of the calyx equal in length the

Sea Pink.

Sabbatia stellaris.   Sabbatia gracilis.

GENTIAN FAMILY. *Gentianaceæ.*

lobes of the corolla (rarely they are appreciably shorter).
The style is about half-cleft. 1–2 feet high. Marshes,
Nantucket, Mass. to N. J., south to Fla. and La.

Large Marsh Pink
Sabbatia chloroides
Crimson-pink
July–August

The largest-flowered and most beautiful member of the genus. The basal leaves blunt-tipped and tapering toward the base, the upper light green leaves diminishing to lance-shape and linear. The few crimson-pink flowers are nearly two inches
broad, with generally ten obovate corolla lobes (an equal
number of linear calyx lobes), each marked with a
three-pointed ochre-edged, green-yellow base which
contributes to the beauty of the central star-figure of
the flower ; the stamens are golden yellow, and the style
is deeply two-cleft. The flower is visited most frequently by bees and the flies of the genus *Syrphidæ*.
The wiry stems, simple or branching very little, are 1–2
feet high. Rarely the flowers are white. On sandy
margins of brackish ponds from Mass. to Fla. and Ala.,
near the coast.

Fringed Gentian
Gentiana crinita
Pale violet-blue
September–October

The most famous member of the beautiful Gentian group, remarkable not so
much for its blue color as for the delicate,
misty quality of that color, and the ex-
pressiveness of the flower-form. The
plant is an annual with a leafy, perpendicular, branched stem, the branches erect,
somewhat four-angled, and each bearing a single terminal flower. The flower is deep vase-shaped with four
rounded, light violet-blue lobes deeply fringed and
spreading horizontally only in the sunshine ; the color
varies from pale to deep violet-blue, with occasionally a
ruddy tinge, but never with a suspicion of true blue,
though lines of a deeper blue-violet appear on the outer
surface of the corolla. The large four-pointed calyx is
four-sided, and generally a bronzy, yellow-green. The
yellow-green leaves are ovate-lance-shaped or narrower,
and they are conspicuously opposite. 1–3 feet high. In
low moist ground from Me. to the Daks., south to Iowa,
and in the mountains of Ga.

Rose Pink.   Sabbatia angularis.

GENTIAN FAMILY. *Gentianaceæ.*

Gentiana serrata
Light violet-blue
July–September

A similar annual species with lance-linear or linear leaves, a stem but little branched with a few blunt wedge-shaped leaves at the base, and violet-blue flowers nearly as large as those of the preceding species with the fringe at the summit of the corolla short, or reduced to mere teeth. 4–18 inches high. Moist ground from western N. Y. to Minn. and Iowa.

Ague-weed
Gentiana quinqueflora
Light violet-blue
August–October

Also an annual; the stem ridged and four-sided. The leaves, in general, ovate, sharply pointed at the tip, slightly clasping at the base, and with 3–7 ribs. The very light violet-blue or lilac flowers clustered at the apex of the branches in groups of 2–7 but generally 5. The flowers smaller, scarcely an inch long, tubular, and terminating in five triangular small bristle-pointed lobes. A common species in the west, attractive but not so beautiful as the Fringed Gentian. 8–22 inches high. Moist hillsides from Me., south, and west to Mich. and Mo., generally in the mountains ; it is found at an altitude of over 6000 feet on the peaks of N. Car. Occasional in Vt., and absent in central N. H.

Downy Gentian
Gentiana puberula
Blue-violet
August–October

A handsome perennial species with usually a single stem, generally minutely hairy and rough, and with narrow, rigid, lance-shaped light green leaves, the uppermost nearly linear. The blue-violet flowers are bell-shaped with five triangular lobes, rather open-spreading. The calyx has five linear lobes quite rough to the touch. The flowers are borne in terminal clusters or at the bases of the leaves, and are seldom if ever solitary. 8–17 inches high. On prairies and in fields from western N. Y. and Ohio to S. Dak. and Kan., south to Ga. and Ky. Common in the vicinity of Minneapolis, the Minnehaha Falls, and on the dry borders of the great wheat-fields of Minnesota.

Downy Gentian.　　　Gentiana puberula.

**Soapwort
Gentian**
*Gentiana
Saponaria*
**Pale blue-
violet**
**August–
October**

A familiar species of the Middle and Western States closely resembling the Bottle Gentian. The pale blue-violet, or light lilac-blue flower is only partly open, the five lobes are blunt, erect, slightly cut at the tip, and the flower-cup is club-shaped, the anthers within cohering in a ring. The light green leaves are commonly ovate lance-shaped, three-ribbed, and pointed at either end, the edges rough. The flowers form a terminal cluster; a few grow from the leaf-angles. They are frequented by honeybees and bumblebees; *Bombus americanorum* is a common visitor. Both this Gentian and the preceding one ripen their pollen before the stigma is receptive and cross-fertilization is therefore inevitable. The smooth and slender stem is 12–27 inches high. The juice of the plant is soapy. In wet woodlands from N. Y., west to Minn., and south.

**Bottle or
Closed Gentian**
*Gentiana
Andrewsii*
Violet=blue
**August–
October**

A perennial. In the east this is the commonest of all Gentians; it is remarkable for its tight-closed bottle-shaped corolla, which is contracted by plaits white-striped, white at the base and an intense violet-blue at the apex; sometimes the blue approaches ultramarine. The medium (sometimes rusty) green leaves are smooth, ovate lance-shaped, pointed at the tip, and generally narrowed at the base. The flowers are mostly crowded in a terminal cluster, but some grow from the leaf-bases; all are set close to the leaves, which are conspicuously arranged in pairs. Bumblebees not infrequently force an entrance into the corolla, and self-fertilization is sometimes questionable. The smooth, round stem 1–2 feet high. Rich woodland borders, Me. to S. Dak., south to Ga. and Mo.

*Gentiana
linearis*
**Light blue-
violet**
**August–
September**

A much less common Gentian frequenting mountain bogs. It is a smooth, slender-stemmed perennial, with light green linear or lance-linear leaves with three ribs, acute at either end. The pale blue-violet flower-cup is contracted to a funnel-form with rather scallop-shaped lobes; the light green,

Bottle Gentian.   Gentiana Andrewsii.

simple, round stem is 10–24 inches high. Wet situations among the mountains of N. Eng. and N. Y., south to Md. Found at high elevations of the Adirondack and Green Mountains.

Gentiana ochroleuca
Greenish white
September–November

A greenish white-flowered species with a corolla narrowly open, displaying within stripes of magenta-lilac on a greenish veined background, the lobes somewhat triangular and with a tooth. The flowers are mostly in terminal clusters. The medium green leaves are obovate, the uppermost acute at the tip, the lower ones blunt and short, all narrow at the base. Slender stem 8–16 inches high. Shaded woodland borders from southern N. J. and Pa., south.

Gentiana angustifolia
Light ultra-marine blue
August–October

A smaller and exceedingly delicate and pretty species mostly confined to the pine barrens of the Southern States, with a simple or sometimes branching stem, and with solitary, bright light ultramarine blue flowers (often speckled within) at the apex of the stem or its branches; they are much larger than bluebells. The five lobes of the corolla are deeply cut, ovate, and open-spreading. The small linear leaves are less than 2 inches long. 6–15 inches high. In moist situations from southern N. J., south.

Yellow
Bartonia
Bartonia tenella
Greenish yellow
July–September

An attenuated, slender, stiff-stemmed little plant, simple or with a few erect branches, *destitute of leaves*, but with small awl-shaped opposite-growing scales closely hugging the stem, which is a trifle angled, all a yellow-green. The lower scales are close together, the upper become more and more separated. The yellow, bell-shaped flowers of a greenish tone, with four blunt (often slightly toothed) lobes, are arranged oppositely on the plant-stem, the peduncles (flower-stems) about as long as or longer than the flower. The flowers are mostly terminal but inconspicuous on account of their uncertain coloring. 4–14 inches high. In thin woods, pastures, and dry cranberry bogs, but mostly in damp soil, from Me., south, and west to Mich.

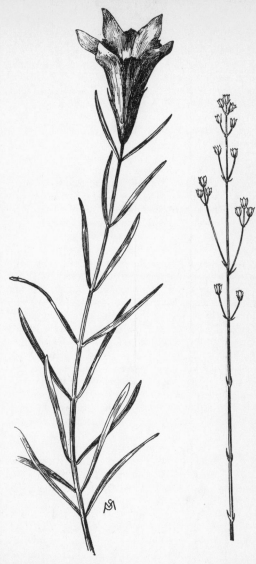

Gentiana angustifolia.   Bartonia tenella.

DOGBANE FAMILY. *Apocynaceœ.*

Chiefly a tropical family with few representatives in our range. Plants with an acrid, milky juice, closely related to the Milkweed Family. Leaves opposite (generally) and toothless. Flowers perfect, five-parted; stamens as many as the lobes of the corolla (flower-cup), the latter rolled up in the bud. Fertilized mostly by butterflies and bees.

Spreading Dogbane
Apocynum androsœmifolium
White-pink
June–July

A somewhat tall and shrublike plant, with a smooth, slender, branching stem, generally reddish on the side exposed to sunlight. The opposite growing, lustreless light blue-green, ovate leaves are toothless, and ruddy short-stalked. The delicate and beautiful little bell-shaped flowers are white-pink, five-lobed, and lily-of-the-valley-like, striped with pink on the inside of the cup. The clusters are small and terminate the branches; their most frequent visitors are bees and butterflies, and among the latter are the ever-present little yellow *Colias philodice* and the handsome monarch (*Anosia plexippus*). Müller says the flower is fertilized by butterflies, and cements its pollen to their tongues. An insect inseparable from the dogbane is the so-called dogbane beetle (*Chrysochus auratus*), jewellike and resplendent in metallic red and green of incomparable lustre; it is scarcely ⅓ inch long (see *Familiar Features of the Roadside*, p. 178). 1–4 feet high. Common in half-shaded field borders, or in thickets throughout the north, and south to Ga.

Indian Hemp
Apocynum cannabinum
Greenish white
June–August

A far less attractive species with greenish white, tiny flowers erectly five-pointed. Similar to the above in other respects, but less spreading and more upright. The leaves narrower and abruptly acute. 1–3 feet high. On sandy river-banks, in fields, and in thickets everywhere. Both species found in Campton, N. H. The name is Greek in origin — ἀπό, from, and κύων, a dog.

Spreading Dogbane.
Apocynum androsæmifolium.

Indian Hemp.
Apocynum cannabium.

MILKWEED FAMILY. *Asclepiadaceæ.*

Milky-juiced plants with large leaves, and flowers deeply five-parted, the sepallike corolla segments turned absolutely back at the time of bloom ; the so-called corona within with its five concave parts thus fully exposed ; the anthers and stigma remarkably connected, and the pollen cohering in waxlike, granular, pear-shaped masses not unlike those of the Orchids. The masses quite frequently become attached to the feet of bees, and the entanglement causes their death. The flowers are almost exclusively fertilized by bees and the beelike flies (see Müller's *Fertilization of Flowers*).

Butterfly Weed or Pleurisy Root
Asclepias tuberosa
Light orange
June–September

The handsomest member of the genus, with brilliant light orange or orange-yellow flowers, in erect flat-topped clusters at the termination of the branches. Leaves light olive green, narrow oblong, or lance-shaped, hairy beneath, and veiny, nearly or quite stemless. The juice is very slightly if at all milky. The stem somewhat rough. The slender pods are borne erect on a short stalk with an S curve. 1–2 feet high. Common in dry fields everywhere, especially south. Found on Cape Cod.

Purple Milkweed
Asclepias purpurascens
Magenta-crimson
June–August

A misnamed species, as its flowers are pure crimson or else crimson-magenta; but they are never purple. The stem is usually simple, green, and magenta-tinged at the leaf junctures. Leaves ovate, and finely hairy beneath ; smooth above. The flowers are ¼ inch long, with broad horns abruptly pointed inward. 2–3 feet high. Common in dry fields and thickets. Me., south to Ga., west to Minn.

Swamp Milkweed
Asclepias incarnata
Dull light crimson
July–September

A similar, rather smooth species, the stem with two downy lines above and on the branches of the flower-stalks. The leaves narrow, or lance-shaped ; all short-stalked. The small flowers in small terminal flat-topped clusters, dull light crimson or dull crimson-pink. 2–4 feet high. Common in swamps throughout our range.

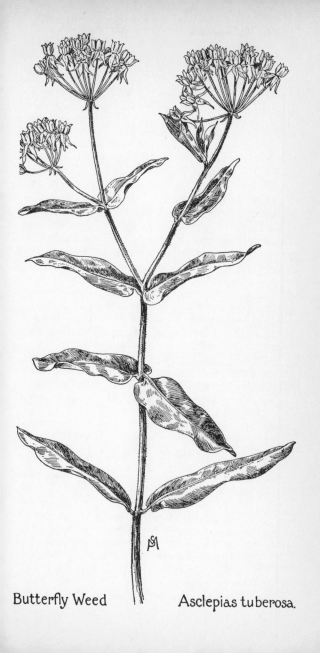

Butterfly Weed   Asclepias tuberosa.

The var. *pulchra* is more or less hairy, has broader, shorter-stalked leaves, and dull crimson or pink or even pink-white flowers. Common north, south to Ga.

**Common
Milkweed**
*Asclepias
Cornuti*
**Pale brown-
lilac**
July–August

The commonest of all the *Asclepias*, and remarkable for its cloyingly sweet, somewhat pendulous flower-cluster, which is most æsthetic in color ; it varies from pale brownish lilac to pale lavender-brown, and from dull crimson-pink and pink-lilac to yellowish (the horns particularly) and brownish lavender. Gray's and Britton and Brown's "green-purple" is a misleading color description ; the authors of *Wild Flowers of the Northeastern States* (p. 434) are quite correct in their description of this flower-color and all others. The broad oblong leaves and stem of the plant are very finely hairy, the color is light yellow-green, and the ribs are yellowish. The rough-surfaced seed-pod is filled with the silkiest of white down, attached to flat yellow-brown seeds, overlapping each other like the scales of a fish. The flower-clusters are borne at the junction of leaf-stem and plant-stem. The flowers are mostly fertilized by bees, who not infrequently lose their lives by their feet becoming inextricably entangled with the pollen masses, or caught in the fissures of the corona (described fully in William Hamilton Gibson's *My Studio Neighbors*, p. 232). 3–5 feet high. Common everywhere.

*Asclepias
obtusifolia*
Lilac-green
July–August

Pale magenta-purple-stained green flowers in a solitary terminal cluster. The oblong, wavy leaves with a clasping base somewhat heart-shaped. Rather uncommon northward, but frequent in the south. Found in sandy soil near Burlington, Vt.

**Poke
Milkweed**
*Asclepias
phytolaccoides*
Cream white
June–August

A rather tall milkweed with large ivory or cream-white flowers, whose reflexed corolla-segments are green or magenta-tinged on the outer surface ; the flowers loosely clustered and drooping. The rather large leaves are thin and pointed at either end ; the stem is slender and 3–6 feet high. One of our most dainty and beautiful wild flowers. Common on

Common Milkweed.   Asclepias Cornuti.

CONVOLVULUS FAMILY.   *Convolvulaceæ.*

the borders of thickets and woods throughout the north, and south to Ga.   Found near Lake Dunmore, Vt.

Four-leaved Milkweed
Asclepias quadrifolia
Magenta-pink
May–July

An early-flowering species with delicate magenta-pink flowers, the reflexed lobes of which are palest pink.   The stem is slender and generally leafless below, bearing about two circles of four leaves about the middle and two pairs of opposite smaller leaves at the upper part of the stem.   The plant is delicate and small, with few flower-clusters.   1–2 feet high.   Woods and copses, throughout the north, and south to N. Car.

Asclepias verticillata
Green-white
July–September

An extremely small narrow-leaved plant with a slender stem leafy at the summit. The leaves smooth and very narrowly linear, generally grouped in circles of 4–7. Flowers greenish white.   1–2 feet high. Common on dry hills, especially so south.   Me., west to S. Dak., and south.

CONVOLVULUS FAMILY.   *Convolvulaceæ.*

Herbs, in our range, with twining or trailing stems, alternate leaves, and regular, perfect flowers with generally a bell-shaped or funnel-formed corolla, and five stamens.   Flowers visited by the honeybee and bumblebee.   Self-fertilized as well as cross-fertilized.   The name from the Latin *convolvo*, to roll together.

Upright Bindweed
Convolvulus spithamæus
White
June-August

A small, erect or slightly twining plant, scarcely a foot long, with blunt, oval, light green leaves, heart-shaped at the base, short-stemmed, about 1–2 inches long.   Funnel-formed white flowers about 2 inches long, borne singly.   Calyx inclosed in two large leafy bracts.   In sandy or rocky fields, Me., south and west.

Hedge Bindweed
Convolvulus sepium

A smooth-stemmed vine with arrow-shaped, triangular, grayish green leaves, slender-stemmed and acute-pointed. Handsome bell-shaped or funnel-shaped

Poke Milkweed.
Asclepias phytolaccoïdes.

Four-leaved Milkweed.
Asclepias quadrifolia.

CONVOLVULUS FAMILY. *Convolvulaceæ.*

White, pink-tinged
June-August

flowers ranging from pure white to pink-tinged borne singly on long stems; the five stamens cream yellow, the pistil white. The five-parted calyx is inclosed in two pale green bracts. The flower generally closes before noon; it is sometimes over 2 inches broad and 3 long. Vine 3–10 feet long. Along moist roadsides and borders of fields, climbing over shrubbery, from Me., south to N. Car., west to S. Dak. and Utah. Also in Europe.

Trailing Bindweed
Convolvulus sepium, var. *repens*
White or pink-tinged
June-August

A more or less fine-hairy, trailing species, with simple or slightly branched stem, and ovate or oblong leaves, arrow-shaped or slightly heart-shaped at the base, 1–2 inches long. Flowers white or pink-tinged, borne singly on long stalks, and about 2 inches long. Calyx inclosed in two ovate bracts. 1–3 feet long. Common.

Small Bindweed
Convolvulus arvensis
White or pink-tinged
June-September

A smooth-stemmed, very slender species with oblong and arrow-shaped gray-green leaves, the lateral lobes of which are acute. Small flowers not over 1 inch long, white or pink-tinged, and generally borne in clusters of two. The calyx *without* leafy bracts at the base. 1–2 feet long. In fields and waste places from Me., south to N. J. and Pa., and west to Kan.

Common Dodder
Cuscuta Gronovii
Dull white
July-October

A miserable parasite often troublesome in gardens, but found in low, damp, shady situations. It climbs high upon other plants by twining closely about their stalks and exhausting their juices through a thousand tiny suckers. Its threadlike, twisting stem varies in color from dull yellow to dull orange, it is crowded with bunches of tiny dull white bell-shaped flowers having five lobes. The calyx is greenish white. All the dodders start at first from the ground, but finally securing a convenient plant upon which to climb, the root in the earth dies and they become parasitic. Common everywhere.

Hedge Bindweed.
Convolvulus sepium.

Common Dodder.
Cuscuta Gronovii

PHLOX FAMILY. *Polemoniaceæ.*

Herbs with alternate or opposite leaves and perfect, regular or nearly regular flowers with a five-lobed corolla which is rolled up in the bud, the lobes of the mature flower remaining somewhat contorted. Stamens five. Cross-fertilized most generally by butterflies and bumblebees. The name *Phlox* is from the Greek φλόξ, meaning flame.

Downy Phlox
Phlox pilosa
Purple, etc.
May–June
A more southern and western species with soft-downy stem and leaves, the latter deep green, linear or lance-shaped, without teeth and stemless. Flowers from pale crimson-pink to purple and white. The calyx sticky-glandular, the corolla-tube usually fine-hairy. 1–2 feet high. In dry ground from Southbury, Conn. (E. B. Harger), and N. J., south, west to S. Dak., and Tex.

Wild Blue Phlox
Phlox divaricata
Pale lilac or violet
April–June
Another rather western species with a somewhat sticky fine-hairy stem, with spreading leafy shoots from the base. Leaves wider than those of the preceding species, especially those on the sterile shoots; they are deep green, ovate lance-shaped, and acute-pointed. The pale violet or lilac flowers have generally notched lobes, they are slightly fragrant, and are gathered in loose clusters. Often the lobes are without notches. 9–18 inches high. In moist thin woodlands. N. Y., south, west to Minn.

Ground or Moss Pink
Phlox subulata
Crimson pink, etc.
April–September
A very low species with tufted stems, spreading over the ground until it forms compact masses resembling moss. The small, thickish yellow-green leaves sharp-tipped, linear, and close set; the plant mostly evergreen. Flowers few in a cluster terminating the short stems, varying in color from white through crimson-pink to light magenta; the petals notched. The stems fine-hairy or becoming smooth. 2–5 inches high. In sandy or rocky ground. N. H. and Mass., south, west to Mich. and Ky.

Phlox paniculata, which is a tall garden species, in colors varying from pink and lilac to white, with stout,

Phlox pilosa.

Moss Pink
Phlox subulata.

smooth stem, and dark green acute lance-shaped or oblong leaves, has escaped from cultivation in some of the eastern States, and is established permanently in many localities, generally adjoining old dwellings. 2–6 feet high.

Greek Valerian
Polemonium
reptans
Light violet
April-May

A smooth perennial with slender and weak stems finally reclining, and compound alternately growing leaves formed of 5–15 ovate lance-shaped leaflets; the uppermost leaves generally simple; all toothless. Flowers about ½ inch long, light blue-violet or rarely white, in loose clusters and nodding—bluebell-like. 8–12 inches high. In thin woods, N. Y., south to Ga., west to Minn. and Mo.

Jacob's Ladder
Polemonium
cœruleum
Violet
May-July

A much rarer species, found only by the mountain streams and in the swamps of the north. It has a stout horizontal root from which spread numerous rootlets, with erect stems smooth and leafy to the top. Leaves compound like those of the preceding species, the lower ones consisting of 15–19 nearly stemless, ovate pointed leaflets. Flowers numerous in a somewhat long cluster, bright violet, and nearly 1 inch broad, with conspicuous stamens and style, the five lobes of the corolla rounded. 1–2½ feet high. From Vermont and northern N. Y., south to Md. Common only in the far north. Found at Abby Pond, Ripton, Vt.

BORAGE FAMILY. *Boraginaceœ*

In our range annual or perennial herbs with rough-hairy stems and generally alternate, toothless, rough leaves. The blue-violet flower perfect and regular with a five-lobed corolla (*Echium* excepted), and five stamens. Flowers mostly in one-sided spikes, which at first are somewhat rolled up, straightening as the blossoms expand. Cross-fertilized mostly by butterflies and bees.

Hound's tongue
Cynoglossum
officinale
Magenta
June-
September

An ill-smelling biennial with a fine-hairy, stout, branching stem, and with lance-shaped leaves stemless, except the basal ones which are oblong and long slender-stemmed. The small magenta or rarely white flowers, five-lobed, and

Greek Valerian.   Polemonium reptans.

loosely arranged on a fine-hairy curving stem. The fruit, four nutlets set in a four-sided pyramidal shape, surmounted by the withering style. 2 feet high. Fields. Me., south to N. Car., west to Minn. From Asia.

Wild Comfrey
Cynoglossum
Virginicum
Pale violet
April–May

A perennial species with usually a simple hairy stem, without leaves above. The basal leaves deep green, oblong lance-shaped, rough, and short-stemmed, the upper ones clasping the stem by a heart-shaped base. The pale violet flowers on a few long naked stems ; the corolla divided into five rounded lobes. The fruit, four depressed nutlets, convex on the upper face, and hairy. 1–2½ feet high. In thin woods from Me., south, west to Kan. and La.

Virginia Stick-seed
Echinospermum
Virginicum
Lavender-white
June–September

A biennial with a fine-hairy, branching stem, slender and spreading. The basal leaves vanishing, as a rule, at the period of bloom, rather broad ovate ; the stem-leaves light green, ovate and lance-shaped, growing quite small toward the top of the plant, acute at either end. The flower-spikes very slender and bearing tiny white flowers of a lavender tinge. The tiny burlike fruit covered with *barbed prickles*. 2–4 feet high. The name from ἐχῖνος, a hedgehog, and σπέρμα, a seed, referring to the spiny fruit. Common on the borders of dry woods. Me., south to Ala. and La., west to Minn., S. Dak., and Neb.

European Stickseed
Echinospermum
Lappula
Light violet
May–September

An annual species somewhat hairy, with many small light gray-green linear leaves, the basal ones widest at the tip. The tiny flowers light violet, thinly scattered on slender branches. The fruit globose-oval, burlike, and covered with minute slender barbed prickles. 1–2 feet high. In waste places from Me., south to N. J., and westward.

Virginia Cowslip
Mertensia
Virginica
Violet
March–May

A beautiful species frequently cultivated, having rich violet-hued flowers nearly 1 inch long. The stem smooth and erect, sometimes branched. The deep green leaves toothless, ovate pointed or obovate, strongly veined, and scarcely stemmed ;

Wild Comfrey.   Cynoglossum Virginicum.

BORAGE FAMILY. *Boraginaceæ.*

only the lowest with margined stems. The showy flowers trumpet-shaped with five lobes ; rarely they are white. 1–2 feet high. On river meadows and along river-banks from N. Y. and N. J., south to S. Car., west to Minn., Neb., and Kan.

Forget=me-not
Myosotis palustris
Light blue
May–July
The true forget-me-not of gardens, escaped from cultivation, and found in wet ground or marshes. A perennial with slender, sprawling, fine-hairy stems, and gray-green oblong lance-shaped leaves, stemless or nearly so. The small light blue flowers with a golden eye, in small clusters somewhat curved. 6–15 inches high. Beside brooks and in wet places from Me., south to Pa., and west. A native of Europe and Asia.

Smaller Forget=me-not
Myosotis laxa
A species similar in many respects to the foregoing, with the fine-hairiness bending close to stem and leaf, the leaves blunt and oblong, and the very small and pale light blue flowers on long stems, loosely clustered. The calyx lobes as long as the flower-tube. 6–19 inches high. Wet places. Me., south to Tenn., west to Wis.

Spring For-get=me-not
Myosotis verna
White
April–June
An annual or biennial species, with very bristly-hairy stems and leaves, the latter oblong and obtuse. The white flowers small; the calyx unequally five-cleft, bristly, with some of the bristles hooked at the tips. 3–15 inches high. On dry banks from Me., south, and west to Minn. and Tex.

Corn Gromwell
Lithospermum arvense
White
May–August
A rough-hairy annual or biennial, with erect, branching stems and foliage resembling that of *Myosotis*, but a brighter green. The small white flowers scattered on the spikes and stemless or nearly so. 6–18 inches high. Sandy roadsides and fields from Me., south to Ga., and west to Mich. and Kan.

Lithospermum officinale
Cream white
A similar taller species with a much-branched stem, gray-green, few-veined, rough, and stemless leaves rather broad lance-shaped. The cream white flowers with corollas funnel-formed and a little longer than the five-pointed hairy calyx. 1–3 feet high. New Eng.,

Forget-me-not.   Myosotis palustris.

west to Minn.   Both of these last species are naturalized from Europe.   *Lithospermum* is formed of the Greek words *stone* and *seed*, referring to the hard seed.

Lithospermum canescens
Orange-yellow
March–June

An indigenous species, the so-called Puccoon of the Indians.   A perennial, soft-hairy and rather hoary, with obtuse linear-oblong leaves, stemless and hairy. The orange-yellow flowers with a broad corolla, salver-formed and five-lobed, about ½ inch long.   6–18 inches high.   Cross-fertilized by bees and butterflies ; some of the latter are *Papilio ajax*, *Papilio asterias*, *Colias philodice*, and *Osmia cobaltina*.   In dry soil, Me., south to N. J. and Ala., and west to Minn., S. Dak., Kan., and Ariz.   Rare in New Eng.   The roots yield a red dye.

False Gromwell
Onosmodium Virginianum
Cream white
May–July

A densely harsh-hairy perennial herb, the hairs of which lean toward stem and leaf, the stem slender and branching.   The light green leaves oblong lance-shaped. Flowers cylindrical, cream white, with five long sharp lobes ; the style threadlike and extending far beyond the mouth of the corolla ; the calyx with five sharp segments ; the flower-cluster at first curved, finally erect and long.   Flowers ⅓ inch long. The flower matures the stigma before the anthers ; it is mostly cross-fertilized by the butterflies.   1–2 feet high. Banks and hillsides from Me., south, and west to Kan.

Small Bugloss
Lycopsis arvensis
Light violet
June–September

A rough-bristly annual species, natural-ized from Europe, with a branching stem and lance-shaped leaves.   The light blue-violet flowers in crowded clusters, the calyx nearly as long as the curved corolla. 1–2 feet high.   In fields and on roadsides near dwellings, from Me. to Pa. and Va.   The name Greek, λύκος, a wolf, and ὄψις, a face ; but the flower's face scarcely looks that way !

Viper's Bugloss
Echium vulgare
Blue-violet
June–July
nial with an

Sometimes called blueweed, and in fact a flower sufficiently approaching a blue tone to justify the name ; but the blos-soms actually range between lilac, purple, and violet of a bluish cast.   It is a bien-exceedingly bristly-hairy stem, and hairy-

Viper's Bugloss.   Echium vulgare

silvery light green leaves, linear lance-shaped, toothless, and stemless. The flowers are rather showy, tubular or vase-shaped with five rounded unequal divisions; the four stamens, which, with the pistil, are pink, extend far beyond the limit of the corolla. The flower-spike one-sided, at first closely coiled, but finally long and but slightly curved; the blossoms are pink, but the mature flower is light ultramarine violet. 1–2½ feet high. Roadsides and pastures from Me. to Va., and west to Nev. and S. Dak. Naturalized from Europe. The name Greek, ἔχις, meaning a viper. Rare in central N. H.

VERVAIN FAMILY. *Verbenaceæ.*

Generally herbs (at least in our range) with opposite leaves and perfect, more or less irregular flowers in terminal clusters. The corolla with united petals, uniform in shape, or two-lipped, the tube generally cylindrical and spreading into 4–5 lobes. Four stamens, two long and two short, or very rarely only two. Probably self-fertilized, though cross-fertilization may occur, assisted by the honeybee, bumblebee, and the beelike flies.

European Vervain
Verbena officinalis
Purplish or white
June–September

A troublesome annual weed with a four-sided, slender, nearly smooth, branching stem, and minutely hairy leaves, deeply cleft and sharp-toothed; the upper ones lance-shaped and toothless, the lower ovate and sharply divided; all deep green. The small pale purple or white flowers in branching spikes about 5 inches long, inconspicuous and uninteresting. 1–3 feet high. In waste places everywhere. Naturalized from Europe.

White Vervain
Verbena urticæfolia
White
July–September

A similar perennial species with white flowers; usually with erect slightly rough-hairy stem four-sided and grooved, and coarsely toothed, deep green leaves, all or nearly all with distinct stems, acute, and slightly hairy. The flower-spikes at length very long, the white flowers very small. 3–5 feet high. In fields and waste places, from Me., south, and west to Minn., S. Dak., and Tex.

White Vervain.   Verbena urticæfolia.

VERVAIN FAMILY. *Verbenaceæ.*

Narrow=leaved Vervain
Verbena angustifolia
Pale violet
June–August

A small, rough-hairy species with a slender, often simple stem. Leaves linear and lance-shaped, the lower ones broad at the tip and wedge-shaped at the base, all more or less toothed and veiny. Flower-spikes few or single, densely clustered with pale violet flowers about ¼ inch wide. 8–22 inches high. Dry borders of fields. Mass., south, and west to Minn. and Ark.

Blue Vervain
Verbena hastata
Deep purple
July– September

One of the handsomest yet commonest members of the genus. The stem erect, stout, four-sided and grooved, roughish, and dull green. The short-stemmed leaves dark green, lance-shaped or oblong lance-shaped, acutely incised with double teeth, and with a rough surface ; the lower leaves are more or less three-lobed. The flower-spikes are numerous and branch upward like the arms of a candelabra ; the flowers bloom from the foot of the cluster upward, a few at a time, leaving behind a long line of purple-tinged calyx ; the tiny blossoms are deep purple or violet — either one hue or the other. The flowers never approach blue or any hue allied to it, so the common name is misleading. *Verbena hastata* is a special favorite of the bumblebee, and it is also closely attended by the honeybee and the bees of the genus *Halictus*. The smaller butterflies are also occasional visitors, among them the white *Pieris protodice*. 3–7 feet high. In fields everywhere. Rare in central N. H.

Lopseed
Phryma leptostachya
Crimson= magenta
July–August

A tall plant. The stalk is four-sided, hollow, and strong-fibred, branching divergently above. The deep green leaves are thin, coarsely toothed, and arranged in pairs, each pair set at right angles with the next ; the upper leaves nearly stemless and ovate pointed ; the lower oval. The slender flower-spike bears little two-lipped flowers (the lower lip is three-parted) set in pairs at right angles with each other. The flowers are crimson-pink with a magenta tinge. The blackish seed-receptacle hook-pointed. In woods. Me., south, west to Minn. and Kan.

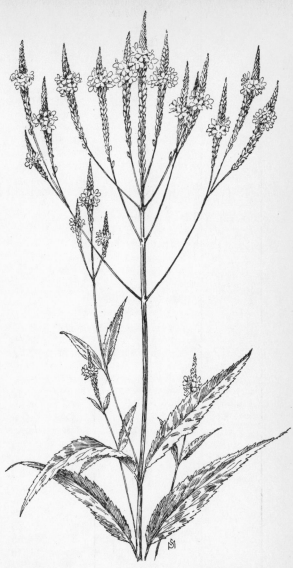

Blue Vervain.　　　　Verbena hastata.

MINT FAMILY. *Labiatæ.*

A large family of aromatic herbs, the foliage of which is covered with tiny glands containing a strong-scented volatile oil of a peppery character; the different species superficially resemble one another. The flowers are usually small, tubular, with an entire or two-lobed upper lip and a three-lobed lower lip. The stem is generally *square*, and the leaves grow opposite each other. The tiny flowers are gathered in more or less conspicuous spikes, or are clustered at the base of the leaves; they are honey-bearing, and are almost exclusively cross-fertilized by honeybees, bumblebees, and the smaller bees. The name from *Labiæ*, the lips.

Blue Curls or Bastard Pennyroyal
Trichostema dichotomum
Pale violet or magenta
July–September

This is an annual species whose light violet, magenta-pink, or rarely white flowers are generally in pairs at the terminating branchlets of the somewhat woolly-sticky stiff stem. The leaves are narrowly oblong or lance-shaped, and a trifle sticky, with an aromatic pennyroyallike odor. The flowers are too scattered to form a panicle or cluster, and they are remarkable for the *extraordinary length* of the violet stamens which extend in a curving line far beyond the five-lobed corolla, or flower-cup—hence the name Blue Curls. The Latin name also refers to the hairlike stamens. After the corolla fades and falls, the little nutlets within the calyx are in plain view. 6–20 inches high. In dry sandy fields, from Me., south, and west to Pa. and Ky.

Trichostema lineare
Pale violet, etc.
July–August

A very similar species with a slender woolly stem, ascending branches, and very narrow linear leaves, stemless and smooth. In sandy fields and dry pine barrens near the coast, from Long Island and Conn., south to La.

False Pennyroyal
Isanthus cœruleus
Pale violet
July–September

A slender branching annual with lance-shaped, toothless or slightly toothed, conspicuously three-ribbed leaves, and extremely regular-lobed flowers (for one of the family *Labiatæ*), with five nearly equal, obovate, spreading divisions. The

Blue Curls.   Trichostema dichotomum.

pistil greatly exceeds the stamens in length, the latter
scarcely extending beyond the corolla; it is evident,
therefore, that the flower is cross-fertilized. The most
frequent visitors are the bumblebees, the honeybees,
and the smaller butterflies, chief among which are
Pieris rapœ, white, and *Colias philodice*, yellow.

**American
Germander
or Wood Sage**
*Teucrium
Canadense*
**Pale purple
or magenta**
**July–
September**

A downy perennial with a stiff perpendicular stem, and light green, unevenly
toothed leaves, lance-shaped and fine-
hairy, particularly underneath. The rather
long flower-spike with the large nearly $\frac{3}{4}$-
inch-long flowers arranged in circles, purple, deeper or paler, and sometimes magenta, or a pinkish white. The lower lobe
of the flower broad and prominent, forming a convenient
landing for visiting bees. 1–2 feet high. Moist thicket
borders, or marshes. Me., south, and west to Minn., S.
Dak., Neb., and Kan.

**Horse Balm
or Rich Weed**
*Collinsonia
Canadensis*
Pale yellow
**July–
September**

A stout-stemmed, yellow-flowered perennial species, tall and branching, with
large ovate sharply toothed leaves and a
nearly smooth stem. The pale yellow
flowers with 2 long divergent stamens and
a prominent pistil, strongly lemon-scented.
Flower-cluster very loose. Named for
Peter Collinson, an early amateur botanist. 2–4 feet
high. In damp rich woodlands, from Me., south, west
to Wis. and Kan.

*Perilla
ocymoides*
White
**July–
September**

A coarse and aromatic perennial species
introduced into the gardens of this country from China and India, and escaped to
roadsides near dwellings. The large, ovate,
coarsely toothed leaves deep purple-tinged
beneath, and with a bronze tone above, the green completely suffused with the other color. Strongly scented.
Flowers tiny, in terminal clusters, and dull white or pale
magenta. 1–3 feet high. In waste places, southern N.
Y. to Ill.

Note the long lower lip of the
corolla and its slightly
fringed edge.

Rich Weed.   Collinsonia Canadensis.

MINT FAMILY. *Labiatæ.*

The genus *Mentha* is a tribe of odorous perennial herbs with little tubular flowers mostly in close clusters ; the plant-stems square. Almost all the species are naturalized from Europe, and there are many hybrids. Name from Μίνθη (of Theophrastus), a Nymph. The mints are commonly fertilized by the order *Diptera* (the flies), and particularly by the genera *Syrphidæ* and *Bombylidæ*.

Horse Mint
Mentha
sylvestris
Pale purple
July–August

Flowers in rather crowded, slender, leafless spikes, sometimes disconnected. Leaves ovate-oblong and ovate lance-shaped, almost stemless, sharp-pointed and sharply toothed, often smooth above, but the whole plant generally finely white-haired. Plant-stem square. 18 inches high. Roadsides and field-borders. Pa. and N. J. The var. *alopecuroides* with larger leaves, stemless, broadly oval and obtuse, often approaching heart-shape, coarsely toothed and more veiny. Southern N. Y., Pa., and N. J., west to Mo.

Spearmint
Mentha viridis
Pale purple
July–August

Flowers variable in depth of color ; clusters crowded like those of the preceding species, but especially narrow and pointed. Plant-stem green, square, and *nearly* smooth. Leaves oblong or ovate lance-shaped, unevenly toothed and stemless or very nearly so. 12–20 inches high or more. Wet places and roadsides in cultivated ground, everywhere.

Peppermint
Mentha
piperita
Pale purple
July–August

Flowers in narrow, loose, disconnected, leafless, terminal spikes, and often on a rather long stem proceeding from between the plant-stem and leaf-stem. Leaves long-ovate, deep green, smooth, and regularly toothed, slightly rough beneath, and very hot-tasting. Plant-stem purplish, 18–36 inches high. Along brooks and in cultivated ground everywhere.

Water Mint
Mentha
aquatica
Pale purple
August–
September

The flowers in a roundish or nearly oblong terminal cluster ; frequently there are one or more clusters between the plant-stem and the upper leaf-stems. Leaves ovate or round-ovate. The plant is characterized by downy hairs (rarely it is smoothish) which generally point *downward*. Wet

Mentha sylvestris.

Mentha viridis.

Peppermint.

Mentha piperita.

places from N. Eng. to Pa., Del., and Ga. Not common. 18–28 inches high or more. In the var. *crispa* the plant is smooth, but the green flower-cup is hairy; it has also *torn-toothed* leaves somewhat curled. Swamps and roadside ditches. Southern N. Y., N. J., and Pa.

Corn Mint
Mentha arvensis
Light purple
July–August

The tiny bell-shaped flowers clustered *in circles* about the plant-stem at the junction with leaf-stems. Leaves ovate, blunt-toothed, and distinctly stemmed. Not a common species. 6–20 inches long. Found in moist fields. N. Eng., N. Y., and Pa., south.

Wild Mint
Mentha arvensis var. *Canadensis*
White or lilac=white
July–September

The only *native* mint. The lilac-white or white flowers oblong bell-shaped, with a short-toothed edge; the clusters arranged as in the preceding species. Leaves conspicuously tapering from the centre toward both ends, coarsely toothed, ovate-oblong or lance-shaped, and roughish, or nearly smooth. The plant is more or less hairy throughout, and has the odor of Pennyroyal. In wet places south to Va., and through the northern United States across the continent. 10–28 inches high. This mint, according to Prof. Charles Robertson, is visited in Illinois by the fly *Jurinia smaragdina.*

Bugleweed
Lycopus Virginicus
White
July–September

A mintlike weed with small white flowers remotely suggesting a bugle shape. Stem slender, four-angled, and generally smooth. The light green leaves ovate lance-shaped and *very coarsely* toothed. The tiny flowers clustered at the bases of the leaves have but two *perfect* stamens; the other two, if present, are quite abortive. Fertilized mostly by the beelike flies, and the small bees of the genus *Halictus.* 6–24 inches high. Common.

Cut-leaved Water Hore-hound
Locopus sinuatus
White
June–September

A similar species, with some leaves so deeply toothed that they appear incised, and others incised to an appearance of lobes. The stiff stem generally smooth, simple or branched. The flower-cup tiny and but little larger than its green calyx. 1–2 feet high. Common.

Wild Mint. Mentha arvensis var. Canadensis.

Leaf of M. arvensis.

MINT FAMILY. *Labiatæ.*

Hyssop
Hyssopus officinalis
Pale violet
June–September

A coarse, stiff, aromatic perennial naturalized from Europe. Slender-stemmed and lance-leaved; the leaves stiff and pointed at either end. The tubular flowers with projecting stamens, crowded at the angles of the leaves at the upper part of the plant. 1–3 feet high. Waste places and roadsides near dwellings, from Me., south to N. Car., and west.

Mountain Mint
Pycnanthemum lanceolatum
White purple-dotted
July–September

This is a stout and stiff-stemmed species with a slight fragrance of mint; but unlike the latter its tiny flowers are borne in a somewhat flat-topped cluster. Leaves stemless or nearly so, lance-shaped, toothless, and slightly aromatic; stem smooth or very slightly hairy, and very leafy. The flowers lilac-white, purple-spotted, standing out from the globular heads. 1–3 feet high. In dry fields, or pastures, or on the borders of thickets, from Vt. and Mass., south to Ga., west to Minn. and Neb. The name meaning crowded flower-clusters.

Pycnanthemum linifolium
White purple-dotted

A similar species, with smooth linear leaves, sharp-pointed and light green. The stem and leaves stiff. The tiny flowers white, speckled or dotted with purple. 1–2 feet high. Dry fields, N. H., south, and west to Minn. and Tex. Found in Campton, N. H., but rare; occasional in Vt.

American Pennyroyal
Hedeoma pulegioides
Pale light violet
July–September

A small annual, exceedingly odorous, usually found in dry pastures. The stem erect, finely hairy, with upward-reaching branches; the small light olive-green leaves with few teeth, ovate lance-shaped, blunt-pointed, and narrowed at the base. The tiny pale violet or lavender, tubular flowers with a three-lobed under lip. Fertilized mostly by bumblebees, honeybees, and the smaller bees. 6–15 inches high. Common in dry fields everywhere, but not found in Campton, N. H., nor anywhere in the vicinity of the White Mts. The essential oil of Pennyroyal is said to be efficacious in driving away mosquitoes.

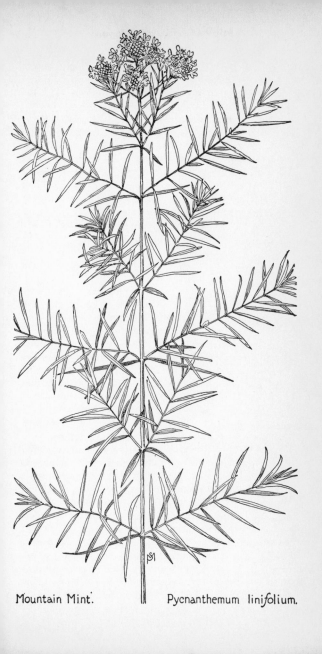

Mountain Mint.   Pycnanthemum linifolium.

MINT FAMILY. *Labiatæ.*

Lyre-leaved Sage
Salvia lyrata
Light violet
June–July

A slightly rough-hairy, slender plant, with conspicuous light violet flowers nearly an inch long, which are cross-fertilized mostly by the bumblebees ; *Bombus vagans* and *Bombus pennsylvanicus* being frequent visitors. The lower leaves are somewhat lyre-shaped, the upper pair (sometimes two pairs) mid-way up the stem, similar but less cut, or lobed ; the tubular flowers with a broad three-lobed lip which furnishes a convenient landing-platform for insect visitors ; 1–2 feet high. In dry woodlands, and beside thickets. N. J., south, and west to Ill. and Ark.

Oswego Tea or Bee Balm
Monarda didyma
Scarlet-red
July–September

A brilliant and showy wild flower whose scarlet-red color is strongly relieved by its usual background of shady woodland. Commonly found beside streams on the border of the woods.

The *Monardas* are peculiarly adapted to the visits of butterflies, although they are also commonly visited by bees, the bumblebee in particular. The two anther-bearing stamens are prominent, as well as the two-parted stigma, and neither can be passed without friction by butterfly or bee, both of which have the long tongue necessary to reach the nectar. The bumblebees mentioned as visitors of the foregoing species also frequent this flower, together with the butterflies *Colias philodice*, yellow, and the large *Danais archippus*, black-and-tan. The sombre dark green leaves are broad lance-shaped, sharply toothed, and stemmed ; the small leaves just beneath the flower are often tinged ruddy. The stem, rather hairy-rough and square, is about 2 feet high, or more. Moist ground, N. Eng., south to Ga., and west to Mich.

Wild Bergamot
Monarda fistulosa
Magenta-purple
June–September

A similar species with a smooth or sparingly downy, slender stem, and deep green leaves, the upper ones somewhat stained with the pure pale lilac or whitish tint which characterizes the flower-bracts. The flowers with a less expanded throat, paler or deeper magenta-purple. 2–3 feet high. Dry ground, Me., south, and west to Neb.·and S. Dak.

Wild Bergamot.

Monarda fistulosa
var. rubra.

MINT FAMILY. *Labiatæ.*

Monarda fistu-losa var. *rubra*
Crimson-pink
A rather smooth form with handsome crimson-pink or rose red flowers finely hairy over the tube and upper lip, and thin leaves rather smooth. On the borders of moist thickets, Me. and N. H., south along the mountains to Pa. and Va. The var. *media*, with deep purple flowers. Alleghany Mts., and west to Minn. The var. *rubra* is locally plentiful in parts of N. H., notably south of New-found Lake. It is unfortunately classified as Purple Bergamot, *Monarda media*, in Britton and Brown, which is manifestly confusing. *Monarda mollis* is a less common species; flowers flesh pink and lilac; in S. Dak.

Downy Blephilia
Blephilia cili-ata
Light purple
June–August
A woodland species rather similar in many respects to *Monarda*. The small tubular flowers about ½ inch long, with a three-lobed under lip, light purple or violet, and fine-hairy. The lance-shaped leaves almost toothless (except the lower ones), white-downy beneath, and quite stemless, or nearly so. The stem downy and mostly simple. 1–2 feet high. Mass., south to Ga., and west to Minn. and Kan.

Catnip
Nepeta Cataria
Lilac=white
July–October
An exceedingly common weed to which many of the animals of the tribe *Felis* are greatly attached. A favorite Manx cat of mine would walk a mile every other day or so, from my Campton studio to a spot where it grew in plenty, notwithstanding the way was through the woods and over a hill of no small difficulty! The stem is densely downy as well as the deeply round-toothed leaves, and both are sage green in color. The pale lilac or lilac-white and spotted flowers are also downy, and gathered in small terminal clusters, which are rarely 4 inches long. Leaves strongly aromatic. 2–3 feet high. Common everywhere. Naturalized from Europe.

Ground Ivy or Gill=over=the=Ground
Nepeta Gle-choma
Light purple
April–May
A small creeping plant, adventive from Europe, common in all moist shady places; it takes the place of our Trailing Arbutus, in the moist fields of England in April. The pale purple flowers, spotted darker near the throat, and often with the calyx magenta-tinged, has two lips, the upper

1·Catnip.
Nepeta Cataria.

2·Gill-over-all-the-ground.
Nepeta Glechoma.

one two-cleft, and the lower, three-cleft; the deep green leaves, scalloped and rather heart-shaped, are often stained with magenta, as well as the stem; the latter takes root at the joints, and reaches out sometimes fully 18 inches. Me., south to Ga., and west to Minn., Neb., and Kan.

Mad-dog Skullcap *Scutellaria lateriflora* **Pale purple July-August** A bitter perennial herb, not aromatic, with two-lipped tubular flowers, the four stamens located under the upper lip, which is arched. Name from *scutella*, a dish, in allusion to the peculiar hump on the upper section of the green calyx, which, however, does not even remotely suggest the shape of a dish. The little flowers, about a quarter of an inch long, light or pale purple (rarely white), are borne in succession along the delicate stems which terminate the branches or spring from between leaf-stem and plant-stem. The flowers borne on one side of the stem which later is decorated with the odd little hoodlike green calyxes containing four white seeds. Plant-stem smooth, square, and sometimes slightly twisted, upright and much branched. Leaves narrowly ovate, veiny, coarse-toothed, pointed, rounded at the base, and slender-stemmed. 1–2 feet high. Common in damp and shady places, throughout the country The *Scutellarias* are fertilized by the smaller bees, *Halictus*, and the leaf-cutter bee, *Megachile*.

Scutellaria versicolor **Light violet July-August** Light violet flowers almost an inch long, the whitish lower lip sometimes purple-stained. Leaves heart-shaped, very veiny, rough, round-toothed, rather blunt, and long-stemmed. Plant-stem soft-hairy. 1–3 feet high. Banks of streams, Pa., south, and west to Minn. and Ark.

Scutellaria serrata **Light violet May-June** Flower an inch long, narrow, and its upper lip only a trifle shorter than the lower one. Leaves ovate or long-ovate, toothed, tapering at both ends, and smooth. Green and nearly smooth, slender plant-stem, 1–2 feet high. In woods, southern N. Y. and Pa., south to N. Car., and west to Ill. The most showy of all the genus.

Mad-dog Skull-cap.   Scutellaria lateriflora.

MINT FAMILY. *Labiatæ.*

Scutellaria canescens
Light violet
July–August

The flowers, stems, and under sides of the leaves covered with soft white down; flower nearly one inch long. Leaves ovate or narrow-ovate, stemmed, and some slightly heart-shaped at the base. 2–4 feet high. River-banks from Ontario to Ill., and south among the mountains to N. Car.

Scutellaria pilosa
Light violet
May–July

Flowers half an inch long or a trifle more. Leaves distant, oval or long ovate, veiny, round-toothed, the longer-stemmed lower ones sometimes slightly heart-shaped, the upper on short, margined stems. Plant-stem with spreading hairs. Dry or sandy ground, or woods. 12–30 inches high. Southern N. Y. and Pa., south, and west to Mich.

Scutellaria integrifolia
Light violet
June–August

Flower bright light violet, and an inch long, in a striking terminal cluster. Leaves oblong lance-shaped, or narrower, mostly toothless, o b t u s e, short-stemmed, and downy together with the plant-stem. 6–20 inches high. Dry ground, borders of fields, woods. The seaboard States from R. I. south. A handsome species.

Scutellaria parvula
Violet
May–July

A low species with flowers ¼ inch long, borne on very short stems at the junction of leaf-stem with plant-stem. Leaves opposite-growing, toothless, round to lance-ovate or slightly heart-shaped, about ½ an inch long. Stem spreading, 3–10 inches high. Sandy banks and moist places, from N. Y. and N. J., south, and west to S. Dak., Minn., Neb., and Tex.

Scutellaria galericulata
Blue-violet
July–August

Flowers ¾ inch long, growing in the same position as those of the foregoing species. Leaves ovate lance-shaped, the lower sometimes with a slight heart-shaped base, toothed, and acute. Stem smooth and slender. 1–2 feet high. Common in wet shady places and along streams, especially in the north, west to N. Dak.

Leaf of
Scutellaria parvula.

Leaf of
Scutellaria pilosa.

Skullcap. Scutellaria integrifolia.

MINT FAMILY. *Labiatæ.*

Scutellaria nervosa
Pale blue-violet
June–August

Flowers a trifle more than ¼ inch long. Leaves about an inch long, roundish or ovate, slightly toothed, and the lower ones slightly heart-shaped. The floral leaves toothless. Stem smooth and slender, 1–2 feet high. Moist woods and thickets, N. Y. and N. J., south to N. Car., and west to Mo.

Self-heal or Heal-all
Prunella vulgaris or *Brunella vulgaris*
Purple, light or deeper
June–September

A very common low perennial with generally a single stem, and tubular, two-lipped, hooded flowers proceeding from a spike or head of closely set, sometimes rusty colored green, floral bractlike leaves. The name (of uncertain origin) said to be from the German *braune*, a throat disease. Flower tiny, purple, but sometimes flesh color or white, the lower lip slightly fringed. Generally fertilized by the bumblebee, *Bombus pennsylvanicus* being a frequent visitor; the common yellow butterfly *Colias philodice* is also a constant attendant. Leaves ovate-oblong, narrowing toward the tip, slightly or imperceptibly toothed, stemmed, with generally two small bractlike leaves at the base of the stems. Plant-stem slightly hairy. 6–13 inches high. Very common along roadsides, and on the borders of woods and fields. Across the continent.

False Dragon-head
Physostegia Virginiana
Pink-lilac or lighter
July–August

A smooth perennial with upright, slender stem, stemless lance-shaped leaves mostly toothed, and large, 1 inch long, showy flowers crowded in terminal, leafless spikes. Flower pinkish pale lilac, often variegated with white, and funnel-shaped, the upper lip a little hooded, the lower three-parted; the throat inflated. Plant-stem smooth, 1–4 feet high. Wet grounds, from northern Vt., westward and southward. Very variable. The var. *denticulata*, slender and generally low, with scallop-toothed, or imperceptibly toothed leaves, and very slender flower-spikes. Moist situations, Vt., south, and west to S. Dak. and Neb.

Self-heal.   Prunella vulgaris.

MINT FAMILY. *Labiatæ.*

Horehound
Marrubium vulgare
White
August–September

A white-woolly, bitter, and aromatic perennial, branched at the base, with small tubular dull white flowers circled about the plant-stem at the leaf junctions. Leaves round-ovate, stemmed, and scallop-toothed. 1–2 feet high. Cultivated, and escaped into waste places. Naturalized from Europe. The name from the Hebrew *marrob*, a bitter juice.

Motherwort
Leonurus Cardiaca
Pale lilac
June–August

Perpendicular-growing decorative herbs, without any particular odor, with deeply cut leaves, and tiny flowers encircling the plant-stem at the point of junction with the leaves. The name from λέων, a lion, and ὸνρά, tail — lion's tail, alluding to the form of the flower-spike, but a poor simile. The upper lip of the tiny, tubular but shallow, pale lilac flower bearded. The green calyx characterized by five thornlike points; the base of the calyx, when the flower is gone, marked with a cross upon examination with a glass. The small leaves about the flower-clusters conventionally arranged around the tall stems, wedge-shaped toward the stem, and three-pointed at the tip. The lower leaves rounded, slashed, and long-stemmed. 2–4 feet high. A familiar perennial naturalized from Europe, and common everywhere in waste places about dwellings.

Dead Nettle
Lamium amplexicaule
Pale purple-magenta
April–September

Low spreading herbs found on waste grounds. With tubular, bell-shaped flowers, and *small* long-stemmed leaves below, heart-shaped ones in the middle of the stem, and others above directly connected with the circling flower-clusters; all round-toothed. The upper lip of the flower is bearded, the lower one spotted; all magenta or pale purple. A honey-bearing flower, cross-fertilized mostly by honeybees and bumblebees, and frequently visited by *Bombus bifarius*, commonly called the orange-banded bumblebee. The foliage of the dead nettle is *not* stinging to the touch. 6–18 inches high. Naturalized from Europe.

Motherwort.　　　Leonurus Cardiaca.

NIGHTSHADE FAMILY. *Solanaceæ.*

Lamium purpureum
Magenta
May–
September

Like the foregoing, also naturalized, the leaves more heart-shaped, roundish, or oblong, and all of them stemmed. Flowers magenta. Less common, from N. Eng. to Pa.

Hemp Nettle
Galeopsis Tetrahit
Magenta-
purple
July–
September

An annual, with spreading branches, and several circling clusters of small pale magenta flowers (the lower lip purple-striped) gathered at the stems of the floral leaves. Name from the Greek, *weasellike*, from the fancied resemblance of the flower to the head of a weasel. The tiny flowers white-hairy, the flower-cup bristly. Leaves ovate, toothed, hairy, and pointed. Plant-stem square, very hairy, with hairs pointing downward, and conspicuously swollen below the joints. Cross-fertilized by the bumblebees and smaller bees, *Bombus vagans* a most frequent visitor. 10–18 inches high. Common in waste places and gardens, everywhere. Naturalized from Europe.

Hedge Nettle
Stachys palustris
Magenta-pur-
ple, or paler
July–
September

Hairy perennial herbs, with tubular bell-shaped flowers, clustered in circles, 6–10 in each circle, and forming a terminal spike. The upper part of the light magenta-purple flower and its green cup (calyx) hairy. Leaves stemless, or the lower ones short-stemmed, ovate lance-shaped or longer, scallop-toothed, downy-hairy, rather obtuse, and rounded at the base. Plant-stem square, 1–3 feet high. Wet grounds, N. Eng. to Pa., and west.

Stachys aspera
Magenta-
purple
July–
September

Like the foregoing, but with mostly smooth flowers, leaves sometimes smooth, and nearly all distinctly stemmed; the plant-stem taller, commonly smooth on the sides, but stiff-hairy at the angles. The flower-spike slender. Stem 2–4 feet high. Common on wet grounds, everywhere.

NIGHTSHADE FAMILY. *Solanaceæ.*

Mostly herbs with alternate leaves and regular, perfect flowers ; the five-lobed corolla with generally five stamens and a very small stigma. Foliage strongly scented.

Bugle-weed.
Lycopus Virginicus.
(See page 394)

Hemp-nettle.
Galeopsis Tetrahit.

NIGHTSHADE FAMILY. *Solanaceæ.*

The fruit, though often narcotic and extremely poisonous, is sometimes harmless and edible ; usually a many-seeded round berry with the calyx generally adhering to its base. The potato and the tomato are the widest-known members of the family.

Nightshade or Bittersweet
Solanum Dulcamara
Violet, purple
June–September

A tall, almost shrublike plant with variable dark green leaves from ovate to triangular in outline, some lobed and others formed of three leaflets, the two lateral ones quite small, all without teeth. The small flowers in diminutive loose clusters, with deeply five-cleft corolla, violet or purple, or sometimes lilac-white, the yellow conic centre colored by the five stamens. The fruit (at first green) an oval, translucent ruby red berry, hanging or drooping in small clusters. The flower is visited by honey-bees and the beelike flies. 2–8 feet high. In moist thickets and by waysides. Naturalized from Europe. Me., south to Del., and west to Kan. and Minn.

Black Nightshade
Solanum nigrum
White
July–September

A native species, with an erect, smooth, branching stem, and ovate, wavy-toothed, thin-stemmed l e a v e s slightly unequal-sided. Flowers white in small side clusters, the corolla deeply five-lobed ; the calyx adhering to the globose berry, which is black when fully ripe, and clustered on thin drooping stems. 1–2½ feet high. In waste places, or near dwellings in cultivated ground, from Me., south, and west to the Northwest Territory and Tex.

Clammy Ground Cherry
Physalis heterophylla
Green-yellow
July–September

A tall, and late in its season a reclining or sprawling species resembling *Solanum*, with spreading, sticky-hairy stem, and broad heart-shaped leaves coarsely toothed and pointed. Flower greenish yellow, brown in the centre, with five triangular short lobes ; anthers and berry dull yellow, the latter enclosed within the enlarged calyx. 1–3 feet high. Common in rich soil from Me., south, and west to Col. and Tex. A variable species, not yet satisfactorily defined, but including perhaps more than one species. Found at Manchester, Vt., by Miss Mary A. Day.

Black Nightshade.   Solanum nigrum.

NIGHTSHADE FAMILY. *Solanaceæ.*

Virginia Ground Cherry
Physalis Virginiana
Pale yellow
July–September

A branching and erect-stemmed species, mostly smooth. The ovate lance-shaped leaves tapering toward both ends very slightly shallow-toothed and light green. The flower dull pale yellow with five brown-purple spots; anthers deep yellow. The stigma matures before the anthers, and extends beyond them. Fertilized by the honeybee and the bees of the genus *Halictus; Halictus pectinatus* is a common visitor (Prof. Robertson). The reddish berry enclosed within the enlarged calyx. 1-3 feet high. Rich soil, Vt. and N. Y., south to La., and west to Minn. *Physalis pubescens*, the strawberry tomato, is downy, with angular leaves. The flower light green-yellow, brown-spotted at the throat, with violet anthers. Fruit green-yellow. Escaped from cultivation eastward.

Thorn Apple or Jamestown or Jimson Weed
Datura Stramonium
White
July–September

A rank-smelling annual weed with a smooth, green, stout stem, and thin ovate, acute, angularly coarse-toothed leaves, slim-stemmed. The white trumpet-shaped flowers about 4 inches long, with a light green calyx less than half the length of the corolla, which has five sharp-pointed lobes. The green fruit-capsule, ovoid, about 2 inches long, and covered with stout prickles, the longest of which are at the tip of the capsule. 1-5 feet high. In waste places and vacant city lots, from Me., south, and west to Minn. and Tex. Naturalized from Asia.

Purple Thorn Apple
Datura Tatula
Magenta-lavender
May–September

A similar species with a slenderer stem, and darker green leaves both more or less stained with magenta. Flowers like those of the preceding species, but the flaring tips of the corolla stained with magenta or lavender, or the tube nearly white. All the prickles of the capsule nearly equal in length. 1-5 feet high. In waste places from Vt., N. Y., and Minn., southward. Rare in Vermont.

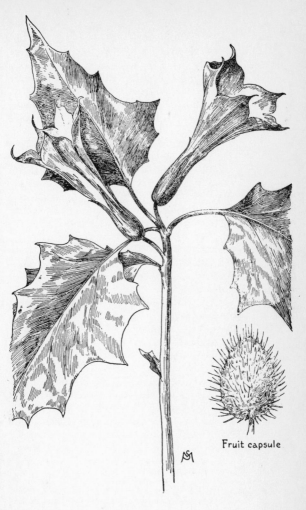

Fruit capsule

Purple Thorn Apple.   Datura Tatula.

FIGWORT FAMILY. *Scrophulariaceæ.*

Commonly herbs with opposite or alternate leaves, and perfect, irregular flowers with two sets of stamens, 2–5, longer and shorter ones; corolla two-lipped or nearly regular. Fruit a two-celled and generally many-seeded capsule. A large family of bitter-juiced plants; some are narcotic-poisonous. Cross-fertilized by moths, butterflies, and bees.

Great Mullein
Verbascum
Thapsus
Yellow
June–
September

A very common, picturesque, velvety-leaved weed of rocky pastures and road-sides, naturalized from Europe. The basal leaves at first in the form of a rosette, large, ovate, thick-velvety, and white-green. The stem stout and erect, with a few smaller, acute-pointed leaves; the terminal flower-spike cylindrical, woolly, and dotted with scattered light yellow flowers; corolla five-lobed, and anthers golden yellow. Rarely the flowers are white. 2–6 feet high. In barren fields and waste places, from Me., south, and west to Minn. and Kan.

Moth Mullein
Verbascum
Blattaria
Yellow, white
June–
September

A smaller species with smooth stem and thin, light green, glossy leaves, mostly oblong with deeply cut, notched, and toothed margins; the upper leaves lance-shaped and clasping at the base. The flowers, similar in shape to those of the preceding species, are light yellow or white, tinged on the back with lavender, and set on slender stalks; the five stamens are fringed with ruddy hairs, and the anthers are deep orange. The slender flower-spike is 1–2 feet long, and a trifle woolly. 2–5 feet high. In waysides, waste places, and pastures. Me., south, west to Minn. and Kan.

Blue Toad=flax
Linaria
Canadensis
Lavender
June–
September°

An extremely slender and smooth annual or biennial species with few small, thickish, linear, light green leaves, tooth-less, stemless, smooth, and shining. The small pale violet or lavender flowers about $\frac{1}{3}$ inch long, two-lipped, and spurred; the lower lip large and three-lobed, with a white, convex, two-ridged palate; the upper lip with two acute divi-

Great
Mullein.
Verbascum Thapsus.

Moth Mullein.
Verbascum Blattaria.

sions; the spur curving and threadlike. 5–30 inches high. Common in dry, sandy soil, from Me., south, and local west to the Pacific coast. The name from *Linum*, flax.

Toad=flax or Butter-and- Eggs
Linaria vulgaris
Yellow and orange
July-October

A very common but beautiful perennial weed naturalized from Europe, with erect smooth stem, and gray-green linear, stemless and toothless leaves growing alternately but near together. The flowers are about an inch long including the slender spur, and two-lipped, the upper lip two-lobed, light yellow, the lower lip three-lobed and pouch-shaped, tapering to the tip of the slender spur, and furnished above with a protruding gold-orange palate which nearly closes the throat of the corolla; the four stamens are tipped with ochre yellow anthers; the style is greenish. The flowers are assisted in the process of fertilization by bumblebees and butterflies; among the latter, *Colias philodice* (yellow) and *Melitœa phaëton*, the Baltimore (brown), are frequent visitors. 1–3 feet high. In fields, pastures, and city lots, everywhere.

Small Snap- dragon
Antirrhinum Orontium
Light purple
June-August

A smooth annual with erect stem and light green linear leaves. The flowers light purple or white, showy, solitary, and with a sac-shaped, two-lipped corolla; the upper lip two-lobed, the lower three-lobed. About 1 foot high. In fields and waste places near dwellings, New Eng. and N. Y. Adventive from Europe.

Figwort
Scrophularia nodosa, var. *Marilandica*
Green- magenta
July- September

A smooth perennial with a slender four-sided, grooved stem and slender-stemmed, ovate lance-shaped, toothed, light green leaves. Flowers small, sac-shaped, and clustered on long, nearly leafless branchlets; the two-lipped corolla green without, and shiny brown-magenta within. 3–7 feet high. In thin woods and thickets, from N. Y., south to N. Car. and Tenn., and west to Kan.

Butter-and-Eggs.
Linaria vulgaris.

Blue Toad-flax.
Linaria Canadensis.

FIGWORT FAMILY. *Scrophulariaceæ.*

Turtle=head
Chelone glabra
**White, pink=
tinged**
**July–
September**

A smooth-stemmed plant superficially resembling the Bottle Gentian, with smooth, bright deep green, toothed, short-stemmed, lance-shaped leaves 3–6 inches long. The flower not unlike a turtle's head, about an inch long, white, and delicately tinged at the tips with magenta-pink or crimson-pink ; the corolla two-lipped, the upper lip arched over the lower one. The stamens dark and woolly. 1–3 feet high. On wet banks, in swamps, and beside brooks, from Me., south, and west to Minn., Kan., and Tex.

**Pentstemon or
Beard=tongue**
*Pentstemon
pubescens*
**Magenta=
white**
May–July

A perennial with slender and straight stem woolly almost to the base. Leaves light green, slightly woolly, oblong to lance-shaped, slightly toothed, the upper ones toothless, the lower ovate and stemmed. The flowers whitish, tinged with dull magenta, the corolla trumpet-shaped, two-lipped, two lobes on the upper, three on the lower lip, and the throat nearly closed by a palate on the lower lip covered with long hairs. There are four stamens and a sterile stamen or so-called filament, which is hairy or bearded a little more than half its length. Cross-fertilized mostly by butterflies. 1–3 feet high. Me., south, and west to Minn. and Tex. Found in Campton, N. H., by Carroll S. Mathews.

**Pentstemon
lævigatus**

A very similar species, smooth *except* the somewhat sticky-hairy top of the stem bearing the flowers ; the latter ¾ inch long, whitish with a magenta-tinged base, the corolla as in the foregoing species, but the throat wider open, and scarcely or not at all hairy ; the sterile filament hairy on the *upper side* only. The stem ruddy, and the light green leaves more or less so at the edge. 2–3 feet high. In thickets or moist fields, from Pa., south, and west to Ky. and La., where according to Gray the common form is the var. *Digitalis*, with stem-leaves ovate lance-shaped, the lower longer and wider. The flowers white, larger, and the corolla abruptly inflated. 2–5 feet high. Me. and N. Y., south to Va. and Ark., and west to Ill. Probably escaped from cultivation in the west. *P. pubescens*

Turtle-head. Chelone glabra.

and *P. lævigatus* have been found in the fields and rocky hills of Vermont by Wild, in Roxbury, Conn., by C. K. Averill; *P. lævigatus* has been found by H. G. Palfrey in Haverhill, Mass.; and *P. lævigatus* var. *Digitalis* has been found in Middlesex Co., Mass., by Mabel P. Cook.

Monkey-flower
Mimulus ringens
Purple
June–September

A smooth perennial with an upright square stem often considerably branched, and light green, smooth, lustreless leaves with irregular obscure teeth, lance-shaped or oblong, opposite-growing and clasping the stem. The flowers are a rich clear purple; the corolla two-lipped, the upper lip erect and two-lobed, the lower with three wide-spreading lobes; there are two yellow spots near the narrow throat. The pistil and four stamens are white; the five-pointed, green calyx is stained with dull purple. The few flowers are long-stalked and spring from the angles of the upper leaves. 1–3 feet high. In swamps and beside brooks, generally in meadows, from Me., south to Va. and Tenn., and west to S. Dak., Minn., Neb., and Tex. Rarely the flowers are white. Found near Langdon Park, Plymouth, N. H. The name from the Greek for *ape*, or *buffoon*, in allusion to the fancied grin on the face of the corolla.

False Pimpernel
Ilysanthes riparia
Pale dull lilac
July–September

A branching and spreading little annual with rounded ovate or oblong, smooth leaves, scarcely toothed, the upper ones stemless and clasping the plant-stem slightly. The pale dull lilac flowers ¼ inch long; the upper lip of the corolla two-lobed, the lower three-lobed and flaring not unlike *Mimulus*. 4–9 inches high. Common in low, wet ground, everywhere.

Culver's Root
Veronica Virginica
White
July–September

A very tall, smooth, perennial species, commonest in the west, with simple, straight stem, and lance-shaped or oblong leaves growing in circles about the plant-stem, sharply toothed and smooth. Flowers small, white or pale lavender, with rather a long tube to the corolla, and with prominent stamens, in dense terminal spikes 3–6 inches long. 2–7

Pentstemon pubescens.

feet high. In meadows and moist woods. Not recorded in Vermont by Brainerd and Eggleston. N. Y., south to Ala., and west to Mo. and Neb.

American Brooklime
Veronica Americana
Lavender-blue
May–September
A perennial species with a h o l l o w, smooth stem, which creeps over the ground and finally becomes erect and branching. The leaves long-oval or oblong lance-shaped, light green, slightly toothed, with short, flat stems. The tiny flower is lavender-blue violet-striped, with a white centre ; the corolla four-lobed, the lower lobe narrower than the others, the two divergent stamens light purple. The frail, quickly fading flowers are set on slender stems, in loose terminal spikes. 6–15 inches high. On banks of streams and in damp places ; common from Me., south to Pa., and westward. Found in the Catskill Mountains near the Mountain House.

Marsh Speedwell
Veronica scutellata
Lavender-blue
May–September
A similar species. The flowers on rather zig-zag stems, and with linear, acute, shallow-toothed leaves, slightly clasping the stem. Fruit capsule flat, notched, and broader than it is long. 6–20 inches high. In swamps, from Me., south to southern N. Y., and west to Minn. Local in Cal. Also in Europe and Asia.

Common Speedwell
Veronica officinalis
Light lavender
June–August
A woolly species with prostrate but finally erect stem. Leaves light green, oval or obovate, toothed, and narrow at the base. The flowers light lavender, striped with light violet ; corolla four-lobed. The flowers are set closely on slender spikes, rising from the leaf-angles. 3–10 inches high. Common in dry fields and wooded uplands. Me., south to S. Car., west to Mich. Also in Europe and Asia.

Veronica alpina
A small mountain species with the same time of bloom ; the slender stem generally simple, the leaves indistinctly toothed or toothless, elliptical or ovate. Lavender flowers in short clusters. 2–12 inches high. On Mt. Washington and the high mountains of New Eng., also in the Rockies. The seed-capsules of *Veronica* are in effect notched.

American Brooklime.   Veronica Americana.

Thyme-leaved Speedwell
Veronica serpyllifolia
White, pale lavender
April–May

A small species, generally found in the grass, with a slender branching stem and small oval leaves, toothless, short-stemmed, and opposite-growing. Flowers like those of American Brooklime but white or pale lavender with deeper stripes; they are less frail than those of the other *Veronicas*. 2–10 inches high. In fields and thickets, from Me., south to Ga., and westward. Also in Europe and Asia. Named for St. Veronica.

Fern-leaved False Foxglove
Gerardia pedicularia
Pure yellow
August–September

A handsome annual or biennial species with a rather sticky fine-hairy, leafy, branching stem, round in section. The light green leaves are fernlike, and deeply cut into many toothed lobes; they are stemless or nearly so. The showy, pure light lemon yellow flowers are bell-shaped with five broad, spreading, rounded lobes. The blossoms measure a full inch or more in diameter. The outer surface and the throat of the corolla, the stamens, and the toothed lobes of the calyx are fine-hairy. Both flower and fruit are very beautiful, and the plant would be worthy of cultivation if its character permitted ; but the *Gerardias* are more or less parasitic on the roots of other plants. 1–3 feet high. Visited frequently by the bumblebee and the light brown butterfly, *Junonia cœnia*. On the borders of dry woodlands and thickets, from Me., south, and west to Minn. and Mo.

Downy False Foxglove
Gerardia flava
Pure yellow
July–August

A handsome species with a simple stem, and yellow-green leaves, ovate lance-shaped, broadest at the base, slightly coarse dull-toothed or toothless, the edge wavy. Both stem and leaves are velvety downy with soft hairs, the leaves with their stalks magenta-tinged. The showy, pure yellow or light lemon yellow flowers about 1½ inch long, trumpet-shaped like foxglove, with five lobes, the broad throat downy on the inside. Stamens four, two short and two long ; hairy. The flowers set in a close terminal cluster, rather one-sided. Cross-fertilized mostly by butterflies and bumble-bees ; the Peacock butterfly (*Junonia cœnia*), light brown

Downy False Foxglove.　　　Gerardia　flava.

darker spotted, is one of the frequent visitors. 2–4 feet high. Thin woodlands. Me., south to Ga., west to Wis.

Smooth False Foxglove
Gerardia quercifolia

A similar species with flowers a little larger and the same pure yellow; but the whole plant *smooth* and with a slight bloom; the leaves cut or plain-edged, oblong lance-shaped, the lower ones cut quite deeply, with the outline wavy and toothed. 3–6 feet high. New Eng., south, west to Ill. and Minn.

Purple Gerardia
Gerardia purpurea
Magenta-purple August–September

One of the daintiest of the *Gerardias;* an annual with a generally smooth stem, slim, straight, and rigid, the branches widely spreading. The leaves are yellowish green, small, and linear, with acute tips. The downy, lighter or deeper magenta-purple flowers are cup-shaped, with five wide, flaring lobes; there are four stamens bearing rather large deep golden yellow anthers. The flower is commonly visited by various bees, the yellow butterfly, *Colias philodice,* and the brown butterfly, *Junonia cœnia.* Seed-capsule spherical. 12–26 inches high. In moist soil, generally near the coast, or in the vicinity of the Great Lakes, from Me., south, and west to Minn. The var. *paupercula,* not quite as tall, has a smooth, simple or branched stem, and the smaller flower is about ½ inch long; seed-capsule prolate-spheroidal. 6–17 inches high. N. Y. and N. J., west to Wis.

Sea-side Gerardia
Gerardia maritima

A similar and even lower species confined to the salt marshes of the coast. The linear leaves are rather fleshy, and obtuse at the tips; the upper ones are unusually short. The light magenta flowers, about the same size as those of the preceding species, are not downy, but smooth. 4–14 inches high. From Me., south.

Slender Gerardia
Gerardia tenuifolia

A very slender species with linear, acute-pointed leaves. The light magenta flowers have two of the five lobes not so fully expanded as the others; the calyx-lobes are short and acute. 10–20 inches high. In dry fields and along roadsides. Common. Named for John Gerarde, a celebrated herbalist.

Purple Gerardia.   Gerardia purpurea.

FIGWORT FAMILY. *Scrophulariaceæ.*

Painted Cup
*Castilleja
coccinea*
**Scarlet
green-yellow
June-July**

An odd species, annual or biennial, with the flower's corolla almost hidden in the long, cylindrical, two-lobed calyx, which is generally tipped with brilliant scarlet. The plant-stem is ruddy, soft-hairy, slender, and simple. The leaves are light green, parallel-veined, and slightly hairy or smooth, the lower ones oblong or broader, clustered, and undivided, the uppermost generally three-lobed — sometimes five-lobed ; all are stemless, and each looks as if it had been stained on the tip with deep vermilion or scarlet, more or less vivid according to the individual plant. William Hamilton Gibson calls the color of the Painted Cup "the brightest dab of red the wild palette can show." The color of the inconspicuous *flower* is greenish yellow, the corolla is tubular and two-cleft. The blossoms, completely eclipsed by the red floral leaves, form with these a dense terminal cluster. Rarely the red of the leaves is displaced by yellow. Like the *Gerardias*, this plant is also parasitic in nature. 12–20 inches high. Common in low, wet meadows, from Me., south to Va. and Ky., and west to Kan. and Tex. Named for Castillejo, a Spanish botanist.

*Castilleja
pallida*, var.
septentrionalis
**Whitish yel-
low-green
June-Septem-
ber.**

A pale green-leaved species living on the bleak and rocky summits of mountains in the north, or on the north shore of Lake Superior. A slender perennial, generally smooth, except at the uppermost parts, and the stem is usually simple. The light green leaves are (mainly) toothless, stemless, and 3–5 ribs run nearly parallel with each other, meeting at the somewhat acute tips ; the upper leaves are lance-shaped, the lower linear. The floral leaves or bracts are rather obovate with a few broad teeth ; the color is pale or whitish yellow-green, or else green-white tinged with dull magenta. The yellowish flowers are about as long as the bracts, and are inconspicuous. All are crowded at the summit of the stem. 6–20 inches high. In damp rocky places. Alpine summits of New Eng. (Mt. Washington), Minn., S. Dak., in the Black Hills, and the Rockies, Col.

Painted Cup.
Castilleja coccinea.

Castilleja pallida
var. septentrionalis.

FIGWORT FAMILY. *Scrophulariaceæ.*

Eyebright
Euphrasia
officinalis
White, yellow-ish, etc.
July–August

A tiny annual with ovate or lance-shaped leaves slightly resembling *Castilleja* in aspect, confined to the coast of Maine and southern Canada. The pale olive green leaves are indistinctly dull-toothed and small on the lower part of the plant, and the upper, floral leaves are somewhat jagged and bristly toothed. The inconspicuous flowers are whitish or yellowish green. The corolla is two-lipped and a trifle notched, the lower lip three-lobed and spreading, the upper two-lobed (with reflexed sides), beneath it are the four stamens. 4–10 inches high. Possibly introduced from Europe. Found at Great Cranberry Island, Me., by Mr. E. F. Williams. *Euphrasia Oakesii* (*Euphrasia officinalis* var. *Tartarica* of Gray's *Manual*, Sixth Ed.) is a very dwarf form scarcely attaining a height of 2½ inches, with tiny yellowish flowers, and more rounded leaves with rounded teeth, growing in the Alpine regions of the White Mountains (under the crest of Mt. Monroe), and along the north shore of Lake Superior.

Yellow Rattle
Rhinanthus
Crista-galli
Yellow
July–August

A slightly similar taller annual confined to the same situations, with lance-shaped or oblong, dull green leaves coarsely toothed, and growing oppositely, the floral ones deeply cut and with bristle-tipped teeth. The flowers Naples yellow (straw color), and crowded on a one-sided leafy spike. The corolla two-lipped, the upper lip without lobes but slightly toothed on either side part way down, the lower three-lobed. Four stamens. Fruit-capsule round but flattened ; the seeds, when ripe rattle in the inflated pod. 6–20 inches high. Rocky soil, coast of New Eng., and the Alpine regions of the White Mountains, west to Lake Superior.

Beefsteak Plant or Lousewort
Pedicularis
Canadensis
Magenta, dull green-yellow
May–July

Also known as Wood Betony. A very slightly hairy species with simple stem, and soft-hairy leaves, dull dark green, and finely lobed, growing on grassy slopes or in copses. The lower leaves are feather-shaped and often stained with dull magenta, as is also the rather stout plant-stem; the upper leaves are sparse and grow al-

Wood Betony.   Pedicularis Canadensis.

ternately. The flower-cluster is terminal and dome-shaped, the flower two-lipped, the prominent upper lip dull dark whitish-opaque magenta, and strongly curved in a hook-shape with a two-toothed tip; the lower is three-lobed and dull green-yellow. The coarse and hairy, light green calyx is tinged at the edge with dull crimson-magenta. Bractlike leaves are set close in the flower-cluster, which lengthens to an oblong shape as the flowers develop. The four stamens are under the hooded upper lip admirably protected from rain or other pollen-destroying agents; the flower is fertilized mostly by bees; the bumblebees and the bees of the genus *Halictus* are common visitors. 5–12 inches high. Common everywhere. Me., south, west to S. Dak. Found on the Campus of Smith's College, Northhampton, Mass.

Pedicularis lanceolata
Light Naples yellow
A species with less crowded flowers, few of which bloom together, and a simple, nearly smooth light green stem. The deep green leaves are broad lance-shaped and finely cut in the semblance of a fern; they grow oppositely, or nearly so. The upper and lower lips of the corolla are pale dull Naples yellow, and press against each other nearly closing the throat of the flower. The same bees are common visitors. 12–34 inches high. In swampy places, Conn., south to Va., west to S. Dak.

Cow-wheat
Melampyrum Americanum
Greenish white
July–September
A delicate, low annual commonly found in the half-shaded borders of woods especially in the northeastern States, with slender, wiry, gray-green, branching stem, and yellow-green, lance-shaped leaves, the lower ones toothless and the upper with generally 2–4 bristlelike teeth or lobes near the base, all set in pairs, and growing oppositely. The frail greenish white flowers are cylindrical, opening into two lips, the lower lip three-lobed, and tinged straw yellow. The flowers grow singly from between the leaves, and are less than ½ inch long; their common visitors are the yellow butterfly *Colias philodice*, the spotted brown one, *Junonia cœnia*, and the white cabbage butterfly, *Pieris rapæ;* they are also visited by various bees. 4–10 inches high. The name from the Greek, meaning *black wheat.*

Cow-wheat.   Melampyrum lineare.
Melampyrum Americanum. Michaux.

BROOM-RAPE FAMILY. *Orobanchaceœ.*

Fleshy parasitic herbs having yellowish scales instead of leaves; the flowers perfect, or pistillate and staminate on the same plant. Stamens four. The tiny seeds borne in a capsule. Visited by various flies and bees.

Beech=drops or Cancer Root
Epiphegus Virginiana
Dull magenta buff=brown
August-October

A parasitic plant which draws its sustenance from the roots of the beech tree. The stem is tough, straight, almost upright-branched, stained with brown madder, and set with a *few* small, dry scales. The *curved* tubular, dull magenta and buff-brown *upper* flowers are purple-striped; although generally sterile they are complete in every part, the style slightly protruding beyond, and the stamens just within the throat. The tiny lower flowers are cleistogamous—closed to outward agencies and self-fertilized. A few of the upper flowers are cross-fertilized by bees. 6–20 inches high. Beech woods, Me., south and west to Wis. and Mo. The name means *on the beech.*

Squawroot
Conopholis Americana
Pale dull yellow
May–July

A pale parasitic plant, the stem hidden by the overlapping, light tan-colored, lance-shaped or ovate pointed scales; the flowers perfect, set in a many-scaled dense spike, the upper lip hooded, the lower small and three-lobed, the stamens protruding; the lips are pale ochre yellow fading toward the corolla. 3–8 inches high. In rich woods over tree roots, Me., south, and west to Mich.

Naked Broom-rape or One-flowered Cancer Root
Orobanche uniflora
Purplish
April–June

A beautiful little parasitic plant bearing a few brownish ovate bracts near the root, and sending up 1–4 erect, slender, one-flowered stalks; the curved tubular, five-lobed flower is purplish or light violet, or rarely cream white, ¾ inch long, externally fine-hairy, and delicately fragrant. Cross-fertilized mostly by the smaller bees (*Halictus*) and the bumblebees. 3–6 inches high. In moist woods, Me., south to Va.

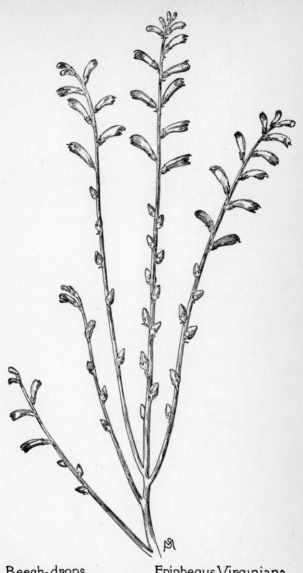

Beech-drops.　　　　　Epiphegus Virginiana.

PLANTAIN FAMILY. *Plantaginaceæ.*

PLANTAIN FAMILY. *Plantaginaceæ.*

Homely herbs—weeds—generally with coarse, strong-ribbed leaves springing from the root, and insignificant flowers in long narrow spikes, perfect, or polygamous—that is, staminate and pistillate on the same plant or different plants—and even cleistogamous—that is, fertilizing in the bud.

Common Plantain
Plantago major
Dull white
May–September

The familar weed of unkempt dooryards and grass-plots, with ovate, dark green, slightly hairy or smooth leaves, the long stems trough-shaped, the ribs conspicuous, and the edge generally toothless, or rarely coarse-toothed. The flowering spikes are cylindrical, blunt-tipped, and closely set with the dull, greenish white, four-lobed, perfect florets which mature the threadlike style *before* the corolla is *fully open*, the former projecting. The four stamens mature much later and thus insure cross-fertilization. Seed-capsule ovoid and opening near the middle, the seeds reticulated. Flowering stalks 6–18 inches high. Common everywhere, indigenous northwestward but naturalized from Europe on the Atlantic seaboard.

Plantago Rugelii
June–September

Similar to the preceding ; the leaves thinner, the flowering spikes less dense and attenuated above, and the seed-capsules cylindrical-oblong ; the latter open below the middle and quite within the four lobes of the calyx. The seeds are *not* reticulated. Common from Vt., south to Ga. and Tex., west to S. Dak.

English Plantain. Ribgrass
Plantago lanceolata
Dull white
April–October

A similar more or less fine-hairy European species, naturalized and very common. The leaves are *long* lance-shaped, nearly erect, generally three-ribbed, acute and toothless ; at the base of the leaves the hairiness is dark rust-color. The flower-spike is dense and *short*, bearing similar dull white flowers. But the conspicuously grooved stalk is 8–22 inches high. Old fields and waste places throughout our range.

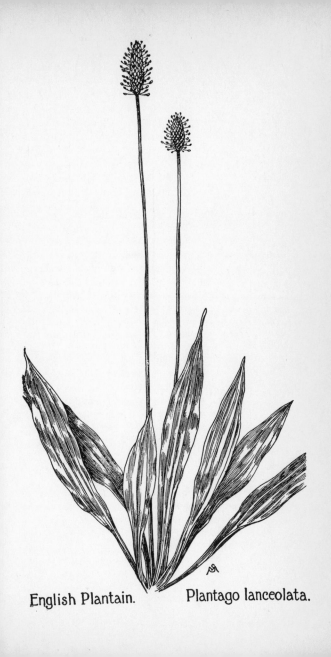

English Plantain.   Plantago lanceolata.

MADDER FAMILY. *Rubiaceæ.*

Shrubs or herbs with toothless leaves growing oppositely or in circles ; the regular flowers perfect, or staminate with rudimentary pistils, or pistillate with rudimentary stamens ; the corolla funnel-formed with 4 (sometimes 5) lobes and as many stamens. Cross-fertilized mostly by bees and butterflies. A large family in the tropics, to which belong the Coffee, the Cinchona tree from which is obtained quinine, and the Madder (*Rubia tinctorum*) whose roots furnish the red dye and the artist's permanent pigment of that name.

Houstonia or Bluets
Houstonia cœrulea
White and lilac, etc.
April–July

A familiar little wayside flower also called Quaker Ladies and Innocence ; communistic in manner of growth and frequently covering large spaces with its white bloom. It is a perennial, and forms dense tufts of oblong lance-shaped, tiny light green root-leaves and slender, thread-like stems sparingly set with minute opposite leaflets. The little four-lobed corolla is about ½ inch in diameter, white, or white tinged on the lobes with lilac, or pale violet (the nearest approach to blue) ; the centre is stained with golden yellow. The flowers are pistillate and staminate as above described. Cross-fertilized mainly by the bees of the genera *Halictus* and *Andrena*, and the smaller butterflies—the Clouded Sulphur (*Colias philodice*), the Meadow Fritillary (*Brenthis bellona*), and the Painted Lady (*Pyrameis Cardui*). 3–6 inches high. In moist grassy places or sandy waysides, from Me., south to Ga. and Ala., west to Mich. Named for William Houston an early English botanist.

Large Houstonia
Houstonia purpurea
Lilac or deep lilac
May–July

A taller southern species. The stem smooth or slightly hairy, the light green leaves pointed broad ovate (the upper ones smaller and narrower), with 3–5 ribs, the largest nearly 2 inches long. The deep lilac or pale lilac, long-tubed flowers in small clusters ; the thin lobes of the calyx longer than the globular seed-pod. 6–16 inches high. In thin or open woodlands, from Md., south (especially

Bluets.   Houstonia cærulea.

in the mountains) to Ga. and Ala., and west to Ark. The var. *ciliolata* has thicker leaves ½ inch long, with the edges conspicuously hairy-fringed, and flowers in small clusters. 5–7 inches high. On the rocky shores of the Great Lakes, and south in woodlands to Pa., West Va., Ky., and Ark.; with various intergrading forms passing to the var. *longifolia*, which has thinner, linear and acute leaves, often a full inch long; the root-leaves are not hairy-fringed. 5–18 inches high. From Me., south to Ga., and west to Minn. and Mo. Frequent in the Lake Champlain Valley.

Partridgeberry
Twinberry
Mitchella
repens
Cream white
pinkish
May–June

A little trailing vine with dark green evergreen leaves green-white-veined and wide, slightly heart-shaped at the base. The commonly four-lobed twin flowers (sometimes conjoined with 8–10 lobes) are cream white and fine-hairy inside, but faint crimson-pink and smooth outside; they terminate the short branches, and are two-formed, i. e., staminate (with abortive pistil) and pistillate (with abortive stamens). Cross-fertilized by the same insects which visit the Mayflower and Houstonia. 6–12 inches long. In woods from Me., south, and west to Minn., Ark., and Tex. Named for Dr. John Mitchell.

Yellow
Bedstraw
Galium verum
Yellow
May–August

A slender, rather erect, perennial herb naturalized from Europe, with a smooth, squarish stem a trifle woody at the base. The narrow, linear, rough, light green leaves, in circles of 6–8, are about an inch long. The tiny, yellow, four-lobed flowers are in small terminal clusters, or at the leaf-angles. 8–30 inches long. In dry waste places and borders of fields. Me., occasional in Vt., south to N. J., near the coast.

Cleavers or
Goosegrass
Galium aparine
White
May–August

An annual species with the usual weak reclining stem characteristic of the *Galiums*, which hangs upon shrubbery by means of the backward-hooked prickles of both leaf and stem. The blunt lance-shaped, light green leaves with roughened edge and rib are nearly 2 inches long, and set in a circle of 6–8. About two tiny white flowers are borne on a stalk. Fruit

Partridgeberry.   Mitchella repens.

burlike, in pairs, and covered with short, hooked bristles which facilitate transportation. 2–5 feet long. Shady thickets and roadsides, Me., south, and west to S. Dak., Kan., and Tex. The following *Galiums* are perennials.

Wild Liquorice
Galium
circœzans
Greenish white
May–July

A smooth or slightly downy species with broad, ovate leaves in fours, three-ribbed, and about an inch long. The greenish white flowers, with four pointed lobes hairy on the outside, are borne on stalks usually forked but once. 1–2 feet high. Common in rich dry woods. Me., south, west to Minn., and Tex.

Northern
Bedstraw
Galium boreale

A smooth species with acute lance-shaped or narrower leaves almost smooth on the edge. The numerous tiny white flowers set in close clusters. 15–30 inches high. Near streams, among rocks. Me., south to N. J., and west to S. Dak., Neb., and Cal.

Small
Bedstraw
Galium
trifidum

A very *small*, delicate, variable species, often much entangled among bushes. The minute stem-prickles are scarcely visible. The linear blunt-tipped or wedge-shaped, deep green leaves, $\frac{1}{2}$ inch long, set in fours. The minute usually three-lobed, white flowers, with three stamens, are in tiny thin clusters. 6–18 inches high. Common in sphagnum bogs and wet woodlands everywhere.

Rough
Bedstraw
Galium
asprellum
White
June–August

A very common, weak, and reclining species, with the usual square stem set with backward-hooked prickles. The light green leaves slightly blunt lance-shaped, and prickly-rough on edge and rib, are set in circles of 4–6. The profuse tiny white flowers are in thin, airy, terminal clusters; they are peculiarly, perhaps unpleasantly, odorous. 2–6 feet long. In damp soil. Me., south to N. Car., west to Neb.

Sweet-scented
Bedstraw
Galium
triflorum

A similar species with the flowers usually borne in clusters of three, and with the same bristly rough stem; the leaves broad lance-shaped, bright shining green, bristle-pointed, slightly rough-edged, and set usually in sixes. The foliage fragrant after drying. 1–3 feet long. Rich woodlands throughout our range; south only to Ga.

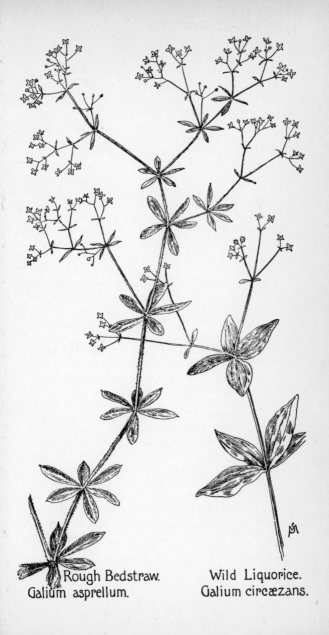

Rough Bedstraw.
Galium asprellum.

Wild Liquorice.
Galium circæzans.

HONEYSUCKLE FAMILY. *Caprifoliaceæ.*

Shrubs, vines, or sometimes herbs with opposite leaves, and perfect regular (occasionally irregular) flowers, with generally a funnel-shaped corolla, five-lobed, or sometimes two-lipped. Cross-fertilized by the larger long-tongued bees, moths, butterflies, and the humming-bird.

Elder
Sambucus
Canadensis
Cream white
June–July

A common smooth-stemmed shrub with a compound deep green, smooth leaf of 5–11, usually 7, fine-toothed, acute-pointed, ovate leaflets. The tiny cream-white flowers, in broad flat clusters (with five prominent white stamens), are fertilized mostly by honeybees who come for pollen, the blossoms yielding little or no nectar. The purple-black berries, in broad clusters, ripen in August. 4–10 feet high. Borders of fields and copses, in low ground, throughout our range.

Red-berried
Elder
Sambucus
racemosa
Dull white
April–May

A similar shrub with twigs and leaves slightly fine-hairy, and warty gray bark. There are 5–7 finely toothed ovate lance-shaped leaflets which are a trifle downy beneath. The fine dull white flowers with yellowish stamens are borne in a sugar-loaf-shaped cluster. The extremely beautiful small, scarlet-red, or rarely white berries, in a compact cluster, ripen in June. 2–12 feet high. In rocky woodland borders. Me., south to Ga. (among the hills), and westward.

Hobble-bush or
Wayfaring Tree
Viburnum
alnifolium
White
May–June

A shrub with coarse, light green, veiny, sharp-toothed, heart-shaped leaves, rusty-woolly on the ribs beneath, together with the young branchlets. The flat flower-cluster is composed of two kinds of flowers ; the marginal dull white broad-petaled neutral—that is, stamenless and pistilless—flowers (the petals are really the five flaring, rounded divisions of the corolla), and the central, smaller, perfect flowers. Fruit a coral red berry, set in a scant cluster. Stem 3–10 feet high, reclining ; the branches often take root and trip up the " wayfarer." The commonest visitors are the bees of the genera *Andrena* and *Halictus*. In low or moist woods. Me., in the mountains to N. Car., west to Mich.

Red-berried Elder.   Sambucus racemosa.

Feverwort
Horse Gentian
Triosteum
perfoliatum
Madder purple
May–July

A coarse perennial, sometimes called Tinker's-weed and often Wild Coffee, common in rich woodlands. The stout, simple stem is rather sticky-fine-hairy, and the opposite-growing, light green or medium green, oval leaves are acute at the tip, and narrowed at the base to a flaring margin either side of the coarse midrib; the edge is toothless and somewhat undulating. The flowers are an inconspicuous purplish brown or madder purple; they grow at the junction of the leaves with the plant-stem; the corolla is five-lobed, tubular, and scarcely longer than the long-lobed calyx, which remains attached to the mature fruit; this is $\frac{1}{2}$ inch long or less, orange-scarlet, densely fine-hairy, and contains three hard nutlets. 2–4 feet high. In rich soil, from Me., south to Ala. and Ky., and west to Minn., Iowa, and Kan.

Twin-flower
Linnæa
borealis
Crimson-pink
June-August

A delicate and beautiful trailing vine common in the northern woodlands, with a terra-cotta-colored, somewhat rough-woody stem, and a rounded, about 8-scallop-toothed, short-stemmed, light ever-green leaf with a rough surface. The fragrant little bell-shaped flowers, in pairs, terminate a 3–4 inches long stalk, and nod; they are delicate crimson-pink, graded to white on the margins of the five lobes. The tiny calyx divisions are threadlike. Branches 6–20 inches long. Common in rich moist mossy woods, particularly in the mountains. Me., to Long Island and Staten Island, N. Y., and N. J., west to S. Dak., Wash., and Col.

Coral-berry or
Indian Currant
Symphoricarpos
vulgaris
Pink and white
July

A shrub with erect, generally madder brown branches very slightly woolly-hairy on the younger growths. The dull gray-green leaves are ovate, toothless (rarely some of the larger leaves are coarsely toothed), and have distinctly short stems. The five-lobed flowers are tiny bell-shaped, and grow in small clusters at the angles of the leaves, or terminally; the corolla pink graded to white, and somewhat filled by the fine hairiness of style and stamens. The small berries in small terminal clusters are first coral red and

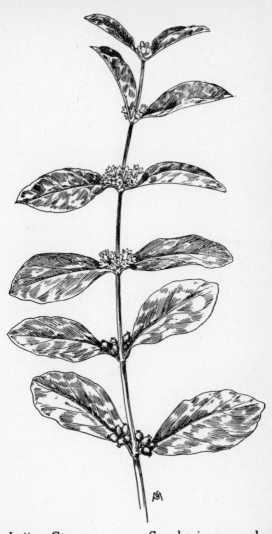

Indian Currant.   Symphoricarpos vulgaris.

finally dull crimson-magenta. The smaller bees and honeybees are common visitors. 2–5 feet high. Rocky slopes. Mass., banks of the Delaware River in N. J., and Pa., south to Ga. and Tex., west to the Daks.

Snowberry
Symphoricarpos racemosus
Pink and white
June–August
A familiar shrub of old-fashioned gardens and door-yards still commonly cultivated, with smooth, erect, gray-brown branches, and oval, dull gray-green leaves lighter beneath, toothless, and a trifle wavy-margined. The young shoots are ochre brown. The tiny, five-lobed, bell-shaped flowers are pink graded to white, and are borne in terminal and leaf-angle clusters. The corolla is conspicuously fine-hairy within ; and the stamens and style almost protrude. The honeybee is a constant visitor, and the flowers continue to bloom even after the large snow-white waxy berries appear ; the latter are a conspicuous feature of the bush in early September. 3–4 feet high. On roadsides, escaped from cultivation, and on rocky banks, from Me., south to Pa. and Ky., and west to Minn., S. Dak., and Cal.

Fly-honey-suckle
Lonicera ciliata
Naples yellow
May–June
A thin straggling bush with smooth, brownish stems. The thin leaves bright light green on both sides, ovate lance-shaped, sometimes very broad at the base, toothless, short-stemmed, and hairy-edged. The Naples yellow or honey yellow, five-lobed flower, about ¾ inch long, is funnel-formed and borne in pairs at the leaf-angles. Fruit two small ovoid red berries. 3–5 feet high. Moist woods, from Me., south to Pa., and west to Minn.

Mountain Fly-honeysuckle
Lonicera cærulea
A similar species but with thickish, blunt ovate leaves fine-hairy beneath. The Naples yellow flowers in pairs, almost united. The ovaries unite and form one two-eyed, gray-black ovate berry. 1–3 feet high. In boggy woods, the same distribution.

Fly-honeysuckle.   Lonicera ciliata.

VALERIAN FAMILY. *Valerianaceæ*.

Trumpet or Coral Honeysuckle
Lonicera sempervirens
Scarlet and yellow
April–August

A scentless, but beautiful species, common in cultivation, twining and climbing high, and evergreen southward. The large deep green oblong leaves are whitish beneath ; the top ones are united, and seemingly perforated by the stem, which terminates in a small cluster of large, tubular, deep Naples yellow flowers, often deeply tinged outside with scarlet. The most frequent and useful visitor is the humming-bird, though many bees and butterflies assist in the transfer of pollen. 8–15 feet high. Copses, Mass. and Conn., south, west to Neb.

Bush Honeysuckle
Diervilla trifida
Naples yellow
May–June

A very common shrubby species with smooth stem and leaves and exceedingly small honey-colored or Naples yellow flowers, with five recurving, rather equal lobes, marked slightly with dull rusty orange. There are five prominent yellow stamens. The deep olive green leaves are ovate, sharp-pointed, and fine-toothed. The flowers grow in small clusters, terminally, and at the junction of leaf- and plant-stem. The fruit is an oblong capsule with beaked tip. 3–4 feet high. In dry woodlands or in thickets, from Me., south to N. Car., and west to Mich. and Minn. Named for Dr. Dierville who carried the plant from Canada to France.

VALERIAN FAMILY. *Valerianaceæ*.

Herbs with opposite leaves, and perfect, or sometimes staminate and pistillate, flowers ; the corolla tube narrow and five-lobed ; stamens 1–3. Commonly visited by bees. The genus *Valeriana* is remarkable for its strong-scented roots.

Swamp Valerian
Valeriana sylvatica
Pale magenta-pink
June–July

An erect, smooth plant, with compound leaves of from 5–11 (rarely less) deep green, lance-shaped, obtuse leaflets, indistinctly shallow-toothed or toothless; the root-leaves are long-stemmed, ovate, and rarely small-lobed. The dull magenta-pink or paler pink or white flowers are tiny, and clus-

Swamp Valerian.　　　　Valeriana sylvatica.

---

tered in a loose terminal spike ; the three stamens *very* prominent. 10–30 inches high. In wet or swampy ground, from Me., south to southern N. Y., west to S. Dak., and in the Rocky Mountains to Ariz.

Garden Valerian, Great Wild Valerian, or Vandal-root *Valeriana officinalis* A common cultivated species, often escaping to roadsides and margins of cultivated fields. A native of Europe. The stem more or less fine-hairy especially at the joints, and the compound leaves with 11–21 lance-shaped, sharply toothed leaflets, the upper ones toothless. The flowers are pale magenta-crimson or white, set in compact, rather rounded clusters terminating the stout stem. The strong-scented roots are medicinal. 2–5 feet high. Mass. south to Del., west to N. Y. and Pa. Name from *valere*, to be strong.

Corn Salad *Valerianella Woodsiana* **Dull white May–July** A smooth forking-stemmed annual with succulent wedge-shaped leaves, and insignificant dull white flowers funnel-formed and five-lobed, gathered in small terminal clusters. 18–34 inches high. In moist places, from N. Y., west to Ohio and Tex. *Valerianella olitoria*, a species from Europe, naturalized in the Middle States and south, has similar leaves, but pale violet flowers. 6–12 inches high. Southern N. Y., and southward.

GOURD FAMILY. *Cucurbitaceæ.*

Climbing vines generally with tendrils, and with lobed leaves growing alternately. The flowers staminate and pistillate on the same plant or different plants. Stamens mostly three. Cross-fertilized by bees and flies in general, and possibly by many beetles and butterflies.

Climbing Wild Cucumber or Wild Balsam Apple *Echinocystis lobata* **Greenish white July–September** A beautiful, rapid-growing, and luxuriant annual climber ; the light green, thin leaves, with 3–7 (mostly five) sharply angular lobes, are rough on both sides. The small, sharply six-petaled staminate flowers are borne in many loose clusters, and the pistillate flowers singly or in twos, at the angles of the leaves ; the petals and the three prominent stamens with

Climbing Wild Cucumber. Echinocystis lobata.

yellowish anthers are greenish white. The spiral tendrils are three-forked. Cross-fertilized mostly by bees
and wasps. The cucumberlike fruit is 2 inches long or
less, green, ovoid, and thickly covered with slender,
weak prickles. 15–20 feet long. Beside rivers and in
waste places. Me., south to Pa. and west to S. Dak.,
Kan., and Tex. Found in the Pemigewasset Valley at Plymouth and Campton, N. H. The name (Greek), means
hedgehog and bladder ; in allusion to the armed fruit.

One-seeded
Bur-cucumber
Sicyos
angulatus
Greenish white
July–
September
Also an annual climber with branching
tendrils and a five-lobed, far less deeply
cut light green leaf; the stem is sticky-
hairy, angular, and coarse. The small
five-lobed flowers are likewise staminate
and pistillate ; the former are borne, five
or six, in a cluster on a long stalk, the
latter are almost stalkless ; both are set in the angles of
the leaves. The yellowish fruit, 3–10 together, is armed
with fine tough bristles ; a single fruit contains but one
seed. 15–25 feet long. In moist places and along
rivers, from Me., south, and west to Minn., Kan., and
Tex. The name is Greek, for Cucumber.

BELLFLOWER FAMILY. *Campanulaceæ.*

Herbs, in our range, with alternate leaves and acrid,
generally milky, juice ; the perfect flowers in a spike or
solitary. The corolla usually bell-shaped and five-lobed.
Stamens five, alternating with the corolla-lobes. Fruit
a many-seeded capsule. Cross-fertilized mostly by bees
and the beelike flies (*Syrphidæ*). A tribe now included
in *Lobeliaceæ* by Engler and Prantl, but one which, *in
our range*, lacks those connecting links which make the
close relationship evident.

Venus's
Looking-glass
Specularia
perfoliata
Magenta-
purple
June–August
An annual with a simple, wandlike stem,
weak and disposed to recline, and small,
curved, shell-shaped, light green, scallop-
toothed leaves clasping the rough, angled
plant-stem. The purple-violet or magenta-
purple flowers, set at the hollows of the
leaves, have deeply five-lobed corollas

Leaf of
Sicyos angulatus.

Venus's Looking-glass.   Specularia perfoliata.

BELLFLOWER FAMILY. *Campanulaceæ.*

with five stamens and a three-lobed pistil. There are also earlier flowers which are cleistogamous — closed to all outward agencies and self-fertilized. Stem 5–22 inches long. Common in poor soil on hills and in dry open woodlands. Me., south, west to Ore. and Utah.

Bellflower
Campanula
rapunculoides
Purple
July–August

A common garden perennial, naturalized from Europe, and a frequent escape from cultivation. The simple, erect, and rigid stem is light green and slightly rough-hairy; the leaves are thin, fine-hairy, and light green, the upper ones broad lance-shaped, the lower arrow-head-shaped with a heart-shaped base; all are irregularly scallop-toothed. The bell-shaped purple flowers have five acute lobes, and hang downward mostly on *one side* of the stem; the pistil is white and protruding; the stigma three-lobed and purple-tinged; the linear lobes of the green calyx are strongly turned backward. The common visitors of the flower are the honeybee and bumblebee. 1–3 feet high. In fields and on roadsides. Me., to southern N. Y., Pa., and Ohio.

Harebell or
Bluebell
Campanula
rotundifolia
Light violet
June–
September

A most dainty and delicate perennial plant, yet one so remarkably hardy that it survives the cold and storms of mountain-tops over 5000 feet above sea-level. It is common in the Chasm of the Ausable River and on the summits of the White Mountains. In spring the plant displays a tuft of round leaves (hence the name *rotundifolia*), small and sparingly toothed; these wither before the time of flowering (rarely they remain until that time), and are succeeded by a tall wiry stem, with linear, pale olive green leaves and a succession of airy blue-violet bells depending from threadlike pedicels (flower-stems). The corolla is five-lobed, and graded in color from light violet or pale lavender to white at its base; the prominent pistil is tipped with a three-lobed stigma, which is at first green and finally white; the five anthers are a delicate lavender tint. The chief visitor is the bumblebee, who must clasp the prominent stigma before he can enter the inverted bell; in the bustling endeavor to reach the base of the blossom some of the pollen obtained from

Bellflower.

Campanula
rapunculoides.

a previously visited flower is brushed off and cross-fertilization is effected. The harebell is also visited by the bees of the genus *Halictus* and the beelike flies. 6-18 inches high. On rocky cliffs, dry or moist, in barren, sandy fields or grassy places, and in shade or sunshine, on mountain-top or meadow. Me., south to N. J., west to S. Dak., Neb., and in the Rocky Mountains south to Ariz ; also in the mountains of Cal. A native of Europe and Asia as well, and identical with the bluebell of Scotland. A degenerate mountain form mistakenly thought to be the var. *arctica* is a much smaller plant bearing a single flower.

Marsh Bellflower
Campanula aparinoides
White or lavender
June-August

A species common in grassy swamps, with branching, slender, weak, reclining stems, bristly rough on the angles, like *Galium asprellum*. The light green, linear lance-shaped leaves are rough on edge and midrib ; indistinctly shallow-toothed, and stemless. The single white or pale lavender flowers scarcely ⅓ inch broad, deeply cleft into five acute lobes spreading open like a deep saucer, are arranged terminally. 6-20 inches high. In wet grassy ground everywhere, west to S. Dak., Neb., and Col.

Tall Bellflower
Campanula Americana
Light violet
July-September

A tall annual or biennial with a slightly fine-hairy, erect, slender, green stem, rarely branched. The ovate or ovate lance-shaped, stemless, light green leaves are long and drooping ; the lower ones are narrowed at the base like a stem ; all are acute-pointed and toothed. The dull-toned light violet or nearly white flowers grow from the angles of the leaves and form a slender terminal spike ; the one inch wide corolla has five long, acute, spreading lobes ; the style curves downward and then upward (as in the *Pyrola*), extending far beyond the mouth of the flower. The commonest visitors are the honeybee, the bumblebee, and the "Yellow-Jacket" hornet. Flower-stalk frequently 18 inches tall. In moist shady places, inland, from N. Y., south to Fla., and west to S. Dak., Kan., and Ark. The name is from the Italian *Campana*, a bell, in allusion to the shape of the corolla.

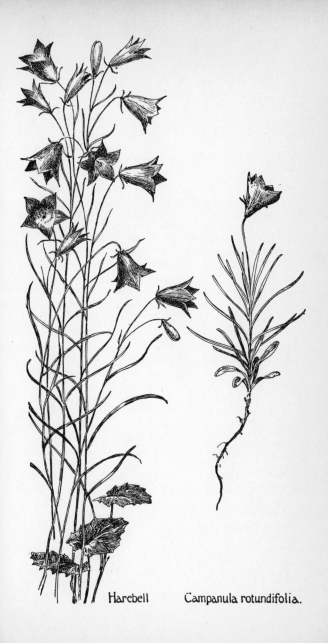

Harebell   Campanula rotundifolia.

LOBELIA FAMILY. *Lobeliaceæ.*

A family of perennial herbs with milky acrid juice. The perfect but irregular flowers with a five-lobed tube-shaped corolla ; the five stamens united in a tube. Cross-fertilized by bees, the beelike flies, and the humming-bird. Named for De L'Obel, an early Dutch herbalist ; it now includes the tribe *Campanulaceæ.*

Cardinal Flower
Lobelia cardinalis
Deep red
August–September

A most beautiful species, remarkable for its rich, deep red which largely influences the color of stem and foliage. The leaves are dark green, smooth or nearly so, oblong lance-shaped, and slightly toothed ; the upper ones are stemless. The showy flower-spike is loosely set with deep cardinal red flowers, the triple-lobed lips of which are a rich velvety color. Rarely the plant produces deep pink or white flowers. Fertilized by humming-birds, and rarely by bumblebees ; but the long tongue of the humming-bird is the only practicable means of cross-fertilization. The length of the flower-tube is too great for the tongue, and the pendant lip too inconvenient for the feet of the average insect. The plant multiplies mostly by perennial offshoots. 2–4 feet high. Common everywhere in low moist ground. Found in Campton Bog, N. H.

Great Lobelia
Lobelia syphilitica
Light blue-violet
July–September

A slightly hairy plant with a stout, leafy, and usually simple stem ; the leaves light green, 2–6 inches long, pointed at both ends, nearly if not quite smooth, irregularly toothed, and stemless. The light blue-violet or rarely white flowers nearly an inch long; the calyx stiff-hairy. 1–3 feet high. Common in low moist ground, from Me., south to Ga. and La., and west to Kan., Neb., and S. Dak.

Downy Lobelia
Lobelia puberula

A similar species with similarly colored flowers in long somewhat one-sided spikes, and with fine soft-hairy leaves. The hairy tube of the corolla is less than ½ inch long, and the lobes of the lip are rather broad and smooth. 1–3 feet high. In moist sandy soil. Southern N. J., south, and west to Kan. and Tex.

Cardinal Flower.
Lobelia cardinalis.

Indian Tobacco. Lobelia. inflata.

LOBELIA FAMILY. *Lobeliaceæ.*

Pale Spiked Lobelia
Lobelia spicata
Pale blue-violet
July-August

A still smaller-flowered species, bearing very long slim spikes of pale blue-violet flowers with a usually smooth short calyx. The stem simple and leafy, the light green leaves nearly toothless, lance-shaped (abruptly so at the base of the plant), or oblong, obtuse, but the upper ones nearly linear. 1-4 feet high. In dry sandy soil from Me., south to N. Car., and southwest to Ark. and La.

Kalm's Lobelia
Lobelia Kalmii
Light blue-violet
July-September

A small species generally found beside brooks, or on wet banks, with slender branching stem, and narrow, blunt-tipped leaves sparingly toothed or toothless; the upper ones linear. The light blue-violet flowers less than ½ inch long and scattered loosely over the spikes. The fruit-capsule not inflated (as *Lobelia inflata*), but small, and top-shaped or nearly globular. 6-18 inches high. On wet meadows and wet river-banks. Me., south to N. J., and west to Ohio and S. Dak.

Indian Tobacco
Lobelia inflata
Light blue-violet
July-October

The commonest species; growing everywhere in dry or wet soil, within the wood or out on the meadow. An annual with a simple or branching slightly hairy stem. The thin light green leaves oval pointed, and sparingly wavy-toothed, the uppermost very small, narrow, and acute. The tiny flowers scarcely ¼ inch long, varying in color from light blue-violet to pale lilac and even white. The calyx smooth, the inflated, prolate-spheroidal fruit-capsule about ⅓ inch long. Very acrid and poisonous to taste, and commonly used in medicine. Me., south to Ga., and west to Ark. and Neb.

Water Lobelia
Lobelia Dortmanna

An aquatic species, smooth, slender, and simple stemmed. Leaves all submerged, thick, linear hollow, and tufted at the *base of the stem.* Flowers in a loose terminal spike, light violet, ⅓ inch long. 6-18 inches high. Borders of ponds. N. Eng. to Pa., and northwestward.

Pale Spiked Lobelia.
Lobelia spicata.

Water Lobelia.
Lobelia Dortmanna.

COMPOSITE FAMILY. *Compositæ.*

Mostly perennial herbs. A great family remarkable for its compound flower-heads which are often radiate in character, with a central disc composed of tiny tubular florets surrounded by brightly colored rays; in some cases the florets are strap-shaped. They are variously perfect, polygamous, and staminate and pistillate on the same or different plants; in chicory and dandelion the florets are perfect and strap-shaped; in coneflower and sunflower the tubular florets of the central disc are perfect and the ray-flowers neutral (without stamens and pistil); in aster and golden-rod the inner tubular florets are perfect and the outer ray-florets are pistillate; in thistle and burdock the florets are all tubular and perfect but lacking rays; in *Antennaria* the tubular florets are staminate and pistillate on different plants, and in ragweed the staminate and pistillate florets are on the same plant. The family is largely dependent upon insects for cross-fertilization.

Tall Ironweed
Vernonia altissima
Madder purple
August-September

A tall smooth-stemmed plant found in moist situations, with lance-shaped, toothed, deep green leaves and a terminal cluster of brownish purple or madder purple flowers remotely resembling bachelor's buttons without petals; the small flower-heads appear hairy or chaffy. 5–8 feet high. Penn., south, and west to Ill. and La.

New York Ironweed
Vernonia Noveboracensis
Madder purple
August-September

The common species eastward, differing from the tall ironweed in its usually slightly rough stem, longer lance-shaped deep green leaves, and acute, bristle-tipped, brown-purple scales of the flower-heads. The æsthetic dull purple (rarely white) flowers resemble petalless bachelor's buttons, or at a distance asters. 3–7 feet high. In moist ground, oftenest near the coast, from Mass., south to Ga., and west to Minn. and eastern Kan. Found near Englewood, N. J. Named for Wm. Vernon, an early English botanist.

New York Ironweed.   Vernonia Noveboracensis.

COMPOSITE FAMILY. *Compositæ.*

Climbing Hempweed or Boneset
Mikania scandens
White flesh pink
July-September

An attractive, twining vine generally climbing over bushes on damp river banks. The light green leaves triangular heart-shaped, and the bristly, dull white or flesh-colored flowers resembling those of bone-set. 5–15 feet long. Mass., south, and west to Ind. and Tex. Named for Prof. Mikan of Germany.

Joe=Pye=Weed
Eupatorium purpureum
Magenta-crimson
August-September

A familiar, tall plant with a stout stem on which the roughish, pointed ovate, toothed, light green leaves are grouped in circles at intervals. The dense terminal flower-clusters with many soft-bristly, æsthetic-toned dull magenta-crimson florets, lighter or deeper, or sometimes dull white. Frequented by the honeybee. 3–12 feet high. Common everywhere on borders of swamps or low damp ground. Named for Eupator Mithridates, and for a New England Indian who used the plant in some concoction for the cure of fevers.

White Thoroughwort
Eupatorium album
White
August-September

A similar, but small, rough-hairy species with white flowers, the scales of which are very long and white. The light green, veiny leaves are stemless or nearly so. 1–3 feet high. In sandy soil and pine barrens, from Long Island, N. Y., to Fla. and La.

Upland Boneset
Eupatorium sessilifolium
White
August-October

A hillside species with generally smooth, opposite, ovate lance-shaped, horizontally spreading leaves tapering to a sharp point. The white flowers, with long, slender but blunt scales, are in flat clusters. 2–6 feet high. In woods or on wooded banks. Mass., south, and west to Ill.

Boneset or Thoroughwort
Eupatorium perfoliatum
Dull white
July-September

The common, familiar species whose leaves have been used in a bitter tonic decoction or tea. Leaves very light green, pointed, opposite, and so closely joined that two appear as one perforated by the plant-stem, which with the leaves is remarkably wool-hairy. The very dull white

Boneset
Eupatorium
perfoliatum.

White
Snakeroot.
Eupatorium
ayeratoides.

florets, in terminal clusters, furnish an abundance of
nectar for the visiting honeybee — the rule with all *Eu-
patoriums* and *Vernonias*. 2–5 feet high. Common
everywhere on wet ground.

**White
Snakeroot**
*Eupatorium
ageratoides*
**White
July–
September**
The most attractive and graceful mem-
ber of this generally coarse genus. The
large-toothed leaves are deep green,
smooth, thin, slender-stemmed, and nearly
heart-shaped. Flowers white (not dull)
and peculiarly downy, like the garden
Ageratum. 1–4 feet high. Rich woods
and copses. Me., south to Ga., and west to S. Dak.,
Neb., and La.

*Eupatorium
aromaticum*
A very similar species with short-
stemmed leaves, dull-toothed and blunt-
pointed ; the flowers a trifle larger. Near
the coast, from Mass. to Ga. The name is misleading—
it is not aromatic.

**Tall Blazing
Star**
Liatris scariosa
**Magenta-
purple
August–
September**
A tall, stout, handsome species belonging to a beautiful genus. The showy
flower-spike set with magenta-purple to
pale violet, tubular, perfect flowers, the
heads sometimes $\frac{7}{8}$ inch broad. Leaves
deep green, hoary, narrow lance-shaped,
and alternate-growing. The flowers ex-
hibit many æsthetic and variable tints. 2–6 feet high.
In dry situations, by roadsides and in fields. Me., south,
and west to S. Dak. and Tex.

*Liatris
squarrosa*
A lower species (beginning to bloom in
June) with smooth or often hairy, stiff,
linear leaves, and with the few flowers on
the spike bright magenta-purple and fully an inch long ;
the scales enveloping them are leaflike with sharp, spreading tips. 6–22 inches high. Pa., south, and west to S.
Dak. and Tex.

*Liatris
spicata*
A commoner species, smooth or nearly
so, with linear leaves and a closely set
flower-spike sometimes fully 14 inches
long ; the flowers, about $\frac{1}{3}$ inch broad, range from purple to violet or rarely to white. 2–5 feet high. Moist
low ground. Mass., south, and west to S. Dak. and Ark.

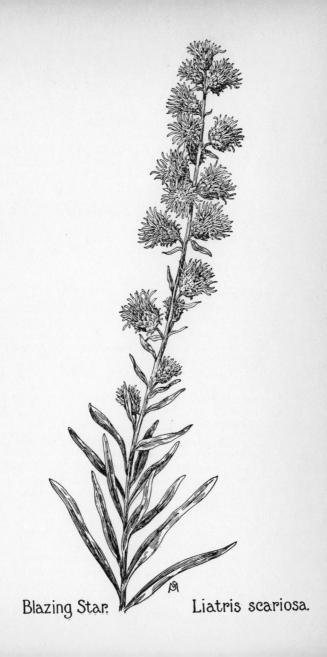

Blazing Star.　　　Liatris scariosa.

COMPOSITE FAMILY. *Compositæ.*

Grass-leaved Golden Aster or Silver Grass
Chrysopsis graminifolia
Golden yellow
August–October

An asterlike but golden yellow flower growing in dry soil generally near the coast. The shining leaves linear, soft, and grasslike, but silvery green-gray with fine-hairiness, the lower ones long. The small flowers $\frac{1}{2}$ inch broad, solitary at the tips of the branches, the ray-flowers pistillate, the disc-flowers perfect. The slender stem 1–3 feet high. Del., south, and southwest to Tex.

Curved-leaved Golden Aster
Chrysopsis falcata
Golden yellow
Late July–August

A much lower species with larger flowers, also found in the coastwise States. The stems very woolly, and the small linear leaves gray-green and crowded together. The pretty, rich golden yellow flowers are an inch broad. 4–10 inches high. From Cape Cod, Mass., to the pine barrens of N. J. Found on Nantucket.

Chrysopsis Mariana
Golden yellow
August–September

A stout, showy species, the stem and leaves of which are silky with soft hairs when young, but become smooth with age. The gray-green leaves are lance-shaped and stemless, and the golden yellow flower-heads are nearly an inch across, the scales below somewhat sticky and hairy. The commoner golden aster of New York and the south, found on dry sandy roadsides near the coast. 1–2 feet high. From southern N. Y. and Pa., south.

The genus *Solidago* includes about 85 species, of which about 25 are commonly found throughout the northern United States. These are readily distinguished by differences in stem, leaf, and flower ; the stem may be rough, smooth, covered with hairs, or with bloom, or angular, or round ; the leaf may be triple-ribbed, feather-veined, or more or less distinctly ribbed or toothed ; the flowers may have few or many large or small rays. The central tubular florets are perfect, and are cross-fertilized by many insects of many orders, chief among which are the butterflies and the beelike flies ; the flowers furnish an abundance of honey for all. The Latin name, *Solidago*, means to make whole, alluding to some curative quality of the plant. There are some hybrid forms.

Golden Aster   Chrysopsis Mariana.

COMPOSITE FAMILY. *Compositæ.*

Stout Golden-rod
Solidago squarrosa
Golden yellow
August–October

A not very common species, the stem hairy above and rarely branched, with large, broad, coarsely toothed, feather-veined leaves, and with rather showy flowers ; the 10–16 rays nearly ⅓ inch long, the tubular florets 15–24 in a single flower-head the scales of which are strongly curved outward. The flower plume generally straight. Plant 2–5 feet high. On rocky hillsides, and the margins of woods. Me., south to the mountains of Va., and west to Vt., the Catskills, N. Y., Penn., and Ohio.

Blue-stemmed Golden-rod
Solidago cæsia
Late August–October

A late-blooming, graceful, slender, woodland golden-rod, with a distinct bluish or purplish, plumlike bloom on the bending stem. The leaves dark green, feather-veined, smooth, sharply toothed, lance-shaped, and sharp-pointed. The flowers in small oblong clusters at the junction of leaf-stem with plant-stem, and *not* in a distinct terminal cluster ; 3–5 rays in a single flower-head, $\frac{1}{16}$ inch broad, quite long, and very light golden yellow. 1–3 feet high. Common on shaded banks, and margins of woods, everywhere.

Broad-leaved Golden-rod
Solidago latifolia
August–September

A similar species, but with broad, olive green, feather-veined leaves pointed at both ends ; the stem lighter green, zig-zag, angled in section, and rarely branched. The light golden yellow flowers in small clusters (like *S. cæsia*), with but 3–4 rays. 1–3 feet high. Rich, moist, wooded banks. Me., south to Ga., west to S. Dak. Found in the Catskill Mountains.

White Golden-rod or Silver-rod
Solidago bicolor
August–September

A very common species ; the only one with white flowers. Leaves elliptical, feather-veined, rough-hairy, very lightly toothed, and dark olive green above, the ribs beneath hairy. Stem simple or branched, upright, and gray-hairy. Tubular florets cream yellow, surrounded by 3–12 *white* rays ; flower-clusters mignonettelike, small, and at the leaf-junctions or crowded in a cylindrical terminal spike. 10–30 inches high. On dry barren ground. Me., south to Ga., and west to Minn. and Mo. A yellow-flowered

Feather-veined leaf
as in S. rugosa.

Three-veined leaf.
as in S. serotina

Solidago cæsia.

form, var. *concolor*, has yellow rays, and densely woolly stem and leaves. Commoner far north, south to Ga., Wis., and Minn.

Large=leaved Golden=rod
Solidago macrophylla
July– September

A northern species mostly confined to damp, rocky woods. The deep green leaves are ovate, thin, sharply toothed, feather-veined, and very long-stemmed. Leaf- and plant-stem usually smooth, but the latter sometimes fine-hairy at the top. Flower-heads nearly ½ inch long, with 8–10 long golden yellow rays. 1–4 feet high. Wooded hillsides. Me. (Aroostook Co.), to northern N. H. and N. Y., south to the Catskill Mountains, and west to Lake Superior.

Alpine Golden= rod
Solidago Vir- gaurea var. *alpina*
August– September

A dwarf alpine form confined to moun- tain-tops and about 8 inches high. The large flowers, thickly clustered at the sum- mit of the stout simple stem, with about 12 rays. Leaves usually obovate and finely toothed. Mountain summits of Me., N. H. (Mt. Washington), and N. Y., and shores of Lake Superior.

Seaside Golden=rod
Solidago sempervirens
August– November

A species frequenting salt-marshes and sea-beaches. Stem stout and smooth ; flower-cluster large, leafy, short, and straight, with large showy flowers having 7–10 deep golden yellow rays. Leaves lance-shaped, smooth, toothless, and with 3–5 obscure nerves. 2–8 feet high. Me. to Fla.

Bog Golden=rod
Solidago uliginosa
August– September

The stem stout and smooth ; leaves smooth, lance-shaped, obscurely seven- veined, slightly toothed or toothless ; those at the root very long. The flowers are light golden yellow, with 5–6 small rays, and are crowded on the wandlike or straight stem. 2–4 feet high. Me. to northern N. J. and Pa., west to Minn.

Showy Golden=rod
Solidago speciosa
August– October

A handsome, stocky plant with a ruddy, stout, smooth, round (in section) stem, and large, smooth, firm, feather-veined, olive green leaves, rough-edged or obscurely toothed ; the upper ones oblong lance- shaped, the lower ovate. Flower-heads

Seaside Golden-rod.   Solidago sempervirens.

with about 5 large golden yellow rays and prominent stamens ; the showy flower-cluster is dense, branched, and somewhat pyramidal in outline. 3–6 feet high. Rich ground and copses. Me., south to N. Car. and Ky., and west to Minn. and Neb.

Sweet Golden=rod
Solidago odora
August– September

An anise-scented species, very odorous when crushed. Leaves bright green, smooth, indistinctly three-ribbed, shining, and dotted. The slender stem, often re-clining, is usually smooth, and nearly cylindrical in section. Flower-heads small, with 3–4 golden rays nearly ⅓ inch long. The flower-cluster one-sided. 2–3 feet high. In dry sandy soil. Me., south, and west to N. Y., Ky., and Tex.

Spreading Golden=rod
Solidago patula
August– October

Very common in swamps ; with stout stem (angled in section) and spreading branches. The large, rough, fine-toothed, feather-veined leaves smooth beneath. Flower-clusters small ; the rather large flowers with obtuse green scales and small rays. Me., south to Ga., and west to Minn., Mo., and Tex.

Rough– stemmed Golden=rod
Solidago rugosa
July– September

An exceedingly hairy or rough golden-rod, very common on wooded roadsides and margins of fields. Leaves dark green, feather-veined, very hairy, and deeply toothed. Stem hairy, straight, cylindri-cal, and thickly set with leaves. The flower-clusters small, weak in color, and terminating several branches also thickly set with leaf-lets ; the flower-heads light golden yellow ; 6–9 rays and 4–7 tubular florets. The plant often branched like an elm at the top, but presenting a variety of forms. 1–7 feet high. Dry ground everywhere.

Elm–leaved Golden=rod
Solidago ulmifolia

A like species with but few differences, viz.: Stem slender, smooth or woolly at the summit, leaves thin, pointed, and ta-pering toward the base. Flowers with about four deep yellow rays, the scales long lance-shaped. 2–4 feet high. Common in low moist copses or woods, from Me., south to Ga., west to Minn., Mo., and Tex.

Solidago rugosa.

Swamp Golden-rod
Solidago neglecta
August–September

A smooth species common in swamps in the north. The upper leaves long lance-shaped, few-veined, and nearly toothless, the lower ones sharply toothed, broader, and tapering to a stem. The flower-clusters rather thick and short, with crowded flowers of 3–8 small rays. 2–4 feet high. Me., south to Md., and west to Wis. and Ill.

Sharp-leaved Golden-rod
Solidago arguta
July–September

A common and very graceful species; one of the earliest golden-rods, with very light golden yellow flowers having 5–7 large rays and small, light green, obtuse scales. The flower-cluster plumelike and reclining. The stem angled, smooth, and angular in section, sometimes ruddy brown. Leaves deep green, indistinctly feather-veined, large, thin, and sharply coarse-toothed, generally elliptical lance-shaped, the upper ones nearly if not quite toothless. 2–4 feet high. Copses and rich thin woods, from N. H., south to Va., and west to S. Dak.

Early Golden-rod
Solidago juncea
July–September

Another very common, slender species often found in company with the foregoing and blooming a little later. Leaves smooth, yellow olive green, and slightly three-ribbed, the upper ones toothless, the lower broad lance-shaped, with sharp and spreading teeth; a tiny leaf-wing grows at either side of each leaf-stem. The flower-clusters are spread somewhat like an elm in larger plants; but in the smaller ones they are one-sided. The golden yellow flowers about $\frac{1}{8}$ inch long, with 8–12 small rays. 2–4 feet high. On dry rocky banks and roadsides. Me., south to N. Car., west to Mo.

Late Golden-rod
Solidago serotina
August–October

A common but by no means a late-flowering golden-rod, generally distinguished for the plumlike lilac bloom (but sometimes light green) of its straight, smooth, dignified stem, which is perfectly cylindrical in section. Leaves dark green, plainly three-ribbed, smooth, and toothed only along the upper half of the edge, narrow and sharp-pointed. The stems of the flower-heads are covered with tiny white hairs;

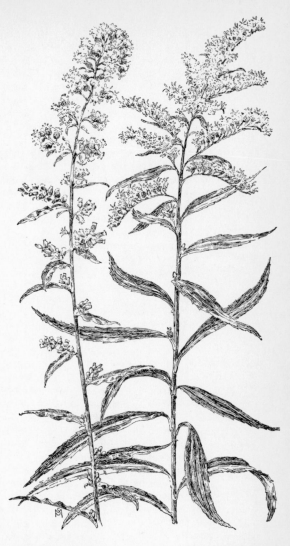

White Golden-rod.   Late Golden-rod.
Solidago bicolor.   Solidago serotina.

the flowers small, light golden yellow, 7–15 long rays. The flower-cluster is generally cylindrical, but bending at the top of the unbranched stem. 3–7 feet high, but seldom tall. Copses and dry roadsides, everywhere.

Canada Golden-rod
Solidago Canadensis
Golden yellow
August– October

A tall, stout, coarse species with lance-shaped, dull olive green, sharply toothed, triple-ribbed leaves, rough above, a trifle woolly beneath, and tapering to a point at either end, the uppermost leaves nearly toothless. The flower-heads are small, with 5–15 short rays; the greenish golden yellow clusters plumelike and large, but not striking. 3–7 feet high. Common everywhere (except at the seaside) in copse borders and on roadsides in dry situations. Quite variable; the var. *procera* with slightly toothed or toothless leaves rather gray-woolly beneath, and the var. *scabra* (N. Y. and Pa., south) also with leaves sparingly toothed or toothless, very rough above and hairy-veined beneath, the flower-heads somewhat larger.

Gray Golden-rod
Solidago nemoralis
August– October

One of the most brilliant of all the golden-rods. A rather low, late-flowering species remarkable for its rich deep golden yellow flowers and its simple, unbranched, green-gray stem, which with the leaves is covered with minute grayish hairs. The leaves are three-ribbed, dull olive green, rough, thick, dull-toothed, and generally broad lance-shaped, somewhat wider at the farther end, the lower ones tapering to a stem; little leaflets are on either side of the bases of the larger leaves. Flowers with 5–9 rays, the cluster generally forming a thickly set one-sided plume. 6–25 inches high. Common everywhere, beside sandy roads and in dry pastures, except at the seaside.

Hard-leaved Golden-rod
Solidago rigida
August– October

A less common species distinguished for its spreading, *flat-topped* cluster, which is usually quite thick. The stout, leafy stem is covered with dense fine hairs; the rough, thick, narrowly oval leaves, feather-veined and extremely rigid, the upper ones broad at the base and clasping at the stem, toothless or nearly so. The large flower-heads with about 30

Canada Golden-rod. Solidago Canadensis.

tubular florets and 6–10 large rays. 2–5 feet high. Dry soil, Mass., south to Ga., and west to Minn. and S. Dak.

Lance-leaved Golden-rod
Solidago lanceolata
August–early October

A slightly fragrant species, distinctly different from all the foregoing. The very small flowers in a *flat-topped* cluster, and the *very small*, toothless, lance-shaped, narrow willowlike, light green leaves with 3–5 ribs and very rough edges. The stem is straight, angular in section, with the ridges minutely rough, and terminates in a thin, wiry-branched flower-cluster not at all showy in color; the tiny flower-heads in small crowded groups; 12–20 minute rays. 2–4 feet high. On river-banks, borders of damp woods, or in moist situations, everywhere.

Slender Golden-rod
Solidago tenuifolia

A somewhat similar, resinously fragrant species; the difference apparent in the slenderer, smoother stem and the very narrow, linear, dotted leaves, commonly one-ribbed. The tiny flower-heads, with 6–12 rays, in numerous groups of 2–3, forming a flat-topped cluster 15–18 inches high. In dry sandy soil mostly near the coast. Mass., south, and west to Ill.

The genus *Aster*, named from ἀστήρ, a star, is a varied and beautiful, late-flowering tribe which, with *Solidago*, monopolizes the roadsides and byways in autumn. The species are distinguished apart in much the same way as in *Solidago*. The ray-florets are pistillate, the tubular florets (upon the disc) perfect, with a five-parted yellow corolla, which with age turns dull magenta. Fertilized mostly by honeybees, bumblebees, and the beelike flies. All the asters yield an abundance of nectar.

White Wood-land Aster
Aster divaricatus
White September–October

A small white aster, not showy but common in thin woods. The stem is rather smooth, a trifle zig-zagged, and quite slender; the olive green leaves are coarsely toothed, slender-stemmed, heart-shaped, sharp-pointed, and smooth. The white flowers, as broad as a "nickel," have only 6–9 rays; the disc-flowers turn madder purple with age. 1–2 feet high. Me., south to Ga., and west.

Lance-leaved Golden-rod. Solidago lanceolata.

COMPOSITE FAMILY. *Compositæ.*

Large-leaved Aster
Aster macrophyllus
Lilac
August–September

A stout, stiff, purplish-stemmed species with few, rough, large, 4–8 inches long, closely toothed, basal leaves, the upper ones ovate, almost stemless, and sharp-pointed. Flowers about an inch broad, with 10–16 bluish lilac, or rarely lilac-white, rays; disc-flowers turning madder brown with age. 2–3 feet high. Common in damp thin woods or on dry banks. Me., south to S. Car., west to Minn.

Showy Aster
Aster spectabilis
Violet
August–October

A very handsome species found only near the coast, with but few showy, deep blue-violet flowers about as broad as a fifty-cent piece, with 15–25 rays often ¾ inch long. The olive green leaves, mostly toothless, are oblong lance-shaped and rough. The stiff, generally simple stem, 1–2 feet high, is slightly rough below. Sandy soil. Mass. to Del.

Rough-leaved Aster
Aster radula
Violet
August–September

A low slender species with few large, violet-blue flowers and a rough stem and leaf, the latter dark green, stemless, sharply toothed, strongly veined, and oblong lance-shaped. The upper leaves closely clasp the stem. The flowers with about 22 rays nearly ⅓ inch long. 1–2 feet high. In wet situations and moist shady copse borders. Me., south to Del. and the Pocono Mts., Pa., generally near the coast. A dwarf form, var. *strictus*, has nearly entire leaves and usually solitary flowers; White Mountains, N. H.

New England Aster
Aster Novæ-Angliæ
Purple or magenta
August–October

A familiar and common species with numerous handsome flowers about an inch broad, which vary from light violet to light purple or white, and in the var. *roseus* to magenta. The stem stout, branched, and rough; the olive green, soft-hairy leaves lance-shaped, toothless, thin, and clasping the stem by a broad base rounded at either side. The flowers, rarely larger than a silver quarter, have usually 30–40 narrow rays, and terminate the branches in large clusters. 2–6 feet high or higher. Frequently cultivated; common northward, and south to S. Car.

Aster spectabilis   Aster radula.

COMPOSITE FAMILY. *Compositæ.*

Spreading Aster
Aster patens
Light violet-purple
August-October

A common species on dry ground, with ovate-oblong, stemless leaves, heart-shaped at the base and clasping the main stem, toothless or nearly so, but rough on the edge and on the upper surface. Stem rough-hairy, slender, and widely branched. Flowers with 20–30 light violet-purple rays nearly ½ inch long, and spreading, pointed, green tips beneath. 1–3 feet high. In dry open places, from Mass., south, and west to northern N. Y. and Minn.

Wavy-leaved Aster
Aster undulatus
Light violet
September-October

An aster easily recognized by its remarkable *broad-stemmed* leaf, which is heart-shaped where it clasps the plant-stem; some leaves are pointed heart-shaped, and the upper ones have an undulating margin. Stems stiff and very rough. Flowers light blue-violet, with 9–15 rays. 1–3 feet high. In dry places and on shaded roadsides. Common everywhere.

Heart-leaved Aster
Aster cordifolius
Lilac or lighter
September-October

A familiar, *small-flowered* aster with variable leaves. Stem slender, smooth, and much branched; the light green leaves rough or fine-hairy, and usually pointed heart-shaped with large sharp teeth; the upper ones short-stemmed or stemless, ovate or lance-shaped. The lilac or blue-lavender flowers, about ⅝ inch broad, with 10–20 rays, are crowded in dense clusters like those of the lilac; the disc-florets turn magenta or madder purple with age. This aster presents a great variety of forms; there is one among the foothills of the White Mountains, Campton and Plymouth, scarcely 8 inches high, with white flowers and smooth, narrow, lance-shaped leaves; the established var. *Furbishiæ* (Fernald) is distinguished for its long soft-hairy stem and leaf-stalks, the leaves somewhat so beneath; northern Maine. Also Dr. Britton recognizes several other varieties. 1–4 feet high. Common everywhere.

Heart-leaved Aster.   Aster cordifolius.

Arrow-leaved Aster
Aster sagittifolius
Light violet
August-October

A rather northern species. The stem stiff, erect, and with nearly upright branches. The light olive green leaves thin, broad lance-shaped, and sparingly toothed toward the top of the stem, but somewhat arrow-shaped lower down. The small, light violet flowers are not showy; there are 10–14 rays about $\frac{1}{4}$ inch long. 2–4 feet high. In dry soil. Me., south to Ky., west to Pa., and N. Dak.

Smooth Aster
Aster lævis
Light violet
September-October

Variable but handsome, with light violet or paler blue-violet flowers about an inch broad, and nearly if not entirely toothless, smooth, light green leaves, lance-shaped, stemless, and clasping the plant-stem with a somewhat heart-shaped base. The flowers with 15–30 rays. Stem 2–4 feet high, smooth, and sometimes covered with a light bloom. Dry soil, roadsides, and borders of woods; common everywhere.

Michaelmas Daisy or Heath Aster
Aster ericoides
White
September-November

A tiny white aster common in southern New York, New Jersey, and Pennsylvania. Stem generally smooth and closely set above with tiny, heathlike, linear, light green leaves, the few basal ones blunt lance-shaped and slightly toothed; all are rather rigid. The tiny white flowers with yellow discs are like miniature daisies; there are 16–24 narrow rays sometimes lightly tinted with magenta. This aster has spread beyond its original limits through cultivation by bee-keepers; its yield of nectar is large, and it is an especial favorite of the honeybee. 1–3 feet high. Common in dry fields and on roadsides, from Me., south, and west from south N. Eng. to Wis. and Ky.

Many-flowered Aster
Aster multiflorus
White or lilac-white
September-November

Another tiny-flowered aster, with hairy, often brownish stems. The tiny, linear, light green leaves are fine-hairy or rough. The dense flower-clusters are crowded with white or lilac-white flowers scarcely $\frac{1}{2}$ inch broad, with 12–20 rays. Stems bushy. 1–4 feet high. Common in dry open places, from southern N. Eng., south and west. Rare in Me., and absent in northern N. H.

Aster ericoides.

Bushy Aster
Aster dumosus
White or lilac=white
August–October

A similar species with fine linear leaves, and loose-flowering branches, the stem slightly fine-hairy, and sometimes brownish, or the whole plant quite smooth. The little flowers, with 15–25 white or pale lilac rays, are rather larger than those of the next species. 1–3 feet high. Dry sandy soil. Mass., and Conn., south and west to S. Dak. and Mo.

Small White Aster
Aster vimineus
White
August–September

A white-flowered species with larger linear, or narrow lance-shaped leaves, the largest ones slightly sharp-toothed. Stem and leaves nearly if not quite smooth, the stem often reddish, its branches *almost horizontal*. The tiny flowers with numerous white rays. The flowering branches very short, and minutely leafy. 2–4 feet high. Common in moist places and on river-banks, from southern N. Eng., south, and west to Minn., and Ark. The var. *foliolosus* is very leafy and the branches turn *upward;* the linear leaves are toothless, and nearly 2 inches long. The flowers in a *very* loose cluster. 2–5 feet high. From Jaffrey, N. H., south to Va., and west to Mo.

Calico Aster
Aster diffusus
Light purple or white
August–October

An exceedingly common and variable species, with a smooth, slender, sometimes magenta-stained stem, with straggling branches. The light green, lance-shaped leaves sparingly toothed, and larger than any of those of the species immediately preceding. The little flowers scarcely $\frac{1}{2}$ inch across, with numerous light purple or lilac or white rays ; the disc-florets a deeper purple. 1–5 feet high. In dry fields, and copses. Me., south to N. Car., west to S. Dak. and La.

Tradescant's Aster
Aster Tradescanti
White
August–October

A slender-stemmed, much-branched white aster, with numerous flowers about $\frac{5}{8}$ inch broad, and with long lance-shaped leaves, the lower ones slightly toothed, smooth on both sides, thin, and tapering to a sharp point. The small flowers with white or lilac-white rays clustered about the short upward-turned branches. 2–4 feet high. In wet fields and swamps, Me., south, and west to Minn.

New York Aster.
Aster Novi-Belgii.

Tradescant's Aster.
Aster Tradescanti.

Panicled White Aster
Aster paniculatus
White
August–October

A very tall species with white or lilac-white flowers a trifle larger than a "nickel," borne in somewhat flat-topped, loose or scattered clusters ; the leaves dark green, very nearly if not quite smooth, long lance-shaped, and obscurely toothed ; the upper ones toothless. The stout, much-branched stem is 3–8 feet high. Common on low moist ground and borders of copses, in half shade, everywhere.

Long-leaved Aster
Aster longifolius
Light violet
August–October

A northern species with remarkably narrow, toothless (or nearly so) leaves 3–8 inches long, and pale violet or light purple flowers as large as a silver quarter. The flower-envelop is encircled with many little acute scales strongly curled backward. 1–3 feet high. In swamps and low ground. Northern N. Eng., west to Minn. and Mont.

New York Aster or Willow-leaved Blue Aster
Aster Novi-Belgii
Lilac or blue-violet
August–October

Flowers large pale violet, lilac or blue-violet, with 15–24 rays, nearly $\frac{1}{2}$ inch long. The stemless, usually toothless light green leaves are thin, long, and smooth, or the small upper ones clasping the stem, the lower very slightly toothed. 10–35 inches high. Gray calls this the "commonest late-flowered aster of the Atlantic border, and very variable" ; but throughout New Hampshire *A. puniceus* is far commoner. The variations of *A. Novi-Belgii* are—var. *lævigatus*, smooth throughout, with the upper leaves clasping the stem by an abrupt base ; N. Eng. and east.: var. *litoreus*, rigid, low, with thick, smooth leaves, the upper ones clasping the stem by a heart-shaped base ; salt marshes south to Ga.

Aster prenanthoides
Pale violet
September–October

A northern species. The upper part of the stem is hairy in lines, and occasionally brownish ; the rough (but smooth beneath), ovate lance-shaped leaves are contracted at the base to a long wide-stemlike figure finally heart-shaped at the plant-stem. The flowers, about as large as a silver quarter, are pale violet or nearly lilac-white. 1–3 feet high. Margins of woods and banks of streams. Newfane, Vt. to Pa., Iowa, and Wis.

Purple-stemmed Aster.　　　Aster puniceus.

COMPOSITE FAMILY. *Compositæ.*

Purple-stemmed Aster
Aster puniceus
Light purple
August–October

A common species with usually *madder purple stem*, rough-hairy and stout. The light green leaves, lance-shaped or narrower, sparingly and coarsely toothed, clasp the upper branches. Flowers about the size of a silver quarter or larger, light violet or light lilac-purple with 20–24 rays, the tubular florets yellow. 3–7 feet high. In moist places and swamps everywhere, and quite variable ; var. *compactus* (Fernald) is stout, hairy, the thick leaves a trifle diamond-shaped but very narrow, coarsely toothed. The flowers compactly clustered ; West Somerville, Mass., also New Haven, Conn. Var. *firmus*, with smooth, green stem, slightly rough above. Var. *lucidulus* smooth, with lance-shaped toothless (nearly so), shining leaves.

Aster umbellatus
White

A common aster in moist thickets, and the borders of damp woods. With few narrow white rays which are generally curved backward. The flowers are borne in flat-topped clusters. The small flowers numerous but not showy, the tubular florets purpling with age. The veiny leaves, long lance-shaped and sparingly toothed, extend to the top of the plant. 2–7 feet high. Common northward in shaded and moist places.

Aster linariifolius
Light violet
September–October

A small species with linear leaves, one-ribbed, rough-edged, without teeth, and rigid. The rather large solitary flowers light violet or rarely lilac-white. 1–2 feet high. Common everywhere in dry situations.

Sharp-leaved Wood Aster
Aster acuminatus
White or lilac-white
August–September

A low *woodland* species with large, scrawny flowers having 10–16 narrow white or lilac-white rays, and generally magenta tubular florets. The large, sharp-pointed, coarse-toothed dark green leaves, thin, and broad lance-shaped, tapering to both ends, often arranged nearly in a circle beneath the few long-stemmed flowers. 10–16 inches high. In cool rich woods. Me. and N. Y., south in the mountains to Ga. In the White Mountains.

Aster acuminatus.

COMPOSITE FAMILY. *Compositæ.*

Aster tenuifolius
Lilac=purple
September–October

A species confined to the salt marshes of the coast from Massachusetts southward. Stem very smooth and generally zig-zagged. The few leaves long linear, taper-ing to both ends, toothless, and thick or fleshy. The rather large flowers an inch broad or more, lilac-purple or paler, borne on a generally simple or slightly branched stem. 8–25 inches high.

Aster subulatus
Pale purple
August–October

A species similarly confined. The leaves linear lance-shaped, toothless, and flat, those on the branches very small and awl-shaped. The numerous, very small pale purple flowers with *very short rays* scarcely extending beyond the disc; the disc-florets purplish. 6–24 inches high. N. H. and Mass. to Va.

Horseweed or Butterweed
Erigeron Canadensis
White-green
June–October

A very common annual *weed*, and the most unattractive member of the genus. The white and green flower-heads are ex-tremely small, ¼ inch long; the rays do not spread, but connect in the form of a cylinder. The dark green leaves are lin-ear, remotely toothed or toothless, and the upper ones are often cut-lobed. The bristly hairy stem is 1–7 feet high. In barnyards and waste places everywhere.

Sweet Scabius or Daisy Fleabane
Erigeron annuus
White or lilac
June–September

An annual and asterlike species with a spreading - haired stem and coarsely toothed, lance-shaped leaves, the lower ones broader. The white or pale lilac flower-heads are about ½ inch broad, with a green-yellow disc. 1–4 feet high. A common weed northward in waste places. Me., west to S. Dak., and south to Va.

Daisy Fleabane
Erigeron strigosus
White
May–September

A singular common species; the hairs not spreading but close to the stem. The light green leaves are linear and toothless or nearly so, the lower ones broad at the tip. The little daisylike flowers are ½ inch broad, with a large green yellow disc; oc-casionally the white rays are lilac-tinged, and sometimes they are extremely short or altogether absent. 1–2 feet high. Common in fields and on roadsides everywhere.

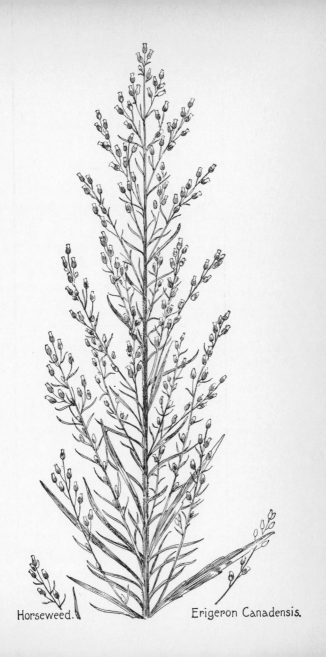

Horseweed.   Erigeron Canadensis.

COMPOSITE FAMILY. *Compositæ.*

Robin's Plantain
Erigeron bellidifolius
Lilac or pale violet
May–June

A rather large-flowered plant which is frequently communistic, tinting the roadside or field with its delicate lilac. The light olive green stem and leaves are *very* soft-hairy, the basal leaves broad at the tip and indistinctly toothed. The showy flowers, 1 inch broad, vary from lilac or magenta to a violet-purple; the somewhat green-yellow disc is broader than the fine rays are long. Fertilized by bumblebees and honeybees (the most frequent visitors) and butterflies. 10–22 inches high. Common everywhere.

Common Fleabane
Erigeron Philadelphicus

A similar but taller plant with light magenta or pale pink flowers and a soft-hairy (rarely smooth) stem; 1–2 feet high. Common throughout our range, but less frequent than *E. bellidifolius*, and blooming to August.

Everlasting or Pussy-toes
Antennaria plantaginea
White
May–June

A small plant with short white hairs; the three-ribbed basal leaves broad near the tip, the stalks nearly as long as the leaf. Upper stem leaves lance-shaped. The linear scales of the small, ¼ inch long flower-head are green or tawny at the base, and white or purplish at the tip. The outer bracts blunt and the inner ones acute. 4–18 inches high. Mass., south to La., and west. The var. *petiolata* is lower and slenderer, with ovate, blunt-pointed basal leaves on slender, long stalks. The calyx is more purple-tinged, with the bracts shorter and narrower. A familiar type of southern N. Eng., very common in eastern Mass. on dry slopes and open woods; also in dry fields of southern N. H.

Antennaria fallax
May–June

A species with larger flower-heads. The basal leaves gray soft-hairy above, and the *greenish* or *tawny* scales of the calyx have rather dry petallike tips. Northern N. Eng., south to La., and west.

Common Fleabane

COMPOSITE FAMILY. *Compositæ.*

Antennaria neodioica
May–middle July

A slender - stemmed and exceedingly *woolly* plant with very leafy basal shoots. The basal leaves about 1 inch long, blunt at the tip but with an abrupt sharp point, one-ribbed or indistinctly three - ribbed ; stem - leaves small and narrow. The flower-bracts with green or tawny bases and dry tips, the outer ones short and obtuse, the inner acutish or blunt. 6–16 inches high. On wooded slopes and dry shady places. Me. to Va., and Wis.

Antennaria neglecta
April– early May

The commonest species of southern New England (also in Franconia, N. H., and Farmington, Me.). A small plant with slender stem and runners. The one-ribbed basal leaves (at first silky-hairy above, but soon smooth) wedge-shaped or blunt lance-shaped, and indistinctly stalked ; the few stem-leaves linear. The head of the pistillate plant ⅜ inch long, with linear bracts greenish, brownish, or purplish below, and white at the tip. 8–12 inches high. Dry barren fields and sunny hillsides. N. Eng., south to Wash., D. C., and west.

Antennaria Canadensis
May–July

A common species with small linear lance - shaped leaves ; the *clear green*, smooth basal leaves, shaped like those of *A. neodioica*, a trifle hairy when very young. The white flower-bracts with dry tips. 6–22 inches high. Hillsides and pastures. Northern N. Eng., south to Mass., and west. (Vide *Rhodora*, vol. i., p. 150, article by M. L. Fernald.)

Pearly Everlasting
Anaphalis margaritacea
White
July– September

The most beautiful of the everlastings ; the linear leaves are sage green above and white beneath ; the flowers are globular, with miniature petallike white scales surrounding the central yellow staminate flowers, arranged not unlike the petals of a water-lily. Cross-fertilized mostly by moths and butterflies, though many other insects are common visitors. Staminate and pistillate flowers grow on separate plants. The stem is white and woolly, terminated by a flat cluster, sometimes 6 inches broad, of close-set flowers. 1–3 feet high. Common from Me., south to S. Car., and west to S. Dak.

Pussy-toes.
Antennaria neodioica.

See page 498.
Daisy Fleabane.   Erigeron strigosus.

COMPOSITE FAMILY. *Compositæ.*

Sweet Everlasting
Gnaphalium polycephalum
Cream white
August–September

A much less beautiful species, but one possessing an aromatic odor resembling that of slippery elm. The flowers cream white and ovoid, not expanding to the water-lily shape until the seed is ripe. The stem (much branched at the top) together with the linear leaves is velvety-hairy and delicate sage green. 12–25 inches high. Very common in dry open places and stony pastures everywhere. The name, from the Greek, means a tuft of wool.

Clammy Everlasting
Gnaphalium decurrens
Cream white
July–September

A similar fragrant species, but with a leafy, glandular-sticky stem, woolly and nearly white; the leaves are a little broader—linear lance-shaped, with a dense woolliness beneath; they partly clasp the stem. Flower-scales a yellowish cream white. 2–3 feet high. On dry or moist open hillsides or banks, from Me. to Pa. and Minn.

Low or Marsh Cudweed
Gnaphalium uliginosum
Brownish white
July–September

An insignificant low annual with white-woolly stem and linear, sharp-pointed leaves, rather broader at the tip. Flowers tiny, ovate, with brownish scales. The many-branched stems are 3–7 inches high. Common on low ground. Me., south to Va., and west to Minn. and Ill.

Elecampane
Inula Helenium
Deep yellow
July–September

One of the tall picturesque weeds characteristic of the Composite Family. Leaves olive yellow-green, white-veined, rough above, fine-hairy beneath, toothed, the lower ones stemmed, the upper ones partly clasping the plant-stem, which is woolly and often toned with purple-gray. The snowy but somewhat dishevelled flower, set amid flattish leaflets, has many narrow, curving, deep lemon yellow ray florets, which are pistillate, and a broad disc of central, tubular, perfect florets, at first yellow, and finally tan color. Cross-fertilized mostly by bumblebees, moths, and butterflies. Two or three flower-heads are grouped together at the termination of the stalk. 2–6 feet high. Naturalized from Europe; common northward, and south to Ga.

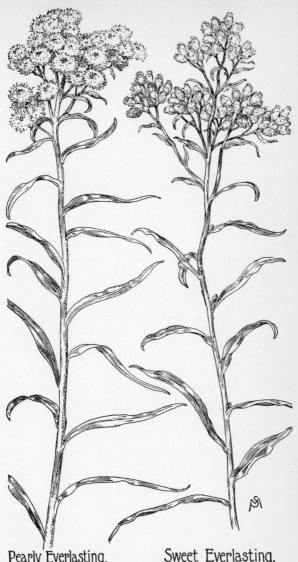

Pearly Everlasting.
Anaphalis margaritacea.

Sweet Everlasting.
Gnaphalium polycephalum.

COMPOSITE FAMILY. *Compositæ.*

Great Ragweed
Ambrosia trifida
Green
July–September

Perhaps the tallest member of the Composite group, not excepting *Lactuca*. Stem stout, hairy or nearly smooth, and filled with a frostlike pith; leaves deeply three-lobed and sharp-pointed, the teeth irregular and acute. The insignificant small flowers form a terminal, pointed cluster (these are staminate), or spring from between the opposite-growing leaves and the stem (these are usually pistillate). William Hamilton Gibson records a ragweed 18 feet 4 inches long. Common in moist soil, occasional in Vt. and N. H.

Roman Wormwood or Hogweed
Ambrosia artemisiæfolia
Green
July–September

A common weed with remarkably ornamental, cut leaves resembling those of *Artemisia* (Composite Family). An annual with a much-branched, fine-hairy stem and thin, lifeless light green, dissected leaves. The slender spikes of the green staminate flowers are numerous and somewhat decorative. The tiny fruit is furnished with 6 short acute spines. 1–5 feet high. Troublesome in door-yards and gardens, everywhere.

Oxeye
Heliopsis lœvis
Yellow
August–September

Like the sunflower, with perfect ray- and disc-flowers, the 10 straplike rays rather showy; the stem and leaves smooth, the latter deep green, broad lance-shaped, three-ribbed, and toothed, growing oppositely. 3–5 feet high. In copses. N. Y., south, west to Ill.

Heliopsis scabra
June–September

A similar species, but distinguished by its rough stem and leaves, which are less narrowly pointed, and its somewhat larger flowers. 2–4 feet high. Me., N. J. to Ill.

Black Sampson or Purple Cone-flower
Echinacea purpurea
Magenta
July–September

A showy western species with handsome flowers whose light or deep magenta petals gracefully droop and are two-toothed at the tip. The disc is madder purple, its florets are perfect; the ray-flowers are pistillate but sterile. The five-ribbed, deep green lower leaves are rough, sharply toothed, and pointed ovate; the upper ones are stemless and toothless. Stem smooth or slightly hairy. 2–3 feet high. Rich soil, N. Y., Ill., Mich., south to Tex.

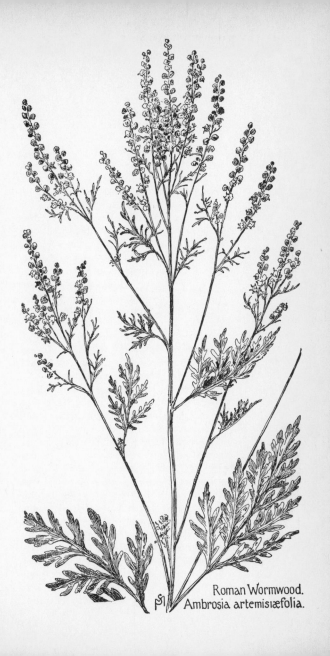

Roman Wormwood.
Ambrosia artemisiæfolia.

*Echinacea
pallida*

A similar species with the same magenta flowers and long lance-shaped leaves, very rough, without teeth, and three-ribbed. The flowers are a deeper color when they at first expand. Rare on roadsides and fields in N. Eng., where it has come from the west; Ill. and Ala., west to Minn., Neb., and Tex. The name from ἐχῖνος, hedgehog.

**Tall Cone-
flower**
*Rudbeckia
laciniata*
Golden yellow

A closely allied species with golden yellow flowers whose rays droop; the central green-yellow cone, at first hemispherical, is finally elongated and brown. Nearly smooth, deep green leaves, the lowest compound, the intermediate irregularly 3–5-parted, the uppermost small and elliptical. Fertilized mostly by the bees; among the bumblebees, *Bombus separatus* and *Bombus americanorum* are frequent visitors. The branching stems 3–10 feet high. In moist thickets, Vt. and N. Y., south and west. Named for Professors Rudbeck.

*Rudbeckia
triloba*
**Golden yellow
August**

Flower-disc purple-brown, at first hemispherical, and afterward oblong-ovoid; about 8–10 golden yellow rays, deeper at the base, and somewhat long-oval. Upper leaves rough, thin, bright green, ovate lance-shaped, lower ones three-lobed, tapering at the base, and coarsely toothed. Stem hairy, much branched, and many-flowered; the flowers small, about 2 inches broad. 2–5 feet high. On dry or moist ground. N. J., south to Ga., west to Mich., S. Dak., and La.

**Black=Eyed
Susan or
Cone-flower**
*Rudbeckia
hirta*
**Deep golden
yellow
June-August**

A biennial. The commonest eastern species, although its seed originally came from the west mixed with clover seed. Both stem and leaves are very rough and bristly; the former *exceedingly tough*, the latter dull olive green, lance-shaped, toothless or nearly so, and scattered along the rigid stem; the lower leaves broader at the tip and three-ribbed. The deep gold yellow rayflowers are neutral without stamens or pistils; they curl backward; the disc is madder purple, and the tiny florets encircle it in successive bloom, creating a zone of yellow when the pollen is ripe; later the stigmas are matured,

Purple Cone-flower. Echinacea pallida.

and cross-fertilization takes place by the agency of insects or the wind. The smaller bees (*Halictus*), the bumblebee (*Bombus vagans*), and the smaller butterflies are constant visitors. 1–2 feet high. Common in dry or sandy meadows. Me., west to S. Dak., and southward.

Helianthus annuus
The common garden sunflower; an annual with generally three-ribbed and heart-shaped leaves, and golden yellow flowers, 1–10 inches broad. 2–12 feet high. Everywhere.

Tall Sunflower
Helianthus giganteus
Yellow
August–September
A tall species with a rough dull magenta stem and rough, bright green, lance-shaped leaves, pointed and finely toothed, nearly stemless, the upper ones quite stemless, and all growing alternately, but rarely some growing oppositely. The light yellow flowers about 2 inches broad, with 10–20 rays; the disc dull yellow, with perfect florets, and the rays neutral, that is, without stamens or pistil. 3–12 feet high. Common in swamps and on the borders of wet meadows, from Me., south, and west to Neb.

Small Sunflower
Helianthus parviflorus
Yellow
July–September
A southerly species with many very small flowers ½–1 inch broad. The stem slender and generally branched; leaves mostly opposite, broad lance-shaped, toothed, rough, and short-stemmed. Flowers with 5–10 yellow rays. 3–6 feet high. Common in thickets and on the borders of woods. Pa., south to Ga., and west to Mo.

Woodland Sunflower
Helianthus divaricatus
A slender, smooth-stemmed species (a trifle fine-hairy above) with opposite lance-shaped, toothed, roughish, three-ribbed, and nearly or quite stemless leaves 3–7 inches long. The yellow flowers, 2 inches broad, are few or solitary. 2–5 feet high. Common in thickets and on borders of woods. Me., south, and west to Neb.

Helianthus strumosus
A species similar in aspect, color, situation, and time of bloom; but the stem very smooth below, and often with a bloom; the leaves rough above, and pale (sometimes minutely hairy) beneath. Flowers with 5–15 rays. 3–6 feet high. Me., south to Ga., but mostly west to Minn. and Ark.

Ten-petaled Sunflower.
Helianthus decapetalus.

COMPOSITE FAMILY. *Compositæ.*

Ten=petaled or Thin=leaved Sunflower
Helianthus decapetalus
Yellow August– September
A rather showy species having 10–12 rays, with many pure yellow or deeper yellow flowers 2–3 inches broad. The slender tall stem is rough above and smooth below; the deep green leaves are broad lance-shaped, a trifle rough, thin, and short-stemmed; they grow oppositely. 2–5 feet high. Borders of copses and low damp woods. Me., south to Ga., and west to Mich. Found in Campton, N. H.

Jerusalem Artichoke
Helianthus tuberosus
Golden yellow September– October
A species extensively grown for its edible roots, now running wild in fence rows and roadsides. The name Jerusalem is a corruption of the Italian *Girasole*, sunflower. Stem stout and rough-hairy; the ovate lance-shaped, three-ribbed, rough leaves grow oppositely (a few upper ones alternately). The golden yellow flowers, sometimes 3 inches broad, have 12–20 rays. 5–12 feet high. Damp soil. Me., south to Ga., and west to S. Dak. and Ark.

Beggar-ticks or Stick-tight
Bidens frondosa
Rusty green July–October
An uninteresting weed with rayless, bristly flower - heads, indeterminate in color, approaching rusty green, surrounded by little leaflets; the branching stem purplish. Leaves of 3–5 divisions, toothed and lance - shaped. Seed - vessels two-pronged (the prongs toothed), less than $\frac{1}{4}$ inch long, and sepia brown; attaching readily to woolly animals or clothing. 1–8 feet high. Common everywhere in moist soil. The name, from *bis* and *dens*, means two-toothed, or a kind of hoe with two prongs.—Virgil. The specific name, from *frondosus*, means *full of leaves.*

Smaller Bur Marigold
Bidens cernua
Yellow July–October
A species with very narrow lance-shaped smooth leaves, coarsely and sharply toothed. The similar, bristly, half globular, rusty flowers generally nod; the rays, if any, are short and small. The seed-vessels are narrower and four-pronged. 6–36 inches high. In wet soil. Me., south to Va., west to Mo. and S. Dak.

Jerusalem artichoke.   Helianthus tuberosus,

COMPOSITE FAMILY. *Compositæ.*

Larger Bur Marigold
Bidens Chrys-anthemoides
Yellow
August–October

A more attractive species with light golden yellow rays, which, when *perfect*, are rather showy. The flowers sometimes over 2 inches broad. Leaves narrow lance-shaped and coarsely toothed. Seed-vessels with 2–4 prongs. 10–24 inches high. In swamps and wet places. N. Eng., south, and west to Minn. All three species are annuals.

Sneezeweed
Helenium autumnale
Yellow
August–September

A nearly smooth plant with toothed, lance-shaped, alternate leaves and decoratively handsome flowers, 1–2 inches broad, with the toothed, golden yellow rays turned considerably backward; the globular disc is yellow and chaffy, the drooping petals pistillate and fertile; cross-fertilized mostly by bees. 2–6 feet high. Common in wet meadows and on river-banks everywhere.

Mayweed or Chamomile
Anthemis Cotula
White
June-October

A daisylike flower about an inch broad, with white, three-toothed, neutral rays (i. e., without stamens or pistils) and a yellow disc, which becomes elongated with age. The small leaves, cut and slashed to absolute formlessness, are remarkable for their disagreeable odor and acrid taste ; used in making a horrible concoction called "chamomile tea." 8–20 inches high. Common about dwellings and on roadsides everywhere ; a native of Europe.

Yarrow or Milfoil
Achillea Millefolium
Gray-white
June-October

A very familiar roadside weed adventive from Europe, with remarkable gray olive green, feathery, dissected, stemless leaves of a rather long-oval outline, and pleasantly aromatic, minute, grayish white flowers in flat-topped clusters. The gray-green, stout, and tough stem is fine-hairy. The perfect disc-florets are at first yellowish, but finally gray-brown ; the 4–6 pistillate rays are white, or rarely crimson-pink. Fertilized mostly by bees and the smaller butterflies ; chief among the latter is the yellow *Colias philodice*. 1–2 feet high. Common everywhere, by the wayside and in fields ; probably native in the west, where it is more fine-hairy and less green.

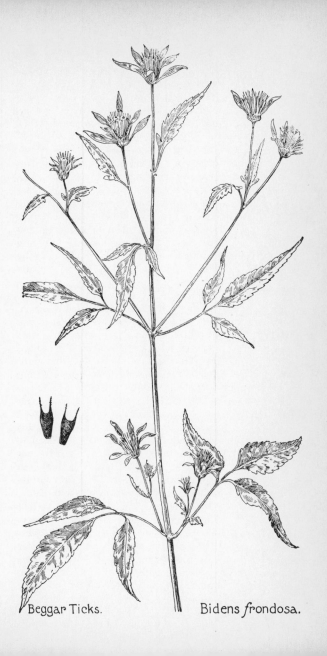

Beggar Ticks.   Bidens *frondosa*.

COMPOSITE FAMILY. *Compositæ.*

Oxeye Daisy
*Chrysanthe-
mum Leucan-
themum*
**White
June–
September**

The commonest of all common weeds of the field and wayside, often called Farmer's Curse, yet a prime favorite with children and artists! The flower's form is a *summum bonum* of simplicity and decorative beauty. The orange-yellow disc, depressed in the centre, is formed of perfect flowers ; the white rays are pistillate. The dark green leaves are ornamentally lobed. 15–25 inches high. The name, from the Greek, means golden flower.

Feverfew
*Chrysanthe-
mum Par-
thenium*
**White
June–
September**

A tall, branching species commonly cultivated, with small daisylike flowers in generous clusters ; the stem smooth, the ornamental leaves broad and deeply lobed. Flowers small, with large yellow discs of perfect florets. 1–2 feet high. Naturalized from Europe, and mostly an escape from gardens. Mass. to N. J., and west to Wis.

Tansy
*Tanacetum
vulgare*
**Orange-yellow
July–
September**

A common weed naturalized from Europe, generally an escape from gardens belonging to old dwellings. The flatly clustered dull orange-yellow flower-heads resemble those of the daisy minus the white rays ; inner florets perfect and marginal ones pistillate. The compound, deep green leaves, ornamentally toothed and cut, are strongly aromatic. 18–30 inches high. Me., south to N. Car., west to S. Dak.

**Tall
Wormwood**
*Artemisia
caudata*
**Green-yellow
July–August**

A seaside weed with inconspicuous, tiny, green-yellow flowers in long slender clusters, the little flower-heads mostly nodding ; the marginal florets pistillate, the central ones perfect. The bitter-tasting, long, linear, deeply cut leaves with threadlike divisions. 2–5 feet high. Me., south, west to Neb.

Mugwort
*Artemisia
vulgaris*

A familiar, uninteresting weed naturalized from Europe, found in all waste places or near old houses. The smooth green leaves deeply cut, and with lobes coarsely toothed at the tips. The inconspicuous green-yellow flowers *erect*, not nodding, in a simple, leafy spike. 1–3 feet high. Me., south to N. J. and Pa., west to Mich.

Ox-eye
Daisy.   Feverfew.
Chrysanthemum leucanthemum. Chrysanthemum Parthenium.

COMPOSITE FAMILY. *Compositæ.*

Wormwood or Absinth
Artemisia Absinthium

A similar species with a similar environment. Leaves small and often deeply subdivided, covered with fine hairs so the color is a somewhat silvery green. The insignificant light yellow-green flowers are gathered in a scattering cluster. The long terminal spikes are rather dishevelled and picturesque. 2–4 feet high.

Arnica
Arnica Chamissonis
Pure yellow
June–September

A delicate, pure yellow, daisylike flower with 10–14 three-toothed rays, found only upon mountain summits of N. Eng. and N. Y., in moist situations. The deep green leaves long lance-shaped, slightly toothed, and stemless — at least the upper ones. The hairy stem 1–2 feet high. Also in the Rocky Mountains. Found in Oakes's Gulf, Mt. Washington.

Golden Ragwort
Senecio aureus
Deep gold yellow
May–July

An early blooming perennial with handsome deep golden yellow, daisylike flowers (8–12 rays) nearly an inch broad, in terminal clusters on the grooved, brown-streaked stem ; the disc-florets perfect, the rays pistillate. The thick root-leaves in early April resemble violet leaves ; they are small, heart-shaped, scallop-toothed, dark green above and magenta-red beneath ; later they become elongated. The long stem-leaves more or less deeply lobed, the uppermost small and clasping the plant-stem. The plant is woolly-hairy when young. 12–32 inches high. Common in wet meadows everywhere. Found at Clarendon Hills, Mass. *Senecio Balsamitæ* is lower, has fewer flowers, and the basal leaves are oblong, with the ruddy lower surfaces sometimes persistently woolly.

Fireweed
Erechtites hieracifolia
White
July–September

A tall, uninteresting, annual weed with generally smooth, rank-odored stem and leaves. The latter are thin, lance-shaped or broader, and irregularly toothed or deeply incised. The stem is full of sap, heavy, and grooved ; the insignificant flowers are brush-shaped, mostly green by reason of the superior flower-envelop, and tipped with the white of the tubular, fertile florets. 1–7 feet high. Common in burned-over clearings or waste places everywhere.

Golden Ragwort.   Senecio aureus.

COMPOSITE FAMILY. *Compositæ.*

Burdock
Arctium Lappa
Light magenta
July–October
A familiar, rank-odored weed, common in all waste places, with large, dull green, veiny leaves, the lower heart-shaped, the upper ovate; woolly beneath. The globular flower-head a hooked-bristled green bur with magenta or often nearly white, perfect, tubular florets with a five-cleft tip. The depth of color can only be appreciated with the aid of a magnifying glass. The stem is generally much branched. 4–8 feet high. About ruins of old dwellings or in waste places. Me. to southern N. Y., and west. Not so common as the next species in the more eastern States.

Smaller
Burdock
Arctium minus
Light magenta
July–October
A smaller species, with smaller, generally narrower leaves, the lower ones deeply heart-shaped, their stems hollow and hardly furrowed; flower-heads almost stemless on the branches, about ¾ inch broad. The inner spines erect and shorter than the lilac pink or light magenta or white florets. 2–5 feet high. Common. Both species are naturalized from Europe.

Common
Thistle
Cirsium
lanceolatum
Magenta
July–October
A biennial species naturalized from Europe, generally found in pastures. The narrow, white-spiny, dark green leaves hug the plant-stem for an inch or so with prickly wings, the upper surface prickly-hairy, the lower webby-woolly with light brownish fine hairs. The green flower-envelop is armed with spreading spines; the perfect, tubular florets, densely clustered, vary from (rarely white) crimson-magenta to light magenta; the pollen is white. Flowers remarkably sweet-scented, rich in honey, and fertilized mostly by the bumblebees (often becoming intoxicated) and butterflies. Heads sometimes 3 inches broad, generally solitary at the ends of the branches. 2–4 feet high. Common, but south only to Ga.

Yellow
Thistle
Cirsium
horridulum
Corn yellow
May–August
A species with light corn yellow (rarely magenta), flattish flower-heads nearly 3 inches broad; it is exceedingly plentiful in the salt marshes of Long Island and New Jersey. The oblong lance-shaped, light green leaves smooth, clasping, and

Small-leaved Burdock.   Arctium minus.

very yellow-spiny; the flower-heads set in the smaller encircling upper leaflets, with *very* narrow, rough, spineless scales. 2-4 feet high. Common in wet or dry sandy soil along the seacoast, from Me. to Tex.

Tall Thistle
Cirsium altissimum, var.
discolor
Magenta
July-October
A rather common species with magenta (rarely white) flowers about 1½ inches broad and weak-bristled, rough-hairy, stemless leaves, deeply cut into linear lobes, white-woolly beneath. The outer scales of the flower-heads are slightly woolly and weak-bristled. Stem downy, 3-6 feet high. Common on roadsides and in fields; south to Ga.

Swamp Thistle
Cirsium muticum
Magenta
July-October
A species with similar leaves and flowers, but the blunt, prickleless scales of the heads glutinous, woolly, and close-pressing. The flower with a naked stem, or with a few tiny leaflets at its base. 3-8 feet high. Common in swamps and moist low woodlands everywhere.

Pasture Thistle
Cirsium pumilum
Light magenta
July-September
The largest-flowered thistle of all, with solitary heads 2-3 inches broad, the florets light magenta-lilac or nearly white; they are exceedingly fragrant, rich in honey, and are frequented by the bumblebee, who imbibes to the point of abject intoxication! The slightly glutinous scales are nearly smooth and tipped with slender prickles; and at the base are tiny leaflets. The light green leaves narrow and frequently cut into three-prickled lobes, the prickles shorter than those of the common thistle and very numerous. Stem only 12-30 inches high. In dry pastures and fields, Me. to Del. and Pa., near the coast.

Canada Thistle
Cirsium arvense
Lilac or pale magenta
July-September
A pernicious weed, naturalized from Europe, with small lilac, pale magenta, or rarely white heads about ⅞ inch broad. The dull gray-green, whitish-ribbed leaves are deeply slashed into many very prickly, ruffled lobes. Flowers staminate and pistillate; also fragrant. 1-3 feet high. Common in pastures, fields, and on roadsides; south only to Va.

Canada Thistle.   Cirsium arvense.

COMPOSITE FAMILY. *Compositæ.*

**Dwarf
Dandelion**
*Krigia
Virginica*
**Golden yellow
May–August**

A small annual species of dandelion with many long, slender flower-stalks rising from a circle of small, irregularly lobed leaves, each stalk bearing a single golden yellow flower scarcely ¾ inch broad ; later it becomes branched and bears a few leaves. The hairy down of the seeds is short. 2–12 inches high. Common in dry soil or on sandy banks everywhere.

*Krigia
amplexicaulis*

A similar but tall perennial species with smooth stem covered with a slight bloom, and smooth basal leaves distinctly stalked, scarcely toothed, but with a wavy outline. A small leaflet clasps the flowering stem about half-way up ; from this proceed 2–5 branches bearing deep golden yellow flowers 1¼ inches broad. 1–2 feet high. Moist pastures and fields. Mass., south to Ga., west to Kan.

Fall Dandelion
*Leontodon
autumnalis*
**Light golden
yellow
July–
November**

A small dandelion, naturalized from Europe, with a long, branching flower-stalk, which is set with tiny bracts or scales about ½ inch apart. The blunt-lobed, narrow, small basal leaves are dull green and smooth. The light golden yellow flower erect in the bud about an inch broad, in twos or threes, or rarely solitary. The slender stalks of these dandelions above described are somewhat wiry, not tubular like those of the common spring dandelion. 7–18 inches high. In fields and along roadsides. Me. to Pa., Ohio, and Mich., and northward. Common in the vicinity of Boston. Name from the Greek for *lion* and *tooth.* The var. *pratensis* is similar, but the flower-envelop and the tip of the flower-stalk immediately below it are very fine-hairy. Me. to Conn., and Nantucket, Mass.

**Chicory or
Succory**
*Cichorium
Intybus*
**Violet-blue
July–October**

A very common but beautiful weed naturalized from Europe, found on roadsides and in waste places particularly about the seaboard towns. Stem stout, tough, and stiff, with generally lance-shaped, dark gray-green, coarse-toothed leaves. The violet-blue flower, similar in form to the

Chicory.
Cichorium Intybus.

Fall Dandelion.
Leontodon autumnalis.

dandelion, closes in rainy or cloudy weather and opens only in sunshine. There are few florets in a single head but these are highly developed with gracefully curved, branching styles; the exposure of the double stigmatic surface thus, in a measure, insures self-fertilization in the absence of insects. The most frequent visitors are the bees—the honeybee, the leaf-cutter bee (*Megachile*), and various species of *Halictus* and *Andrena*, ground bees. 1–3 feet high.

Tawny Hawkweed
Hieracium aurantiacum
Tawny orange
July–September

An odd but attractive plant, naturalized from Europe, with a stout stem, and a flower-cup closely covered with sepia brown hairs, the rusty character of which gave it the common name in England of Grim the Collier. The coarse, blunt, lance-shaped leaves covered with short gray hairs are nearly all at the base of the plant. The tawny orange flowers (with light golden pistils), strap-rayed and finely fringed at the edge, are grouped in a small terminal cluster, and are quite delicately fragrant. Visited by the bees *Halictus* and *Andrena*, and the smaller butterflies—*Pieris rapæ*, white, and *Colias philodice*, yellow. 7–16 inches high. In fields, woodlands, and along roads, from Me., south to Pa., and west to N. Y. Growing to be a troublesome weed in fields and pastures of northern Vermont.

Canada Hawkweed
Hieracium Canadense
Pure yellow
July–September

A generally smooth species; the light green, lance-shaped leaves with coarse and wide-spread teeth, and the dandelionlike, very small yellow flowers in a loose branching cluster terminating the leafy stem. In October the plant is decorated with tiny brown globes of down. 1–4 feet high. In dry woods northward, south only to N. J.

Hieracium paniculatum

A similar northern plant with a drooping-branched loose flower-cluster, generally smooth stem and lance-shaped leaves, and smaller yellow flowers. The thin leaves almost stemless, and very *slightly, if at all, toothed.* 1–3 feet high. South as far as Ga.

Canada Hawkweed.
Hieracium Canadense.

Tawny Hawkweed.
Hieracium aurantiacum.

Rattlesnake-weed
Hieracium venosum
Light gold yellow
June-September

An early flowering species, with deeper yellow flowers closely resembling small dandelions, and generally leafless (or with 1–3 tiny leaflets), few-haired stems, branching to a few-flowered cluster. The light green leaves are dull magenta on the ribs, edges, and under side ; they are hairy, scarcely toothed, and clustered at the root. 12–30 inches high. Common in woodlands and thickets northward, and south to Ga. Only occasional in Vermont and rare or absent in northern New Hampshire.

Hieracium scabrum

The simple stem stout, and remarkable for its hairy character. The obovate or very blunt obovate, almost toothless leaves are rough-hairy and light dull green. The small terminal flower-cluster with several small heads of yellow flowers (the floral envelop a hairy green) is conspicuously irregular and angular in its branching. 1–3 feet high. Common in dry woods north ; south to Ga.

Hieracium Gronovii

A similar plant with a slenderer stem, often ruddy, rough-hairy (slightly so above), and very leafy and hairy *below*. The leaves like *H. scabrum.* The seed-vessels very tapering at the summit. The blossoms open only in sunshine, and very quickly wither. 1–3 feet high. Dry soil ; commoner in the south. North only as far as Mass. and Ill. The name from ἱέραξ, a hawk.

Smooth-stemmed White Lettuce
Prenanthes racemosa
Dull lilac
August-September

A tall weed with inconspicuous, narrow flowers of a dull lilac tint, clustered in a rather narrow wandlike spike. The somewhat thickish light green leaves smooth and with a slight bloom, scarcely toothed, and blunt lance-shaped. The green floral envelop and its stalk are hairy. 2–5 feet high. In moist fields, Me., south to N. J., west to S. Dak., Mo., and Col.

Rattlesnake-root or White Lettuce
Prenanthes alba

A commoner and more interesting species with drooping, dull cream-colored flowers, occasionally touched with pale lilac; the green floral envelop has about 8 magenta-tinged sections; the stamens are

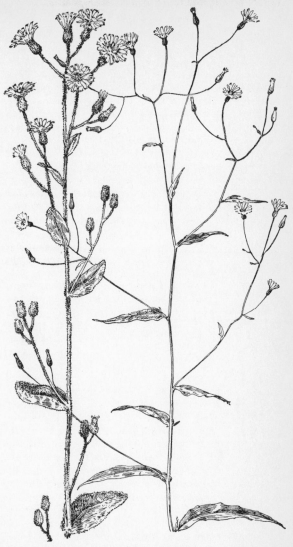

Hawkweed.

Hieracium scabrum.   Hieracium paniculatum.

**Dull cream
color
August-
September**

quite prominent and cream-colored. The smooth, deep green leaves are varied in form, the lower ones broad, three-sided, and remotely toothed, the upper ones deeply cut, and the uppermost lance-shaped with two small lateral lobes or none at all. The smooth stem is stiff, round, and generally dull, deep magenta-tinted, with a bloom. 2–4 feet high. Common in thin woods northward, and south to Ga. and Ky.

**Lion's-foot or
Gall of the
Earth
*Prenanthes
serpentaria*
Dull cream
color
July–
September**

A similar smooth species, the stem of which is green and without a bloom. The leaves also very variable, a trifle roughish, and shaped (but more angularly) like those of *P. alba*. The flower-cluster is inclined to be somewhat flat-topped, and the pendulous, bell-shaped, dull cream-colored flowers are enclosed in a somewhat bristly, hairy, green envelop, which is sometimes a trifle magenta-tinted. The curled branches of the style are slender and prominent, as in all the *Prenanthes*. 1–3 feet high, usually 2 feet. In thickets, or dry sandy ground, Mass. (rare) and N. Y., south to Ala. and Fla. *P. trifoliolata*, var. *nana* (Fernald), confined to alpine summits of N. Eng. (Mt. Katahdin) and N. Y., has deep madder brown flowers and variously shaped leaves. 4–12 inches high.

**Tall White
Lettuce
*Prenanthes
altissima*
Dull cream
color
July–
September**

A tall, generally smooth species, with a green or magenta-tinged stem. The leaves (except the uppermost) variously shaped but long-stalked. The numerous narrow, pendulous, dull cream-colored flowers with a smooth green envelop, are borne in a narrow terminal spike, or in small clusters at the leaf-angles. 3–7 feet high. In woodlands and thickets, northward, and south to Ga.

**Prenanthes
Bootii**

A dwarf species with stout, ruddy stem, large flower-heads, and thick, narrow, variously shaped leaves. Flowers whitish and fragrant, enclosed within a dull magenta-tinged envelop. 4–12 inches high. Alpine summits of N. Y. and N. Eng. Found on Mt. Washington, Oakes's Gulf.

Lion's-foot.　　　Prenanthes serpentaria.

Common Dandelion
Taraxacum officinale
Golden yellow
May–June

The familiar grass-plot, yellow flower of the country and city, naturalized from Europe. The heads are sometimes 2 inches broad, and are supported on a pale green, hollow stem; the perfect flowers are orange-gold in the centre of the head, and light golden yellow on the straps of the margin. The seeds are neutral brown, and spiny at the upper part. The deep green leaves are irregularly and angularly broad-toothed, the jagged edge bearing a remote resemblance to the row of teeth in a lion's jaw, hence the common name, a corruption of the French *dent-de-lion*. 3–14 inches high. The silky down forms a beautiful globe when the seeds ripen and the acute divisions of the flower-envelop are reflexed. Common everywhere.

Red-seeded Dandelion
Taraxacum erythrospermum

A similar but smaller species with flower-heads scarcely over an inch broad, pure yellow, but deeper in the centre; the two-pointed straps or bracts of the floral envelop usually have a thickened point or knob near the tip. The outermost straps are magenta-tinged; the smooth leaves are very deeply cut into thin, irregular, sharp, backward-tending lobes or narrow angular divisions. The seeds are bright *terra-cotta red*, and spiny over the upper half of the surface. Distribution unknown beyond N. Eng., N. Y., and Pa.

Wild Lettuce
Lactuca Canadensis
Pale yellow
June–September

A tall biennial species often 6 feet high, with a smooth, stout, leafy stem branching at the top in a thin, scattered flower-spike with insignificant pale yellow ray-flowers mostly enclosed within the green floral envelop. Both stem and leaves with a slight bloom; the leaves slightly like those of the dandelion, but the upper ones lance-shaped, and the lower sometimes 12 inches long. 4–10 feet high. Common in wet soil, northward, south to Ga. and La.

Lactuca integrifolia

A similar species with a broader flower-cluster, and oblong lance-shaped, smooth, acute leaves, toothless or nearly so. The flower-rays pale yellow or magenta-tinted. 2–6 feet high. In damp places. Me. to Ga., west to Neb.

Red-seeded
Dandelion.
Taraxicum erythrospermum

Common
Dandelion.
Taraxicum officinale.

COMPOSITE FAMILY. *Compositæ.*

Lactuca hirsuta

A less leafy and lower species, found in similar situations. The leaves like those of *L. Canadensis,* but fine-hairy ; the reddish stem hairy at the base ; the scattered flower-cluster with insignificant dull lilac, or dingy pink-white flowers. 2–4 feet high. Me., west to Minn., south to Ala. and Tex.

Tall Blue Lettuce
Lactuca leucophœa
Dull purple or white
July–September

The tallest member of the genus, with a stout, straight, smooth stem, leafy up to the straggling, large flower-cluster of insignificant flowers which are never fully expanded. The green flower-heads tipped with inconspicuous dull purplish or whitish rays. The deeply lobed leaves are large and irregularly wavy-toothed. 3–15 feet high. Damp shady places northward, south to S. Car.

Sow Thistle
Sonchus oleraceus
Light yellow
May–September

A tall annual, naturalized from Europe, with thistlelike prickle-edged leaves, and a stout, hollow, succulent, smooth, grooved stem. The large, decorative, usually lobed leaves are irregularly toothed and armed with soft spines ; the upper ones clasp the plant-stem, the lower are stalked. The light yellow, thistle-shaped flower-heads are grouped in a somewhat loosely spreading flat cluster. The stem is sometimes reddish at the base. 1–6 feet or more high. Common everywhere in waste places or manured soil.

Sonchus asper
Light yellow
May–September

Similar, but with less divided leaves, the lower ones blunt lance-shaped, the upper clasping the plant-stem by rounded lobes, all irregularly toothed and spiny. The light yellow downy, flat-headed flowers are set in a loose cluster ; they are succeeded by a copious white down. The seeds have long ribs, smooth between, while those of the preceding species are laterally rough between. The flowers are assisted in the process of fertilization by the *Syrphid,* beelike flies, and those of the genus *Eristalis.* The honeybee (*Apis mellifica*) is always a common visitor. Formerly the milk-juiced, succulent leaves were used as a pot herb. Waste places everywhere. The Greek name *Sonchus* (Sow Thistle) is a degrading title for such a decorative-leaved plant !

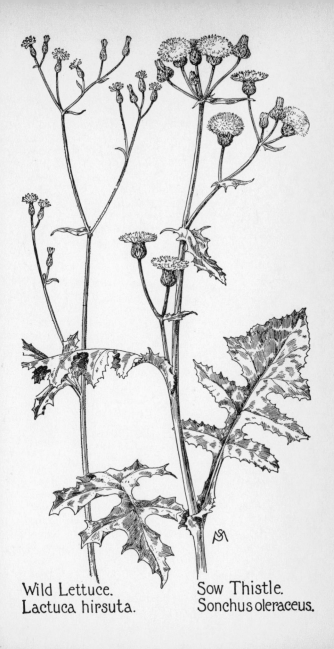

Wild Lettuce.
Lactuca hirsuta.

Sow Thistle.
Sonchus oleraceus.

INDEX.

537

INDEX.

INDEX.

INDEX.

INDEX.

INDEX.

INDEX.

544

INDEX.

INDEX.

INDEX.

INDEX.

INDEX.